okama

HEALING
THE
GENERATIONS

How Understanding Your Family Legacy
Can Transform Your Life

BARRY GROSSKOPF, M.D.

OKAMA

HEALING THE GENERATIONS
OKAMA
P.O. Box 22956
Seattle, WA 98122

Text design by Michael Mendelsohn
Cover design by Maren Costa and Lauren Grosskopf
Cover art by Wendy Lustbader

Manufactured in the United States of America

10   9   8   7   6   5   4   3   2   1

ISBN 0-9662607-1-6

ORIGINALLY PUBLISHED AS
FORGIVE YOUR PARENTS, HEAL YOURSELF

THIS EDITION PUBLISHED BY
AN ARRANGEMENT WITH
THE FREE PRESS
A Division of Simon & Schuster Inc.
1230 Avenue of the Americas
New York, NY 10020

CONTENTS

In memory of my father and mother
Israel Grosskopf, 1911–1991,
Evelyn Grosskopf, 1924–1995

FOREWORD

WENDY LUSTBADER

A ll parents feel vulnerable to their children. Between the longed-for praise—"You did a great job, Mom"—and the dreaded guilty verdict—"You were a lousy mother"—lies an almost limitless area of doubt and self-recrimination. Later in life, when their grown children approach them with questions about the family history, many parents recoil, saying, "Let's just leave the past behind, OK?" The fear of being blamed often supersedes the desire to be close.

The more regretful parents feel, the more watchful they will be for signs of lingering disrespect or long-standing grudges. Hearing that a son or daughter is seeing a therapist may itself feel like an accusation, with the parents worrying that their failings are being subjected to detailed analysis. When a son or daughter asks about the family's earlier years, parents may believe that ammunition rather than understanding is being sought. A flat refusal to talk about the past may result.

The solution to this dilemma is a paradox. It is by approaching parents without recrimination that adult children can finally locate the true source of their grievances. A mother is most likely to bare her soul when she senses that her children have dropped the barrier of previous hurt. When they show her that they are willing to enter into her story with sympathy, leaving behind their own bitter narrative, she may feel safe enough to reveal herself at long last.

Unfortunately, the enthusiasm of blame is at first more compelling than finding sympathy. Holding parents responsible for the pain that they caused is much easier than attending to the patient work of compassion. Decades may pass before an adult son or daughter is ready to hear a parent's story. Most people have to make their own wrong turns and see their own good intentions go awry before they are able to concede that their parents may have faced similar disappointments. The experience is similar to reading a novel at twenty and then reading it again at forty. The reader changes so much in the intervening years that the book seems entirely different. In the second reading, passages that were barely noticed before become utterly moving, and chapters previously skimmed become central. Being humbled by life experience opens us up to a readiness to grant amnesty rather than sit in judgment.

Due to the indispensable nature of such humiliation, it can take a lifetime for us to understand our parents fully. Our comprehension deepens as we are ravaged and rewarded by experience, reaching its peak as we face our own dying. Many people lie on their deathbeds thinking about their parents, finally understanding things that were said or done years ago. In this sense, our parents die twice: first, with their actual deaths, and then again as we relive their dying during our own last days.

Short of dying, other life experiences can rattle us into revelation. For example, becoming a parent generates comprehension of life truths almost as powerfully as approaching the end of life. Each generation faces a similar process of surrender, of bowing to inevitable compromises. A forty-year-old daughter asking her seventy-five-year-old mother about sacrifices she had made for the sake of parenting is likely to be mindful of her own frustrated hopes: "Mom, how come you never went back to school to become a teacher, like you wanted to?" This daughter may have asked the same question twenty years ago, but this time her tone contains a world of acquired understanding. Now the older woman may readily recount the marital conflict that kept her from living out her dreams. If she finds as she speaks that she is looking into the face of a fellow woman rather than that of an angry daughter, she may offer more details about those frustrated years than she ever dared before: "The afternoons before you kids came home from school were so empty. That's when I started drinking."

The ultimate inducement for a mother to speak is to sense that her daughter regards her as a human being who has suffered, rather than merely as the party responsible for pain. This daughter's tender question about a missed opportunity may open a door just as assuredly as an accusatory question, "Mom, why were you drunk every day when I came home from school?" later would have closed it. The shift from fault-finding to compassion is the magic wand of disclosure.

A sympathetic stance cannot be faked. Parental radar for resentment from their children is just too acute. Quick assurances, such as "Mom, I really do want to hear your side of the story," cannot assuage a mother's sensitivity to any residual spite. If beneath seeming commiseration lies a still active eagerness to blame, parents will feel it. Most will withdraw into old self-protections rather than risk exposure. People often complain that their parents will not talk openly to them, without examining the manner in which they are asking their questions. They do not realize that how they are feeling toward the parent while bringing up painful issues is more important than how they word the questions or even which questions they ask. A parent's story always emerges in accordance with the attitude of the listener.

Adult children often insist, "I'm not going to forgive my mother. My childhood was hell and it can't be undone." True, what happened cannot be altered, but the story of what happened can be told in fresh ways. The "length of days" promised in the Fifth Commandment to those who honor their parents has everything to do with the power of this changed perspective. Honoring is not the same as forgiving. Honoring means seeing parents' failings in the context both of their humanity and the story of previous generations. This shift is literally life-giving in that it gives us hope that someone may do the same for us.

The hope of being seen with our own suffering taken into account is no small encouragement. There is no other answer for shame, no other solace for impetuous errors or careless lapses. A daughter who can put herself in her mother's place thirty years ago grants herself consolation. By feeling how urgently her mother blocked out emptiness and disappointment with alcohol, the daughter frees herself to examine her own ways of evading pain. If instead the daughter holds to a rigid condemnation of her mother's conduct, she will be unable to take a compassionate look at herself and thereby allow others to truly know her.

Even small shards of family history can provoke understanding. At fifty-four, a woman learned a single biographical detail about her eighty-year-old father that altered both her view of him and the grievances she had sustained about him all of her life:

> I never even knew that my father once had a brother. He died when my father was twelve. He was only eight years old, stomped to death by a horse. This means my father had grief-stricken parents when he was a teenager. Now I can see where he might have gotten the idea that you have to fend for yourself in life. That was all he ever said to us when we needed help. I always thought he was made of ice. But maybe he's felt alone for a long, long time. That's all he might have known, growing up with heartbroken parents.

A daughter who can imagine her father's lonely grief at the age of twelve begins to liberate herself from the hurt of what seemed like cold fathering years later. By seeing how desperately her father must have tried to cope with his brother's death and his parents' emotional removal, she can finally glimpse him as a father trying to do the best he could with what he knew about life and loss. The once injurious refrain "You have to fend for yourself" is now heard in retrospect as a lesson in survival rendered by a father who never stopped feeling lonely.

No one's hurt is harder to see than a parent's. It requires a great deal of effort to shrink those who once wielded so much power over us to ordinary human dimensions. Initially, many people claim it is impossible for them to approach their parents with a clean emotional slate, even if they know this is exactly what their parents most crave from them. This book leads readers back through the generations, showing how to achieve a cleansing perspective.

Knowing which questions to ask, how and when to ask them, and what to do with the information gleaned will be illustrated in the chapters ahead. Many people think they know their family's history, without realizing that they have misperceived which events were truly central, or they have assembled information without applying emotional textures to the facts. Healing the generations requires information, emotion, and insight mixed together in a special alchemy of grace.

In March of 1984, as a therapist, I needed to look up the psychiatric evaluation of a patient I was seeing at a community clinic. I opened the medical record and found the most unusual psychiatric evaluation I had ever seen. The majority of the evaluation contained information about the patient's grandmother's childhood. I flipped through the pages in frustration, searching for material pertaining to the young woman herself. There was only a brief statement about my patient's current circumstances. I remember thinking, "This psychiatrist is either a madman or a genius."

I married this psychiatrist, Barry Grosskopf, in March of 1987. I have used his approach to healing in my own work for years now, having found that my effectiveness as a therapist grew exponentially as a result. When I teach his approach in workshops for therapists, participants often experience revelations of their own right on the spot. They tell me that they have never looked at their own lives this way, much less their patients' lives, and that they cannot wait to apply these ideas in their work. This book has been long awaited.

PREFACE

This book is about the childhood pain we struggle with all our lives, and is meant as a blueprint for healing, a self-reconstruction process rather than a quick fix. To heal ourselves and protect others from the wounds we carry, we must understand and forgive the pain our parents have passed on to us.

With and without words, emotional lessons from the past are transmitted from parents to children. Unless we understand these forces, we may spend our lives reacting to emotions we have never properly identified. By making the effort to imagine our parents' lives as they were growing up and while they raised us, we can appreciate what they endured as well as what we inherited.

The book challenges the reader to lay aside his own feelings to better understand a parent's. In Chapter 1, we begin as adults revisiting our parents' childhoods. With more mature eyes and a greater depth of imagination, we look again at our old stories. Doing this initiates new insights that may change our perception of our parents as well as give us a new perspective on our own childhood experience and emotional formation.

As we try to imagine our parents' early experiences, we may stumble upon a fact whose significance we had overlooked. The second chapter asks why we so often do not see the reality of others, no matter how empathic or loving we are. We examine the dimensions of our inborn self-centeredness that distorts our perspective and keeps us from understanding other people's emotional experience.

The third chapter explores the biology of grief and trauma. The emotional wounds we carry have biological correlates. We need to understand the biology of our experience and emotional reactions to understand why we act as we do, and why change is so hard. Learned emotional reactions have survival value as well as inherent drawbacks; we need to understand when to ally with, and when to transcend, our biological inheritance.

Chapter 4 examines the roles that consolation and mourning play in healing after we have suffered emotional loss. Unless we heal ourselves, we pass the pain onto our children.

Chapters 5 through 7 focus on shattering events that have multigenerational repercussions. Even if we ourselves have not directly suffered the ravages of war or sexual abuse, or the loss of a parent or sibling in childhood, it is likely that a loved one has. Understanding our parents' wounds allows us to understand the lingering effects that their injuries have on our lives.

Chapter 8 investigates how the painful events of one generation affect the psychology and neurobiology of subsequent ones. Emotions from preverbal experience can haunt and misguide us if we misattribute those earlier feelings to our present circumstances.

We would do well to learn to recognize the emotional forces at play in our lives so that they no longer rule us or dominate our relationships. Chapter 9 examines how buried grief and fear direct us to fashion our own pain. We replay the unhealed painful events in attempts to heal them. Chapters 10 and 11 provide a glimpse of the overt and hidden consequences of honesty and concealment in our relationships.

Chapter 12 explores how the healing marriage transforms conflict into opportunities for healing the unconscious themes that couples play out in repetitive, stylized fights, and the inevitable crises that arise, for good or ill, when intimates expose each other's core wounds.

Chapter 13 discusses how we can refashion painful childhood reactions that damage relationships and hurt intimates. By using the commandment to "Honor your father and mother" as a guide to our own behavior, we can recognize and grapple with the emotional distortions that we learned in reacting to the wounds of our parents.

The last chapters conclude with a challenge to suspend judgment and listen empathically even in the face of a parent's reluctance and hostility. The end of a parent's life is the last of our living opportunities to achieve new understandings and new reconciliation.

The chapters in this book need not be read sequentially; the reader can feel free to decide which are most pertinent to his own family or to the family of someone he is seeking to understand. Throughout, I use the words "we" or "us" to mean our parents, ourselves, or our mates and our children.

"They" or "them" can mean "we" or "us," because we are all fundamentally alike and we play various roles in the family. I use the masculine pronouns as the universal to indicate either sex, and when I speak of marriage, I mean to include gay and lesbian and unmarried couples. Many of the notes at the end of the book are provided for the benefit of therapists.

The aim of this book is to help the reader attain a better understanding of the forces that shaped his parents and himself, to guide him on his journey to deeper healing and self-mastery, and to relieve him from hurt, anger, and bitterness. If we can understand our parents enough to have compassion for them, our conception of them shifts and we release ourselves from the hurt feelings of our childhood. Healing ourselves and healing the generations, we safeguard our relationships and bring a legacy of pain to an end. Maimonedes asks, "If not now, when?"

ACKNOWLEDGMENTS

Alexia Dorszynski passed on January 1, 1999. This book was her last editorial project. I will always be grateful to Alexia for all the work she did. She understood the book, believed in it, and took on the complex task of editing and shaping it. She added many insights of her own. Alexia became my guide, without whom I would have lost my way.

I also wish to thank Susan Arellano, who first envisioned this book and challenged me to articulate my ideas; and Philip Rappaport, my editor at The Free Press, for holding me to a rigorous standard of quality and coherence. This book assumed its final form under his direction, and I am grateful.

I wish to thank Stan Henry for his support and for transforming this book into its paperback edition. His sensitivity has helped me feel all the more at home among these pages.

I wish to thank Carol Glickfeld and Rabbi Leib Kaplan for their teachings; and Edein French, my therapist, for her wisdom; Stephanie Hegstad for challenging me with her clarity; Joseph and Kathleen Sullivan Caggiano for their penetrating questions; Valerie Trueblood Rapport for helping me believe in myself; and my patients, who have given me the gift of their trust and taught me the lessons of their lives.

The following friends have read chapters of the book and have given me helpful commentary: Cliff Barda, Mary Baird, Kathleen Braden, William Braden, Jeff Bridgeman, John and Goldie Caughlan, Keith Claypool, Shirley Crawford, Gordon Davison, Joan Fiset, Johnny Fishman, Bonnie Genevay, Kimberly Hamilton, Rob Henry, David Johnson, Terry and Ira Kalit, Gladys Kinnebrew, Jed Kliman, Lynn Kliman, Fred Lippert, Lani Moore Marquardt, Tracy McAvoy, Douglas Noble, Patricia Rickert, Sarah Ross, Mark Samson, Sharon Sheridan, Lance Sobel, Michael Telson, Patty Thomson, Slim Threlkeld, Beverly Tildon, Sue Tomita, Walter Townes, and Darlene Yuna.

I would also like to thank Tyler Glenn, Barbara Jeaneret, Dean Paton, Rick Rapport, Rachel Rose, and Greg Zachary for their encouragement and moral support.

I wish to thank three friends for being there for me, with no questions asked, since we were fifteen: Johnny Fishman, who taught me laughter and friendship; Douglas Noble, who taught me to speak feelings and be a part of this world; and Michael Telson for his unflagging support. My beloved friend Johnny Fishman passed away in June 1998. Moments of true joy were shared in his company. Now I can see reflections of his light in his children's eyes.

I want to thank my son David and my daughter Lauren for their love, support and tolerance through the years, for forgiving me when I failed them, and for showing me the newness of self-discovery and the diligent honesty of two people courageously accepting the challenges of their lives.

I want to give special thanks to my wife, Wendy Lustbader Grosskopf, who taught me to love again, to respect myself, and for her kindness, wisdom, and honesty. Without her guidance and tutelage, I never would have had the courage or patience to write this book.

INTRODUCTION

In 1972, after I completed my residency in psychiatry, a colleague referred a "difficult patient" to me for treatment. Mary was soft-spoken, intelligent, and pretty, but so suspicious that she could not maintain a relationship, and so angry that she would yell at strangers if she caught their glance. Because she was sensitive to the undercurrents in any conversation, I found myself talking to her as if I were Humphrey Bogart playing Sam Spade—truthful, direct, tough, unambiguous. Mary blamed her parents for her suspiciousness and her fear of letting others get close to her; but her chief injury had occurred before she was born:

> My grandfather was an alcoholic. He raped my mother when she was a child. I know it wasn't her fault, but she became a lousy mother and messed up my life. She gave me no affection at all and wouldn't let my father hug me either. I couldn't even hang out with him because Mom didn't like us spending too much time together.

Mary's mother had blocked her daughter from an intimacy that she desperately needed. Over time, Mary absorbed her mother's fears and became vigilant for potentially dangerous sexual undercurrents. As she grew up, Mary became uncomfortably self-conscious and lonely; she took on her mother's anger and applied it indiscriminately.

It seemed clear to me that if Mary could learn to sympathize with the bind her parents had been in, she would be able to understand the errors they made, why they had failed her. To move on with her life, Mary needed to picture the hurt, frightened little girl her mother had once been and had continued to be while raising her own family. I challenged Mary to imagine herself as a child being raped, and to imagine herself growing up, still frightened, and then trying to shield her daughter. Mary was stunned when she realized how her own vulnerability as a little girl must have reawakened her mother's fears. She began to see the absence of physical intimacy in her childhood as her mother's desperate attempt to protect her rather than as a cruel failure.

When I prompted other patients to learn their parents' stories, those who had previously been in therapy for years with little progress suddenly showed signs of substantial healing. When they were able to look at their parents' pain with compassion, their own pain gradually diminished, along with damaging patterns of expressing hurt and anger. Their intimate relationships improved, and they were better able to love.

Fascinated, I searched the psychiatric literature and could find no books or articles that similarly focused on the experiential world of patients' parents. For example, Swiss therapist Alice Miller[1] speaks for abused children with force and sympathy, but she does not speak for their parents, who were also once children. The books that deeply explore the generational effects of trauma tend to examine the effects of specific traumas, such as the Holocaust's effect on the second generation. Books examining the broader effects of trauma on the generations, such as the literature on genograms and family systems, do ask that we take note of trauma in past generations, but in a way that leads to an intellectual rather than an emotional understanding. We hunger for narratives with true explanatory power.

Great novels, such as *The Bridge of San Luis Rey* and *The Brothers Karamazov,* or the works of modern novelists like Anne Tyler or Pat Conroy, explicate character in vivid, multigenerational portraits, widening and deepening the reader's understanding of family events that shape character and action. Unfortunately, psychotherapy as it is usually practiced does not ask us to learn, much less feel, the events of our parents' and grandparents' life stories. Instead, overlooking the lessons of literature handed down to us from the earliest written civilizations, psychotherapists usually encourage us to tell our life stories with ourselves at the center, rather than as a descendant laden with stories of the previous generations.

Over time, the Fifth Commandment—the commandment to "Honor Your Father and Your Mother," which I'd begun exploring with Mary—became central to my work.

Some patients resisted, asking, "Why should I learn about my family's history?" Some denied problems in the family, seeming to fear unearthing them, as if looking too closely would be an act of disloyalty or as if they were themselves too fragile to see their parents' ordinary humanity. Others acted as if grief or some other dreaded emotion might overtake them. But people condemn themselves to pain by trying to avoid it. In hiding from ourselves, we are fugitives from our own feelings; and in hiding from others, we play-act our lives.

When I reflected back on my own life and tried imagining it from my parents' point of view, and applied the discipline of the Fifth Commandment to guide my own behavior, I began to heal as well.

My parents and I arrived in America from the refugee camps of Europe in 1949 with twenty-two dollars, one good quilt, family photographs, and a set of sterling silverware. Our new country was magic, rich with wonders. A few months after our arrival, we went into a five-and-dime filled with marvels, where I was entranced with a toy airplane. Not quite five years of age, I begged for it, crying till I shrieked, and was elated when my father bought it for me. Then when we got home, he put the airplane under his foot, crushed it, and angrily spanked me for the first time in my life. Later, my mother patiently explained the economics of our survival. I never threw another temper tantrum and rarely asked for anything afterward.

I was seventeen when my father hit me for the second and last time. At the time, I thought he was a raving lunatic. I had borrowed a pair of his socks without asking permission. When I told him, he raged at me: "You have everything and appreciate nothing. You have it too good. Everything comes easy, like money grows on trees...." And on and on he went, with no sign of stopping. Yet, when I'd totaled our car a few months before, all he'd said was "Thank God you're all right!"

My father had billions of socks. How was I supposed to know borrowing one pair would bother him? Finally, I couldn't take his harangue anymore. My voice dripping with contempt, I said, "Drop dead!"

His face turning white, he slapped my face, spun around, and walked away. I turned and marched off in the other direction. But in seeing his ashen face, I felt terrible for what I had said. My mother said, "Talk with your father." I argued my grievance. She repeated, "Talk with your father."

I tried, but he wouldn't talk to me. For three days, he was silent. I begged and pleaded and apologized, and my father finally relented. But I still considered him a lunatic at heart.

Years later, I asked him to take a walk with me on the beach. He said he didn't want to get sand in his shoes. When I suggested that he take them off, he said, "I don't like to go barefoot." I insisted, "Come on, Dad, the sand will feel good on your feet." He then began telling me of a winter he'd spent in Europe when there was no food and people were starving. He sold his shirt and then his shoes in order to survive. All winter, he had to go around with bare feet or rags tied to his ankles. Years later, his feet were still sensitive: going barefoot could never again be a pleasure to him.

Suddenly, my father's earlier words came back to me. "You appreciate nothing! You don't know how good you have it. You have it too easy!" I realized he was right: I'd never done without. Everything necessary to survive had always been readily available. The desperation of starving was and is beyond my experience. For a few moments, even as I recoiled from the image, I saw my father that long-ago winter, half naked and starving, his bare feet freezing on the snow of a Russian winter in wartime.

I think if I went further and really imagined being my father that winter, I would understand more than I'd want. I'd have too many regrets. There were too many times that I had judged him and not understood, times when I lacked compassion and did not listen; too many moments lost in anger and misunderstanding when we might have talked. Had I been more aware of his vulnerability, I'd be much too aware of how I had hurt him over the years.

In the chapters that follow, you will hear the voices of those who have suffered. Each day for the past twenty-five years, I have heard the confessions of wounded people and been privileged to hear many of their previously untold secrets. I relay the knowledge others have given me, passing on their wisdom so we may better understand ourselves and what others have endured. The stories I recount are distillations, with the speakers' identities disguised or combined but with their essence unchanged. We will examine the repercussions of traumatic events throughout life and examine the reverberations of those events through the generations.

To better understand our own lives, it is important that we tell our stories well and tell them truly. Self-centered by our very nature, we manufacture our destinies in ignorance, unaware of how numb we often are to the realities of other people. But insights magnify in imagining the details of a parent or a grandparent's ordeal. When my patients do so, they are humbled by new understandings, softened with compassion, and relieved of the sharpness of old pain with genuine forgiveness. As we shift the focus away from ourselves, it becomes apparent how much we overlook the obvious.

We are made strong by what we overcome;
that man is man because he is as free to do evil as to do good;
that life is as free to develop hostile forms as to develop friendly;
that power waits upon him who earns it; that disease, wars,
the unloosened devastating elemental forces have each and
all played their part in developing and hardening man
and giving him the heroic fiber.

John Burroughs, *Accepting the Universe*

CHAPTER 1

WHEN LIFE DOESN'T WORK

Taking Another Look at Our Life Stories

We weave our memories into narrative,
from which we construct our identities.

Leonard Shengold, *Soul Murder*

Parents want to do well by their children; those who harm their children distort their own hope and intent. To grow beyond the limitations of a painful childhood, we must try to understand the parents who hurt us. But to see our parents clearly, we must acknowledge their love for us and recognize our effect on them.

When parents act in harmful ways toward their children, it is a sign that something harmful once happened to them. What thwarted our parents as they raised us? Was it marital pressures, financial strain, an accident, illness, alcohol or drug addiction, ignorance? Even for parents whose conduct was the worst, there are explanations, reasons that would make sense of the harm they caused. Imagining ourselves living through our parents' experiences allows us to understand them and temper our judgments.

As children and adolescents, we do not understand the sacrifice of freedom, the anxiety, or the depth of love our parents feel for us. Parents want the best for their children and want to be their best for them. But parents have little time for reflection and even less for composure. There is a child to raise, a home to secure, and more work than can be accomplished in a day. There is little time to enjoy former activities and less time to give or receive emotional support from one's partner.

We tend to blame our parents for the emotional problems we have; and unless we make a conscious effort to do otherwise, we also tend to accept the judgments we formed of them in childhood and adolescence. But as children, we did not have the experience to relate to our parents' world; as adolescents we had better things to do; and as adults, we do not automatically use our mature experience to perceive our parents differently. We each have a natural blind spot that gets in the way of seeing our parents accurately and keeps us from imagining the reality of their lives.

In the ordinary course of affairs, we hold on to our longstanding beliefs and dismiss whatever contradicts them. Radical challenges in how we view our lives are too unsettling. We are comfortable viewing our parents according to the emotional bias we carry from childhood, and we interpret events to conform to the familiar feelings that bias us. This circularity of vision makes us overlook the obvious as we cling to attitudes we developed earlier in our lives.

In growing up, we learn our parents' stories in dribs and drabs, and we rarely question those stories in maturity. We string them together to create a diffuse narrative we think we understand. We take so much for granted, we do not notice that we have overlooked obvious gaps in our parents' stories, or have filled them in with faulty or incomplete assumptions. We hear our parents speak in shorthand: "My mother's father died when she was four." The emotional significance of such abbreviated stories is difficult to appreciate, yet we go on reciting what little we remember and presuming knowledge we do not have. New understandings, however, require that we reassess the past.

Ellen, a thirty-six-year-old clinical psychologist, had been in therapy for years before consulting me, so I was surprised at how little she knew about her father. Despite being a therapist, her understanding of his story was poorly developed:

> I didn't have a brother and barely had a father, so I never learned much about being intimate with men. I don't think my father wanted kids. He barely spoke to us. When he came home at night, he'd just sit in front the the TV and read his paper. I used to be angry about this, but I worked it out in therapy.

> No one knows the whole story; but when he was a child, my father's father was murdered. My grandmother never remarried; so I guess

my father never had a father either. The only other trauma I know of was that he fought in the South Pacific during World War II.

Though Ellen had achieved an intellectual understanding of her father, she still saw him largely in terms of the hurt child she herself had been; and from that perspective, Ellen believed that her father didn't want her.

As she spoke, however, I imagined what the expression would have been like on my own son's face upon hearing of my death—or worse yet, of my having been murdered. I imagined him going to school each day and coming home afterwards. I wondered what the following years had been like for Ellen's grandmother. Did she hide the truth of what really happened? Did Ellen's father protect his already burdened mother from his own unhappy feelings by hiding them? Ellen's father had no model to follow for being a father or for expressing masculine emotion.

Ellen's eyes flashed with recognition when I suggested that, emotionally, her father was a hurt little boy who had never stopped crying for his father, and he was probably still a teenager when he was sent into the bloody combat of the South Pacific. How many close friends had he made? How many died? Did the war pound the last nail into the coffin of her father's silence?

After a few sessions, Ellen began reaching out to him, and he responded. Shortly before his unexpected death, he wrote her a letter that she still treasures.

HIDDEN IN PLAIN SIGHT

So much of our family's history is hidden from us in plain sight. As we learn new facts and come to better appreciate the significance of our parents' stories, we are startled into new awareness with each revelation. We are amazed at how much we had previously overlooked or taken for granted.

Matthew, for instance, was in his late thirties before he actively imagined the reality of a story his mother had told him many times before. Until he imagined the feelings of his mother as a little girl, he had not really understood it:

My mom was an unhappy person. Nothing was ever right for her. She complained about everything. I hated the way she whined. Over and over, she told me the story of how she never got the bicycle her father had promised her. She was eight and he died before he could give it to her. I always thought, "So what. Get over it, for God's sake." But now my daughter is about the same age that my mom was when she lost her dad. I started thinking about it. I imagined my mom being eight, excited about her birthday, expecting a new bicycle; and then her father gets killed. It wasn't the bicycle. Her life was never the same or as happy afterwards. The bicycle represents the happiness she never got to have. I realized that my mom still talks about it in the same way she did when she was eight.

When Matthew first heard his mother tell her story, he could only hear an adult childishly complaining about an event long past. Reevaluating the story later as the father of an eight-year-old, however, Matthew began seeing his mother in a different light: he was able to react sympathetically to the hurt little girl his mother had been, and with a bit more patience for the complaining, often immature parent she continues to be.

THE IMPORTANCE OF UNREMEMBERED HISTORY

We identify with events we can remember directly, not with what is passed on to us secondhand. We minimize the importance of what we ourselves cannot remember. We relegate such stories to a nebulous and vaguely understood background and do not imagine the moments of intense life unfolding.

We do not emotionally relate to incidents that we are told happened to us as one-year-olds. Events that have been lost to memory are too removed to feel like a part of ourselves. A piece of our lives disappeared from consciousness, and we neither notice nor feel its absence.

It is the telling of our stories that fixes them in memory. Young children, however, do not have words for anguish. Their vocabulary cannot contain overwhelming and bewildering feelings. Before we learn the right words to explain our early childhood experiences, we may have already forgotten them, remembering only shadows. But the unnamed pain can reverberate throughout our own and our family's history.

For instance, at twenty-eight, Patricia knew her mother's story well and had heard it often, but what she knew did not explain much to her emotionally:

I've heard the story a million times. Mom was four when her father ran off with his secretary. She never saw him again. She was hurt at first, but Grandma fell in love with her childhood sweetheart and everything turned out OK. Mom had a wonderful childhood.

Patricia went on to say:

I love my mother. When I was a kid, I wanted to be just like her. She's so upbeat and sure of herself. But when she left Dad, I was only ten. At the time I was mad at them both, so I decided to take care of myself. Everyone sees me as confident and independent, but I'm insecure: I'm afraid of commitments and afraid of ending up alone. Mom's been divorced three times now. How do you know when someone's right for you? When do you stay and tough it out? When do you go? I'm easygoing and a lot of fun, but I've got this dark side I try not to show. When I'm with anyone too long, I start seeing their flaws and then I'm out the door.

Patricia's mother told a happy-forever-after story about the hurt at the center of her childhood. But that fairy tale, however true it may have been for Patricia's grandmother, was neither complete nor true for Patricia's mother.

Patricia never understood her mother's story because her mother had not really understood it herself. As an adult, Patricia's mother no longer emotionally identified with the anguish of the little girl she had once been. Instead grief became an unexpressed undercurrent of her life, impelling Patricia's mother to try to fill the void of her father's absence. Had she been more aware of how resurgent childhood feelings eventually emerge in the constancy of a relationship, Patricia's mother might have endured the hard times that all couples experience after romance fades.

To understand her mother's story, Patricia needed to imagine the feelings of her mother as a four-year-old girl who adored her daddy. Then she needed to envision the face of that four-year-old who suddenly realised her father had disappeared from her life. The painful childhood feelings we gradually overcome become emotional undercurrent that can cause havoc when they resurface later in our lives. Imagining how she would have felt if her own father had done that to her, Patricia would have, for a moment, felt a pale reflection of the powerful feelings that arose outside her mother's awareness and continued to drive both their lives. Even though her mother no longer actively felt the grief she had buried, the feelings threatened to overwhelm her if she allowed herself to be hurt.

Once Patricia imagined her mother's childhood well enough to *feel* it, she could see how the appearance of strength she had imitated bore the imprint of a sorrow that occurred before she was born. Compassion for the vulnerable child her mother had been, supplanted Patricia's blanket criticism of her, freed Patricia to better accept the strengths as well as the weaknesses of others, and in time opened her up to greater possibilities of commitment, love, and intimacy.

In the telling of their life stories, people often omit the dark times of earliest youth. Adults abandoned by a father in early childhood often mention the fact only as an afterthought. If the mother remarried well, the relationship to the stepfather seems to be the only important one; and the repercussions of unremembered grief and the years of the earlier relationship are accorded little significance. But in order to understand our own life stories, we need to imagine ourselves, our parents, and those we love as they were—growing up—young, developing, and impressionable.

People commonly dismiss the importance of their earliest childhood experience, unable to believe that anything that happened so long ago can still have effects. When terrible things happen and memories are painful, we tend to let a single incident stand in for the hurt of the whole experience. In time, the fragment comes to mean the whole, and even the fragment thins to air in the telling. Details are left out in the retelling of hazy memories, and we are seldom moved to imagine what has been forgotten.

FAMILY SECRETS

As children and adults, we reveal ourselves with the stories we tell, and we keep others away by what we do not tell them. What is missing from our stories—what we don't know or don't appreciate—can hurt us in ways almost too quiet to notice. A sensitive child can carry the sorrows of the whole family and act out emotions that for him may have no context or history.

This was the case for Duane, an adolescent committed to my care after a suicide attempt. He had been drinking, using drugs, and getting into fights since his mother had died three years before. Duane's father was terrified that his son might succeed in a future suicide attempt, and Duane regarded his father with contempt for being weak and distant. But he had no idea what his father had hidden from him:

> Duane's mother had been chronically ill, in pain, and desperately unhappy. Duane's father had taken her to the emergency room time and again after she had overdosed on her medicine. The long effort had worn him down. On the night she died, he knew she had taken another overdose. But he could not bring himself to act. He just went to sleep. He did not intervene.

Secrets usually hurt the very people they are supposed to protect. For years, in protecting Duane from the knowledge of his mother's deep unhappiness, his parents excluded him from their intimacy, leaving him alone with bad feelings that he could only blame on other causes. By hiding her suicide attempts, Duane's mother deprived herself of seeing, firsthand, her son's fear of losing her. She might have found it harder to take her own life had she seen the expression on her son's face. And Duane never saw the depth of his father's loyalty and strength that had kept the family together through the years.

Concealing history inevitably distorts relationships. The secrets behind his mother's death isolated Duane from his father, leaving each of them alone with their grief and bad feelings. Duane lost his mother, then lived without the strength of his father behind him. Appointing himself judge and jury, his father had not only lost the love of his youth but accused himself of killing her and rendered a verdict of "guilty." The story he told himself was that he was tired of caring for a chronically ill, bitterly unhappy woman, sick of her suicide attempts, and selfish and hateful in letting her die. He refused to mitigate his guilt by acknowledging extenuating circumstances.

Ultimately, Duane's father decided that he needed to spend some time talking to a therapist before speaking with his son. I had the sense that until Duane understood what his feelings were truly about, it would take him a long time to heal his life.

Family secrets leave a legacy of puzzling emotions because those who are excluded from them cannot know where their pain is coming from, and those who keep them cannot release the pain that shackles them. The ending of a secret is usually the beginning of healing. Once a family lets go of a secret, the changes set in motion are permanent. Unsettling emotional reactions finally begin to make sense and people can talk honestly.

Our feelings about ourselves and our families change as we come to know our family stories better. Our life stories change as we reassess them in maturity. We learn new facts and new details; our own experiences with life rebuke our arrogance; we empathize more and judge less. We apply our life experience to our parents' stories, then reconstruct our own.

Our thoughts and attitudes do not necessarily evolve as we mature. The understanding of our family and of life that we acquire growing up can leave us stranded as adults with the thoughts and attitudes of our youth. We can learn new things from our own stories if we are willing to look beyond our immediate point of view. We don't notice how young our thoughts and feelings are unless we deliberately step back and review them from a more mature perspective or revisit them in conversation with friends.

"MY PARENTS DIDN'T LOVE ME"

> *Find the pains you have inflicted.*
> *Those you have suffered will keep well enough*
> *without any effort on your part.*
>
> Elias Canetti, *The Agony of Flies*

> *When a father gives to a son, both laugh.*
> *When a son gives to a father, both cry.*
>
> Yiddish proverb

Almost everyone unhappy enough to seek out therapy has complaints about their parents. Those who carry the greatest burden of hurt often say, "My parents didn't love me!"—or at least not enough. A corollary accusation is "If my parents loved me, how could they have been so cold?" Or "favored my brother," "kept on drinking," "let my uncle molest me?"

As children, we calculate our worth in our parents' hierarchy of values. We measure their love for us against their love for a dollar, drink, career, or our other siblings. The impressions we form in those early vulnerable years continue into adulthood, and we treat those impressions as fact, seldom testing them against any hard standard of truth or asking for any clarifying details.

Parents react to their own histories as they raise their children. Unresolved issues from a parent's childhood trigger further turmoil in family life. When their children inevitably thwart or frustrate them, parents find that their frustration becomes a blank screen for the projection of feelings learned in childhood, and they observe themselves, often to their horror, parroting the very words and gestures that their parents used on them as children. The destructive patterns repeat from one generation to another, echoing through the years—unless something happens to break the cycle, to heal the hurt places within.

Those who say their parents didn't love them rarely look at their parents' circumstances at the time the parents were being raised. One woman who left her marriage in search of what she thought she never had, said, "I was alone in an empty soccer field when I realized, 'My mother doesn't love me.' I wept for hours." It was true that her mother had been stingy, unemotional, and unaffectionate; but she had also been raised during the Great Depression. The mother's stoicism and abnegation that she interpreted as a lack of love only reflected the deprivations of her mother's childhood, and not the feelings that her mother had toward her.

Believing that "my parents didn't love me" distorts character, not just from the hurt that develops, but for the patches of empathy that fail to develop. In time, the sympathy that a person fails to develop for a parent's flaws becomes the condemning judgment—a blind spot that prevents that person from understanding others when they seem to be exhibiting similar traits.

Lane, a man of thirty-seven with three suicide attempts and two failed marriages, had been so vigilant for signs of rejection while growing up that he never turned his sensitivity toward the feelings of others. Lane described the turning points in his life in this way:

My dad was a hard worker and he never had much time to spend with me. When I was seven, my uncle told me I was such a spoiled brat no one could stand me. When I was nine, I told my father I loved him and begged him to say that he loved me too. I begged and begged but he never answered. It was then that I realized that what my uncle had told me was true.

Despite years of therapy, Lane had no knowledge of his father's history, and he looked for no other reason for his father's silence than "My father didn't love me." But when Lane told me his story, I wondered what history lay behind the father's silence. I wondered how tormented his father had been to be unable to simply say, "I love you." What must it have been like for Lane's father to face a son who looked at him with eyes so full of hurt and accusation. To have the love he craved, Lane had to learn to fill in the blank of his father's silence with something other than a nine-year-old's conclusions, and he had to become aware of other people's feelings. I urged him to imagine his father's feelings and to pay attention to how others felt.

Given his history, I was surprised at how quickly Lane managed to do this. The benefits were immediate. As he attended to other people's feelings rather than to his own pain, they responded differently to him, and his spirits lifted. To diminish his burden of childhood pain, Lane had to make the effort to learn more about his father. Upon leaving treatment, Lane was determined to return to his family and apply his shift in perspective.

THE FIFTH COMMANDMENT
Clarifying the Parent-Child Bond

"Honor your father and your mother that *your* days be long and *that it may go well with* you *upon the land.*" The Fifth Commandment is a covenant between the generations. Parents and children are bound to one another and are reciprocally vulnerable. Though young children feel their parents are terribly powerful, the Fifth Commandment recognizes that over the course of a lifetime parents are actually more vulnerable than their children.

The discipline of this commandment is central to our maturation and to our ability to be intimate. By healing our relationship with our parents, we heal ourselves. The commandment does not call upon us to love our parents, but it does call upon us to treat them with respect and compassion regardless of how they behave.

Adult children of parents who had abused, neglected, or abandoned them must make a particular effort to go against the grain of their own hurt feelings to understand the pain that drove their parents. This is never easy work. Unless we make that effort, however, we continue to see our parents as the mythical creations we made of them in childhood rather than as ordinary, struggling human beings. When we are hostile toward our parents, we should take it as a sign that something went wrong in *their* lives, or something is wrong with our understanding.

The relationship we have with our parents is the template for all of our subsequent relationships. The way we react to our parents fashions our most intimate reactions to friends, coworkers, and most of all, to our partners and our children.[1] If we were hurt as children, we may continue to react as we did as children all through our lives. The anger, hostility, or contempt we felt toward our parents brims over onto other relationships. Ironically, when we act toward others as we do toward our parents, they begin to react to us as our parents once did.[2] If instead we find a way to treat our parents well, we correct something within ourselves.[3] We become the conscious authors of our own healing story.

IMAGINING ANOTHER PERSON'S EXPERIENCE

Overcoming the Limitations of a Self-Centered Perspective

Where there is no love there is no sense either.
Dostoevsky, *Notes from the Underground*

That's what it was to be alive . . . up and about
in a cloud of ignorance . . . trampling on the feelings
of those about you . . . at the mercy of one self-centered
passion or another.
Thornton Wilder, *Our Town*

By nature, we do not perceive ourselves or others accurately. We magnify the importance of ourselves and diminish that of others. In the beauty of a clear night, however, we look at the stars and feel ourselves small, unimportant, and at peace. On an objective scale, we sense our insignificance. Somehow the realization comforts us. But the moment soon passes and once again we experience our lives as if the planets orbited around us. The return of the illusion hurts us, takes our peace away, allows us to magnify slights, rejections, and humiliations as others challenge the illusion of our self-importance with theirs. It is in our human nature that this be so; it is our task to transcend it.

The Fifth Commandment, "Honor your father and your mother . . . that your days may be long, and that it may go well with you upon the land,"[1] once understood as a compact between the generations, counters the self-centered, emotional reactions that children have to hurtful (and injured) parents with the adult injunction to honor them regardless of their behavior. Overlooking old understandings that had once provided a map for healing the generations, the Fifth Commandment has been mistakenly rewritten in the post-Freudian era, so that it might read, "Honor your children, so that it will go well for *them*." Though there is more than a measure of truth in this—children retain childhood hurts well into adulthood—this contemporary "wisdom" leaves us helpless and hostile in the face of our history. There is a deeper truth in the ancient version, "Honor your father and your mother . . . that it may go well with *you*." Healing the generations requires that we go against the grain of immediate emotions when we are hurt or angry, that we treat our parents well regardless of how we feel in the moment. In adhering to the discipline of the Fifth Commandment, we learn to correct the flaws in our own characters—the habitual emotional responses that cause harm to others. We heal our relationships and prevent our pain from being passed on to the next generation.

As a matter of course, we do not perceive our parents accurately. We know them least when our anger with their faults in raising us blinds us to their pain. Without a special effort to imagine a parent's life, we take too much for granted; we overlook what we do not understand and do not notice the gaps in our awareness. When we were children, our parents' presence or absence loomed so large that as adults we still see them as larger than life, too big for us to understand in ordinary terms. They are not ordinary enough for us to grant them the ordinary tolerance we accord others. Unable to see our parents from the perspective of the adults we have become, we judge them instead, holding them responsible for our wounds and limitations.

IMAGINING ANOTHER PERSON'S EXPERIENCE

When we are young, we can seldom identify with the old. The experiences of age are, as yet, beyond us. Those older than ourselves seem to live in a world foreign to our own, and every generation identifies with its own. Each has a common history and *Zeitgeist*, a spirit of its times. Those who grew up in the sixties may have been on different sides of issues, but everyone had the same president, lived through the same assassinations, and was exposed to the same media. The music and spirit of the times were uniquely theirs, just as the Jazz Age of the twenties was uniquely the flappers'. The camaraderie of common experience makes members of each generation intimate with one another and, in part, strangers to members of every other generation.

On the occasions when we do consider a person's experiences from another generation, our understanding usually only skims the surface or is condescending. By right of youth, vigor, and potential, the young feel superior to their elders, while elders have experience, wisdom, and nostalgia for times past. To understand others, we have to open our emotions to their experience. We have to close our own eyes, imagine looking out of theirs, and put ourselves into their story. Otherwise, thinking we understand another person's life story is like listening to music and being tone deaf.

But how often do we imagine ourselves living our parents' experience? Mark was forty-two years old before he imagined what it was like to be his father. The insight stunned him:

> I used to hang around my dad and he'd tell me stories. I'd always known that when he was a kid, seven or eight, his mom got sick. He was sent to live with his aunts for a couple of years. He came to love them and was bitter when his father made him return home. Dad never forgave him, but when he'd talk about how bad his father was, he didn't sound bad to me. My dad made it sound like he himself was the one in the wrong.
>
> Dad told me a lot about his life and I thought I understood him well, but I didn't—not until in acting class we were asked to imagine the worst day in a parent's life. Each of us had to sit in a chair in front of the group and become our mother or father that day. I imagined being my father, eight years old; they were forcing me to leave home. I had to say goodbye to my brothers and sisters and my mother and father. When I imagined it, I started sobbing so hard I couldn't breathe. I never knew. I mean, I knew, but I never *felt* it before, what the words "I had to leave home" really meant. At that moment, I understood my father like never before.

Mark's acting exercise brought him an epiphany. He felt his eyes open and his perception change. Sympathy brought him closer to his father.

Looking back on his own childhood, Mark had to reappraise what he remembered.

Such emotional insights are transformative. Typically, we limit our understanding because we are reluctant to pierce the comfortable shell of self-centeredness. We recoil at dipping ourselves into the heat of another person's emotions; it's too hot. It is easier to stop at surfaces. And we are usually too absorbed in our own life dramas to send our emotions into the world of another. We feel that we know all we need to know and do not even think to make the effort.

And then, too, there's something frightening about undertaking an experience we sense will change us. Imagining a parent's emotional life is subversive. Something shifts in the very structure of our characters. We may regret not having understood them before, or expose an ugly, shallow, self-centered part of ourselves that we'd rather not acknowledge, much less feel the need to change. Mark, for example, regardless of how much he had gained from it, did not care to repeat the experience of his acting class again.

BLIND SPOTS OF NATURE

Evolution left each of us with imperfect vision. Though we are born with a physiological blind spot, we do not notice it because our brain fills in the blank to give the illusion that nothing is missing. When we learn of this physical phenomenon as children, we play with it, moving a paper with two dots a few inches apart back and forth until, like magic, one of them disappears. We show the trick to our friends and then forget about it. In childhood, this defect in our vision is insignificant. But when we come of age and start driving cars, our blind spot can get us killed if we forget to compensate for it.

We also have a psychological blind spot, one that affects how we see the world. From birth, our brain transforms chaotic stimulation that assaults us into order by making each of us the center of his own perceptual universe. Our senses distort the reality our minds create by giving each of us the illusion that we are central.

This illusion is fundamental to our consciousness, to our passion to survive, as individuals and as members of the human species, to our will to protect what is ours. We love our own and esteem what we love—family and friends, tribe and community; but the grandiose vision of ourselves also makes us small, mean, selfish, and petty. The illusion of our centrality diminishes others while it enlarges ourselves. It cripples our relationships as we think of ourselves first and judge all others by the way they affect us. Young and old, we rage when others puncture our illusion.

Like primitives who believe the sun revolves around the earth, we imagine our parents' lives as revolving around our own. As we grow up, they provide for us and care for us. We believe their love to be our birthright. Our sense of entitlement demands that they live to make the emotional world of our childhood a good one, that they be fair, just, loving, and wise.

In evolutionary terms, the parents' job is to protect and maximize the survival of their offspring. We often feel resentful and cheated if we believe our parents did not do such a good job of it. To mature, however, we need to grow beyond the limited, self-centered views of childhood and try to understand our parents' reactions from their perspective.

It is an illusion to think ourselves the center of the universe, and another illusion to think we know our parents well. Our familiarity with our parents' typical responses to situations and provocations supports the latter illusion, but we do not know them as well as we think. We can live our entire lives unaware of how little we know about them.

As a neurologist, Freud coined the term *agnosia,* Greek for "not knowing." After a stroke or injury to the brain, physicians use the term to describe a patient's frustrating inability to recognize the familiar—the name of an object, the face of a relative, or an article of clothing. The now archaic term *anosognosia* described a similar condition, except that those suffering from it are not aware of not knowing and are quite comfortable. For example, if a person suffers a stroke in an interpretive area (in the parietal area) of the nondominant half of the brain,[2] he can be unaware that he is blind. The brain continues to fill in the blanks to make it appear that nothing is missing. Similarly, when we are driving a car, because of our physiological blind spot, we can look, think we see everything near us, and never recognize that our brain has compensated for what we can't see— until we suddenly see the danger of another car looming.

To a certain extent, we all have *emotional* anosognosia. Perceiving our parents' lives as revolving around our own, we are oblivious to their experience. We expect too much, demand too much, reject too much, and then carry those same attitudes into other relationships. We judge parents on our terms, not theirs. We are predisposed to see them through the eyes of our childhood even as adults. We regard our parents as immutable, a part of our landscape. We are born into their world, and in our childhood their lives seemed etched in granite.

Our parents are so deeply etched in our consciousness that we miss the key events of their lives even as they stare us in the face. The stories we hear about their past can have the unreal quality of ancient myth. Furthermore, what we do learn about these events usually comes out piecemeal—a word here, a nostalgic memory there. These stories become a part of our family's lore, like little fables strung together; but the day-to-day reality of those stories constitutes the bedrock of our emotional formation. We rarely put all the stories together to imagine a parent's whole life evolving. As we get older, we still do not necessarily see that their lives are as fluid and as shifting as our own.

FREUD'S BLINDNESS

Contemporary psychological understanding rests on the foundation of Sigmund Freud's insights. Regardless of subsequent criticism or theoretical diversity, his vision altered how we perceive our own natures. Freud regarded his work as a beginning, a work in progress. The directions he chose opened doors to new exploration and understanding. His concepts of the unconscious as well as the preeminence of the psychological formation of the individual in early childhood are now widely accepted. We owe a debt to the genius of Freud's analysis and the brilliance of his singular perspective.

The restricted focus of self-analysis left Freud with substantial gaps in his own self-understanding. Freud was nineteen months old when his eight-month-old brother Julius died,[3] but in the body of his work and self-analysis, Freud's brother's death appears only as a footnote. Freud's writings record amazement at his awareness of death and the depth of his grief as a two-year-old. He recalls intense feelings of jealousy following his brother's birth, and he describes a lifelong tendency toward self-reproach for the "fulfillment of the evil wishes he had against his rival."[4] Years later, Freud fainted twice while arguing with Jung about the importance of the death wish. Freud attributed his fainting to the death of his brother.[5] But Freud and his biographers write little else about this event. Freud never put his brother's death in adult perspective, nor did he examine the effect of his brother's death on his parents. How can we explain Freud's failure to examine the cataclysmic impact that the death of his brother surely had on his parents and the emotional world of his home?

> *And Jacob rent his garments and put sackcloth upon*
> *his loins, and mourned for his son many days.*
> *And all his sons and all his daughters rose up*
> *to comfort him; but he refused to be comforted;*
> *and he said: "Nay, but I will go down to my son mourning."*
> *And his father wept for him.*
>
> Genesis 37:34–35

> *O my son Absalom, my son, my son Absalom!*
> *would God I had died for thee,*
> *O Absalom, my son, my son!*
>
> 2 Samuel 18:33 (King James Version)

The Death of Jakob and Amalia Freud's Son

When Sigmund Freud was born, his father, Jakob, was forty years old, a widower with two grown sons, already a grandfather. Freud's mother Amalia, Jakob's second wife, was twenty-one. In his biography, Ernest Jones describes Freud's father as aloof:

His father represented to his son the principles of denial, restraint, restriction, and authority. . . . There is no reason to think, however, that his own father was sterner than fathers usually are.[6]

Freud's eldest son, Martin, describes his grandparents differently, however:

Every member of my family loved Jakob and treated him with great respect. He was tall and broad-shouldered, . . . terribly nice with us children. He brought us small presents and he used to tell us stories, mostly with a little twinkle in his great brown eyes. . . .

When he died . . . my father wrote to his friend Dr. Fliess: "By one of the dark ways behind the official consciousness, my father's death has affected me profoundly. I had treasured him highly and had understood him exactly. With his peculiar mixture of deep wisdom and fantastic lightness he had meant very much in my life. . . ."[7]

Grandmother came from East Galicia, . . . these Galician Jews, had little grace and no manners; and their women were certainly not what we should call "ladies." They were highly emotional and easily carried away by their feelings. . . . These people are not easy to live with, and grandmother, a true representative of her race, was no exception. She had great vitality and much impatience; she had a hunger for life and an indomitable spirit.[7]

Adoring his mother and uncomfortably distant with his father, Freud's self-analysis led him to the discovery of the Oedipus complex but not to the family's grief. Were he to have looked back at his brother's death from his parents' point of view, Freud would have realized that he had been bathed in his parents' sorrow throughout his formative years. Their loss would have sapped them of life and laughter. By the time his parents could once again project the joy that affirms children, an ocean of a child's time would have passed.

As an adult, Freud, like so many people, suffered recurrent periods of lassitude. During those times, he felt weak and fatigued; he needed and wanted to do many things, but lacked the motivation and energy. Not imagining his parents' emptiness and sorrow while raising him, Freud believed his "neurasthenia" to be constitutional. Unconsciously, grieving adolescents and adults often try to make themselves feel right by using alcohol and drugs. They may do things they later regret in order to fill an emptiness they don't understand. When Freud discovered the energizing effects of cocaine, he thought it was the answer to mankind's problems, writing his "Cocaine Papers" and encouraging his friends to try it.

The death of Julius must have shattered Freud's childhood home. Losing a child is the worst thing that can happen to parents. The unshed tears for even a stillborn child have major ramifications for a marriage and a family[8] and may affect the next generation.[9] After the death of a living child, most parents believe they have lost touch with reality.[10]

When couples lose a child, they tend to withdraw from each other.[11] Parents often silently accuse themselves and each other for having failed to alter fate; a thousand "if only"'s and life would have been different. In words or silence, this blame divides two people who need each other more than ever.[12]

Families grow stronger when parents talk openly about their feelings. Without continual dialogue, however, a couple in mourning can be at cross-purposes in healing and shear apart with the discordant rhythms of their grief: one parent wants to rise above grief, while the other needs to express it. One spouse feels the other drags him down, while that other spouse feels abandoned. Each parent evokes the other's pain as they interrupt each other's blessed moments of forgetfulness. The infrastructure of the marriage fissures even as external forms appear to be the same. For a painfully long time, both parents need to "talk it out," to restore the intimacy of their marriage.

Sigmund Freud's parents apparently did not talk much. Freud's father spent a lot of time away from the family. Jakob Freud was depicted as distant and aloof in his own home, though less with others. Granddaughter Judith Heller recalls:

> [Jakob] . . . lived somewhat aloof from the others in his family, reading a great deal—German and Hebrew—and seeing his own friends away from home. He would come home for meals, but took no real part in the general talk as the others.[13]

Silence is self-perpetuating. In a marriage of distance, husbands and wives get their emotional fulfillment where they can and defend against further hurt as much as possible. Jakob Freud had a special relationship with his eldest daughter.[14] Sigmund had one with his mother. Freud knew he was his mother's favorite; she doted on and lavished attention on him, more than on his father. About himself, Sigmund Freud wrote, "A man who has been the indisputable favorite of his mother keeps for life the feeling of a conqueror."[15]

In an undivided home, parents work together to avoid showing favoritism toward one child or another. When parents become emotionally distant from one another, however, they divide the children among themselves, designate favorites, and often turn to their children for the love they feel their spouses deny them. Whatever the emotional climate in Freud's home before the death of Julius, experience tells us that there must certainly have been an emotional shift afterward.

Displacing him in his mother's affections left Freud with an uneasy, competitive sense of superiority over his father that he tried to conceal. Dissecting the uneasiness that compelled his attention inward as a child, the Oedipus complex Freud described was less subtle in his family than in most. The feelings left him estranged from his father as a child and hungering for masculine intimacy.[16] Freud's image of his father was in marked contrast to that of Freud's son Martin.

Freud claimed to understand his father totally, but describes his distance from his father as if it were a given, not an occurrence that had its own evolution and equilibrium. Had Freud imagined his father's life, he would have imagined his first wife dying, attending her funeral, and grieving after her death. He would have imagined his parents' joy at marriage, then their inconsolable grief at the death of his brother. He would have understood what it was like for his father to find the oldest son in his second family, his firstborn, so distant and uncomfortable in his presence.

Failure to see through another's eyes causes a fragmentary understanding that can keep a relationship frozen at a superficial, stereotypic level. It is a mistake to hold on to a child's perception when we are capable of reevaluating those we love with the understanding of maturity. When we imagine someone's life before, during, and after an unexpected painful turn of events, the depth of the new understanding can be as healing as it is startling.

Therapeutic worlds have been constructed on the foundation of Freud's legacy, but assumptions implicit in his work reflect the blindfold of biological and cultural bias we all share. Because he did not imagine his parents' experience, Freud overlooked immense forces within his own history, as did his biographers and countless therapists who have followed.

ANCIENT WISDOM

Before Freud and the dawn of psychotherapy, people healed emotional wounds through the counsel of faith and religious wisdom. The wisdom of the past has been circuitously rederived in contemporary therapies, as if it were newly authored or rediscovered. Despite the limitations of its self-oriented perspective, psychotherapy, like the millennial wisdom of religion, urges us to move beyond biology and the harmful illusions of our egocentric reality.

The First Commandment, "I am the Lord thy God," is not a commandment at all but a reminder of our proper place: we are neither supreme nor central in the universe. Biblical wisdom tries to make us see beyond the distortion of our vision to grow beyond our limitations.

Pure biological instinct demands no spiritual or emotional growth. In fact, *our spiritual growth and emotional maturity occur in opposition to instinct—against the grain of our natural inclinations.* Interpretations we make as children do not change unless we get new information or, as we will see later, practice self-confrontation.

Traditional American Plains Indians believe that each of us is born with a particular way of seeing the world, but because our natural viewpoint is incomplete, we must learn the wisdom of other ways of seeing. Everyone in the tribe once understood this. They displayed their strengths and weaknesses in symbols that men exhibited on their shields and on belts women wore around their waists so each member of the tribe could help the others with their strengths and receive help for their weaknesses.[17]

The Jewish scholars of Talmud and Torah, too, believe that we each have a natural way of seeing, a way of responding to the world:

> For someone to realize his potential, he must know his own strengths and weaknesses, and understand . . . that no individual is perfect, but that the community, by melding diverse outlooks . . . gives each of its members opportunities for spiritual growth. . . .[18]

We restrict our lives unless we allow those we care about to witness our vulnerability and help us in our weakness; our lives lack meaning unless we help others with our strengths. In the egocentric world, we are prisoners of a narrow vision. Our sense of centrality causes us pain all our lives: we take everything that hurts us personally, and our view of ourselves makes it difficult to see things otherwise. Habitual emotional reactions steer us into the familiar patterns that evoke familiarly painful responses that keep us from discovering new perspectives.

The wisdom and holy works of the world's major cultures and religions would have us see beyond the limitations of our biological inheritance. They ask us to transcend the self-centeredness of our vision and imagine how we would feel in someone else's situation. Arising from the teachings of Christ, Moses, Muhammad, Plato, and Confucius, the Golden Rule propels us to maturity and exhorts us to "Do unto others as you would have others do unto you." As adults, we mouth the words; and in our minds we hear it in the same singsong voice of childhood.

OUR BIOLOGICAL INHERITANCE
A Reluctance to Imagine Another's Reality

When we are in a conflict with an intimate—a parent, a spouse, a child, a friend—we urgently want the other person to understand why we are right and they are wrong. We do not rest until the other person can understand us. We have neither patience nor compassion for the other's position. Understanding and anger are contradictory emotions. During conflict, our bodies' neuroendocrinological reactions to those we love are the same as the ones we have to our enemies. The surge of adrenaline comes with combat and directs us to fight. The hardness of anger is supposed to exclude the soft vulnerability of compassion. Whether emotional or physical, we fight for survival, not understanding.

In the company of our enemies, we wear armor to protect ourselves, and we are fools to take it off. But the defenses we continue to wear in the company of our intimates reject them by implication. We hurt them, they hurt us, back and forth, the conflict self-perpetuating—until trust intervenes, and we risk revealing ourselves and make ourselves vulnerable.

The blind antagonism that we have toward others maintains the illusion that we see them all too well. But antagonism itself is blind; in the grip of hostile feelings, we know our enemies only for infringing on us. That's all we see, and that's all we want to know. Hurt draws us inward, dominating our consciousness so that other points of view become invisible to us. Long-standing conflicts can go on for years, as we stay entrenched in our own positions.

Within the emotionally reverberating circuits of our relationships, the pain we cause to those we love returns to hurt us again. We need to understand the other person's perspective and broaden our own to resolve these conflicts. To understand our own lives and understand our parents, we must see ourselves objectively. To do this, we must consider the evolution and biology of our emotional formation and return to our first relationship with our parents.

CHAPTER 3

WHY WE CAN'T "JUST GET OVER IT"

The Psychobiology of Wounded People

The dead replay their tragedy on our fleshly stage.
Francine Thompson, *Health and Holiness*

Remembered or not, the intense emotions from our earliest years have enduring effects. Emotions associated with traumatic times may be passed on to children and continue to be passed on for generations. Regardless of whether this assertion strikes us as bold, doubtful, or obvious, science helps us consider the truth of this and, paradoxically, have a better emotional feel for it. To answer questions about our nature, we need to examine ourselves in the broader context of nature. To see ourselves and our parents from a more objective perspective, we must look at how human beings evolved and how our biology causes us to respond.

THE PARENT-CHILD BOND

The love of parents goes to their children,
but the love of these children goes to their children.
Babylonian Talmud, *Sotah* 49a

Parents and children cannot help but love one another; the reciprocity of love between them runs beneath the surface of even the most impaired relationships.[1] Our biology makes our need for love part of our inheritance. If that were not so, children would not survive their parents' intermittent anger, weariness, and longing for freedom.

Sociologist William Graham Sumner, in his classic book *Folkways,* writes:

> Children add to the weight of the struggle for existence of their parents. The relation of parents to child is one of sacrifice. The interests of children and parents are antagonistic. The fact that there are, or may be, compensations does not affect the primary relation between the two. It may well be believed that, if procreation had not been put under the dominion of a great passion, it would have been caused to cease by the burden it entails.[2]

Raising a child triggers parental feelings the way hormone production triggers puberty. Even the most analytic and hardened of people cannot maintain a neutral face when talking about their children. Love for a child comes to exceed a parent's love of his own life: a mother becomes a lioness protecting her cub; a father will kill or be killed for his child. Encoded with evolution's intelligence of a billion years, our biology directs us to survive and perpetuate ourselves, to protect our children with our lives and raise them until they can survive on their own. The whole of our biology is dedicated to that end. Species that are flawed, uncompetitive, or unable to adapt become extinct.

THE EVOLUTION OF HUMAN REACTIONS

The way we act today is the result of successful evolutionary changes insuring the survival of our species. The emotional reactions arising in our brains have been forged in evolutionary stages common to other vertebrates. Like movies using time-lapse photography, newborns emerge from the womb having compressed a billion years of evolution into a nine-month span, growing from a single cell to a multicellular creature that then differentiates into various structures. A primitive neural cord sequentially forms the brain structures of fish, reptiles, mammals, and primates, including humans. Within the womb, our nervous system enlarges with increasingly complex layers that match the patterns set by evolution.[3]

The distinct human ability to assimilate and integrate information and to communicate with others derives from a highly and relatively recently evolved cerebral cortex. Our cortex gives us a capacity to adapt to a greater variety of environments than that of any other vertebrate. This ability has extended the human habitat from the Arctic Circle to the Equator. When we are absorbed in the artificial structures of our daily lives, it is easy to forget that we are a part of nature. Nevertheless, the imperatives of our genes know nothing of civilization or technology.

Reflexes essential to survival are encoded in genes or are branded into the nervous system by traumatic experience. Genetic inscriptions provide for a successful response to a *specific* situation. If the environment changes, however, the responses are generally unvarying and inappropriate. For example, each type of spider is genetically encoded to build its own distinct highly patterned web. If a fly should fall into the web, the resulting vibrations signal the spider to scamper down its web to the fly. The spider, however, has no flexibility of response. If the fly is put in the spider's nest, which is located apart from the web, the spider will flee rather than pursue. It reacts to the fly in the nest as a threat, not as food. The spider cannot generalize.

The human ability to adapt and survive is purchased at the cost of requiring experience to recognize and respond to threat. Situations of danger require immediate response, not complex analysis. Lacking specific genetic inscription, evolutionary survival requires the human brain and body to reflexively recall reactions that allowed us and our ancestors to survive in the past. People "instinctively" recognize threatening situations—dark streets, menacing behavior, general dangers. But in humans, "instinctive" reactions are first learned by generalizing from previous experience or from mirroring a parent's reaction in early childhood. A young child seeing a scorpion for the first time may approach it in all innocence; but it only takes one sting, or a single experience of his mother's terror, to make him jump back from scorpions for the rest of his life. Hearing the backfire of a car while walking down the street, most people turn to look and see what is going on. But the pedestrian who has experienced combat reacts physiologically, readying himself for an attack that does not happen.

When the world is constant, lessons of the past enhance future survival. For example, adults as a whole are safer drivers than teenagers, not only because they are more skilled and less reckless, but because they are also likelier to have had and learned from a greater variety of frightening experiences. But nature never foresaw that the world surrounding us could change so quickly. In only an instant of evolutionary time, we have had to adapt to many different environments; the modern world of man's construction changes far faster than the evolutionary one. When the world changes, old adaptive responses may be maladaptive in the new situation; and nature left no easy mechanism to unlearn lessons that were meant to be permanent. To change traumatically learned maladaptive behaviors, we must go against the grain of our "natural" reactions, and we sometimes have to go against forces of nature that are profound and compelling.

THE PHYSIOLOGY OF FEAR

Scientists believe that the *locus ceruleus,* a collection of nerve cells embedded in the midbrain, triggers the massive physical response necessary for people to survive situations of danger.[4] Dense with norepinephrine, the neurotransmitter responsible for fight-or-flight reactions, the locus ceruleus signals the adrenal medulla, the inner part of the adrenal gland, to release adrenaline in response to a threat. With the release of adrenaline, the heart speeds up and contracts harder. Blood pressure rises; the arteries of the heart open. The arteries of the skin, lungs, digestive system, and kidneys constrict, while the blood supply to muscles increases. The liver releases stored sugar for more energy. Lung muscles relax and allow an easier flow of air. The spleen squeezes itself to push more blood cells into circulation. The body is poised and ready to act, and it learns to associate this response with specific threats.

Memory for traumatic events does not decay like ordinary learning. Norepinephrine and epinephrine (also known as adrenaline) released in traumatic situations intensify long-term memory[5] and leave an indelible mark.[6] Similar physiological states can later trigger memory, and memory in turn can trigger associated physiological reactions. The father who sees a mess and rages at his children for making it is likely to have had a parent who did the same. Once the brain has been sensitized by this kind of learning, even fragmentary cues of potential threat can activate emergency alarm systems[7] passing by the slower processes of thought. Brain function alters,[8] leaving the locus ceruleus hyperresponsive for decades.[9] Adults wounded in childhood often resent their traumatized, neurophysiologically altered parents, unaware that their parents' moods and emotional reactions were not simply learned, but were derived from biological responses beyond their control. Norepinephrine indelibly inscribes trauma on the memory and sensitizes the brain so that we repeat the neurophysiological reactions of a traumatic experience in flashbacks.

"Flashbacks," the sudden, startling intrusions into the present of fragments of feelings, thoughts, or sensations from the past, is a term generally associated with extreme examples of trauma, like the soldier reliving a combat experience, or the woman who reexperiences her rape when attempting to have intercourse. But there are also common, everyday examples of past traumatic events that intrude on everyday life, though we do not necessarily recognize them. These may be the familiar "blue moods" that come on us on cloudy days, or certain times of the year, or for no identifiable reason. Such moods evoke periods of time in our distant past. Like the flashbacks of combat veterans, they are states of being with their own feelings, physiology, thoughts, and expressions.

Flashbacks cause confusion when they are not recognized as feelings from the past. When married couples fight, for instance, triggers to memory often bring past emotions into present-day life, where they complicate marital relationships. As we will discuss at greater length, emotionally charged feelings from childhood often return, seem current, and incite misperceptions. These are the charged reactions that others find abusive.

EMOTIONAL ARREST
Frozen in Time

Years ago, I treated an elderly woman who had a whining quality to her voice that at first left me so hostile that I didn't trust myself to speak. With the inspiration that sometimes comes from desperation, I asked her, "What would your mother do when you talked like that?" She laughed, knowing exactly what I was talking about, then said, "Why, she'd slap me right across the mouth. She never did know how to deal with me." I'm sure my patient's children never knew how to deal with her either.

Consider trauma's neurobiological consequences: if they are blessed with advantages that their parents did not have, children of traumatized parents are likely to mature beyond their parents' emotional age. But growing up with a parent's immature volatility is itself traumatic and lonely for a child. Later, when he encounters someone bearing traits resembling the parent's, he may react with the same immature response he once made to his parent's. Forged in the heat of repeated childhood injury, these reactions persist and only diminish when they are reevaluated at a point of greater maturity, when adult children understand their parents' injury and realize their own advantage.

To understand our parents, we must sometimes think of them as children. The parent who habitually shouts at his children or abuses them is not expressing mature emotions but rather the feelings of a hurt child who was shouted at or abused himself.

A child cannot integrate a traumatic experience at a mature level. An adult who has suffered a great loss at the age of nine retains part of himself that is still nine years old. His character subsequently forms in response to the injury, and part of him is still frozen at the age he was when the trauma occurred.

Loss and trauma require that we adapt, reconcile ourselves to what happened, and then integrate the experience into our lives. To accomplish this, involvement with external life stops for a time. We are drawn inward and pay less attention to the world outside. Then, after enough time and consolation, we take in the experience, make it a part of ourselves. Only then can we truly move on.

WHEN THE LESSONS OF THE PAST OUTLIVE THEIR USEFULNESS
The Attempt to Achieve Balance

When we are helpless and threatened, neurobiological alterations cause symptoms of posttraumatic stress disorder. The heightened physiological arousal that results from trauma causes irritability, an exaggerated startle reflex, hypervigilance, and insomnia. At night, traumatic memories take the form of recurring dreams and nightmares; during the day, fragments of traumatic memories take the form of flashbacks.

After a severe traumatic experience, any trigger to the old neurochemical responses is so disruptive to physical and mental balance that survivors with posttraumatic stress disorder consciously and unconsciously try to avoid thoughts and situations that might recall such reactions. Since there is no adequate cause for these emotions in the present, survivors can make no meaningful responses to them. In order to cope, the brain damps down neurophysiologically to protect itself, resulting in blocks to memory, feelings of emotional numbness, detachment, emotional constriction (such as being unable to feel love), and a dulling of the appreciation of life's vibrancy.[10]

If parents were traumatized, they have nervous systems that underreact in everyday life and overreact when they reach their threshold of stress. When they overreact, they are prone to be impulsive, angry, and quick to fear; and when they underreact, they may be depressed and inattentive. As adults, they tend to be erratic parents who avoid the closeness that their children need because they are unable to sustain, and at times tolerate, the intense feelings necessary for intimacy. Not a few of them abuse substances of one sort or another, looking for anesthesia and relief from pain. As memories erupt as flashbacks, they take precedence over the less-intense present reality. This flood of feelings must then be witnessed and comforted, or it will be repressed and contained once again.

The brain numbs itself to the effects of trauma until the person can consciously accommodate the experience.[11] Until then, however, the numbness makes the sufferer feel as if he were partially dead. Some people will do anything to feel alive again: use alcohol to anesthetize pain, use amphetamines or cocaine to override the bad feelings, or take heroin to relieve the pain and to feel its amniotic warmth. Some people even use a knife to cut their own skin—the numbness is so terrible that piercing it with anything is a relief.

As seen in combat veterans, the phenomenon we call posttraumatic stress disorder is a result of normal emotional learning; posttraumatic stress becomes a disorder only when the lessons of the past become obsolete. When the world changes, the imprint of old, otherwise protective memories may summon reflexive responses that offer nothing useful in the new situation.

Such was the case for Jonathan, a Vietnam War veteran. Recently married and the father of a newborn, Jonathan sought psychiatric help, fearing that he might harm his wife or child in an explosion of rage:

> Before Vietnam, I was just a small-town boy. I was a good athlete, good student, popular; but I never felt like I measured up to my father. My father received a Bronze Star in World War II. I wanted him to be proud of me. After high school, I enlisted and went to Vietnam. I got commendations for bravery and had several field promotions. When I finished my tour, I reenlisted. After my second tour, I couldn't relate to any of my friends or family. I'd been using drugs. Combat was a thrill for me and I was good at it. By the time I left Vietnam, I'd done four tours. I loved it at the time, but I

became a monster. Some of the stuff I got off on was pretty sick. Now I'm no good for the military because I can't take discipline, and I can't take being a civilian either. The other day in a bank, the teller kept doing paperwork and ignored me. My heart started pounding; the blood was beating in my ears. I began to shake. I had to get out of there before I reached over and snapped his neck. I live on an island with my wife and my kid. I stay away from people. I'm afraid of what I might do—and I'm terrified that I might lose it with my family.

Jonathan's reactions were not abnormal under conditions of battle. Actually, in the world of our distant ancestors, he might have been the hero-warrior whose exploits were recounted in an epic poem. In Vietnam, Jonathan's readiness for battle had been honed to perfection—he had learned the ways of jungle fighting, and adaptations at the midbrain quickened his reflexes to keep him alive. When he returned home, however, reactions that were good for him in Vietnam became a danger in society.

The adrenaline surge in response to threat is fundamental to human survival, and once encoded, it triggers rapidly. We see this phenomenon when traffic gets increasingly dense: collisions and near mishaps increase in frequency, subjecting drivers to more frequent norepinephrine spikes and adrenaline rushes. Pressured by time and unreleased emotions, drivers become angry and aggressive. Civility is the result of our habitual restraint of such primal emotions. As we mature, we learn to moderate adrenaline-charged emotions, but we never entirely erase them. Not uncommonly, ordinary people who regard themselves as peaceful use two tons of automobile as a threat. "Road rage," an expression of unconstrained anger in a commonplace situation, is shocking when it occurs, but recognizable.

Perhaps had Jonathan been older, his character more formed and less impressionable, he would have been better able to make the transition back to his own society. But Jonathan was an adolescent when he was sent to Vietnam. He was released from the habitual constraints of civilization during a time when his character was still forming.

Acting without restraint is satisfying. In the quiet confessional of a psychiatric practice, people who have killed enough to no longer be sickened by it describe the cold surge of power that comes from knowing that another person's life is in their control.[12] But those who develop a taste for violence can no longer fit into normal society without putting themselves under continual self-restraint. Without drugs to dampen or situations that call for adrenaline-enhanced emotions—excitement, fear, or anger—their lives become a nightmare of unwanted feelings and disturbing dreams. With time, a teacher, and great effort, Jonathan might have learned to adapt again to a peaceful society, but to do so he would have to struggle to actively oppose his impulse. Evolution expects permanence when the young and still-forming are programmed for battle.

THE ABUSIVE HOME

In a world of threat and war, the child who survives a violent home may have an evolutionary advantage. Abusive parents quicken their children with rage or cripple them with fear. The child watches for dangers, remains alert, reads his parent's mood, and tries to avoid provoking the parent to action. Many adults who were abused in childhood find it hard to live in peace—like Manny, a gravelly voiced man in his late forties. He is the father of a son he rarely sees, and he lives and works where he can. Before being sent to Vietnam at eighteen, Manny already had the hair-trigger reflexes of an abused child. The courts ordered him into treatment after a particularly bad fight:

> I've not done well. I'm always getting into trouble. I get into fights, chop up a neighbor's hose. My father was alcoholic. When he smacked me around, I spit in his face: I knew he was crazy, so I learned to react and run. It stood me in good stead when Death stared in my face.
>
> When I returned from my second tour in Vietnam, I was called a baby killer. It was constant stress. I saw ear trophies hanging from the belts of other soldiers. At first I thought Vietnam was like World War II, then I knew it was an improper war. I don't know what became of my friends. I cry thinking about it. You never really get over it. The alcohol double-crossed me. It used to numb, but now it intensifies my feelings and it's dangerous for me to drink. I don't know who's going to get hurt. The longest I've been clean and sober was 126 days in a treatment center, but I relapsed the day I left. Suicide seems to be the preferred method of going out among my peers. I don't want that, but inside me, the feelings reach a point where I just have to have a drink.

A violent upbringing sharpened Manny's ability to survive combat. Battle quickened his keen reflexes even more. Like so many people whose nervous systems had been ignited by violence, he was unable to adjust to conditions of peace and tried to disarm himself with alcohol. Children who grow up in abusive homes or with depressed parents usually suffer lifelong symptoms of stress and depression as a result.[13]

Until 1995, PTSD was not acknowledged in children under age four.[14] Adults who survived severe abuse as children, however, clearly demonstrate the same symptoms of PTSD that Vietnam War veterans do[15]—flashbacks, nightmares, increased vigilance and reactivity, avoidance of situational reminders. They often become numb to ordinary, everyday experience. Abused children often show signs of a hyperreactive nervous system or have symptoms of depression.[16] Unless they find a refuge with a comforting adult or an absorbing childhood interest to help restore them to balance, the relentless return of bad feelings leaves the survivors of such trauma despairing that they will ever be whole. When they grow up their lives are still dominated by the aftermath of trauma.

Although we can wish that this were not so, the parent who was brutalized as a child has been irrevocably, biologically altered. The brutality is stamped onto the brain and endocrine system, and the damage cannot be fully repaired.[17] When a child watches his mother being beaten with a hammer, his nervous system screams with fear and helpless anger, his locus ceruleus electrifies his norepinephrine-charged brain, and his whole body becomes adrenaline-excited. Afterward, the child's entire neural network flashes fire when, suddenly and again, he is violently beaten for an insolent look, for dropping a glass of milk, or for losing a jacket. When he becomes a parent, his nervous system will electrify again when his own children act insolently, or break a glass, or lose a jacket. When aroused to anger, he, too, may beat his wife.

Abusive parents are usually driven by flashback emotions. Although a father who had been abused as a child may be determined not to inflict the brutality he suffered on his children, small triggers can trip the hammer of the old response. Fear transforms to anger when the threat has passed. No longer afraid or helpless, he may express to his children and intimates the rage he could not express to his parents when he was a child. Now, during the moments of rage, he feels like the master and not the victim. After having such a rage, Alex, a twenty-eight-year-old father, enrolled in an anger-management class:

My father used to beat the hell out of me if I did anything wrong. I promised I'd never treat my kids that way. But once, when my son was six and he lied to me for the fourth time in a day, I had a sudden vision of being unable to believe him as he got older. I had the thought, "I'm losing my son." Everything went black inside me. My son took one look at me, saw my face, and then started to run. When I caught him, I threw him against the wall and started slapping him. He was crying and shrieking, but I kept slapping him. We were both sobbing when I stopped. I felt sick. If I had closed my fists, I would have killed him.

Children do not understand that parents rage out of helplessness, not strength. Rage is a counterfeit, not an outgrowth, of power; but parents in the grip of rage seem immensely powerful to a small and frightened child. Later, that child may also rage at his own children when feeling helpless. Even recognizing that he is acting like a once-feared parent, he may not (or perhaps cannot) stop. Rage is overwhelming and immediately rewarded in its expression, behaviorally as well as neurochemically: a child shuts up, a wife toes the line. When anger-driven action is effective, brain norepinephrine plummets,[18] and adrenaline rapidly deactivates in the liver.[19] The intensity of the emotional flashback driving the rage diminishes and the person returns to balance. People feel more comfortable after expressing strong emotion. Remorse only comes later, when the angry mood ends and rational judgment returns.

Ordinarily, the low-level threats that cause stress and anxiety in everyday life produce less dramatic rises and falls: each time we meet a deadline, resolve an argument, or finish paying the bills, we sigh with relief. Adults abused as children, however, may have trouble coping with even ordinary, everyday stress. A woman traumatized earlier in life may become so overwhelmed as a mother that she alternates between indifference and violence in trying to set limits with her children. Despite her best intentions, she still passes the traumatic effects of her own childhood onto her children, leaving an imprint of her own psychobiological reactions on her child's nervous system.[20]

ORDINARY TRAUMA

As we age, we come to rely more on the "higher" cortical processes of words and thoughts; we rely more on what we think than on what we feel. At birth, however, the human cerebral cortex is still immature. It takes years to fully develop;[21] but the evolutionarily older, emotionally reactive part of the brain is almost completely formed.[22] As young children with an immature cortex, we are all emotionally impressionable in the literal sense. *Synaptic connections between nerve cells grow enormously just at the time when the infant's emotions are most impressionable and actively molded by the environment.*[23] As adults, we are astonished at the sensitivity of animals and children because we become emotionally blunted as we get older. As the cortex develops control over the emotionally reactive part of the brain, it inhibits the raw expression of primary emotion, dampens our receptivity, and then as adults, we no longer even imagine how exquisitely sensitive we once were.

If we fail to respect the vibrant power of a child's experience, we condescend to the children we once were, and similarly shortchange the children our parents once were. We define ourselves and our parents by the familiar moods and feelings we replay, talking in terms of character rather than of the historical events that shape character. We forget that recurring feelings have origins in past experience. Remembered or not, emotions from our early years recur in flashbacks of raw emotion throughout life. They are like mirrors reflecting parental emotions, windows on forgotten events. After a traumatic event, parents reassure themselves with the hope that a small child "won't remember," or will "get over it." But parents are the ones more likely to forget that the child's emotional makeup is still forming.

In *A General Introduction to Psychoanalysis,* Freud wrote:

> An experience which we call traumatic is one which within a very short space of time subjects the mind to such a very high increase of stimulation . . . so that lasting disturbances must result. . . .[24]

But lives are filled with ordinary traumas. Over the great expanse of childhood, our parents, too, absorbed the emotional world around them, and reacted to every event: families moved, leaving beloved family and friends behind; nannies were hired and fired; parents went away for extended absences, divorced one another, or became preoccupied with other involvements.

As adults, we can observe and partially remember, but never again do we experience the exquisite sensitivity of the child. We forget what it was like to be a child, and consequently we misunderstand our parents, our children, and ourselves. Adults require a more intense experience to create an emotional impression as deep and long-lasting as those in childhood, while even common childhood anxieties, such as those about failing school, can elicit nightmares decades later. As children, even small traumas such as a teacher's negative remark, or teasing that is trivial for an adult, make deep impressions on our characters, while the adults who are present only see normal life happening.

RESPONDING TO A PARENT'S EMOTIONS

As we shall see, unstated and outside their conscious awareness, children respond to their parents' emotions and make them their own.[25] The young are forewarned with more than just words. A tone of voice or a look brands the message with the emotion that underlies it. Even though a mother may mute the anxiety in her voice as much as possible, her child will internalize her fear. Intuitively, we know this. For example, parents who felt overprotected while growing up may have strong reactions when they watch their own son or daughter attempt something hazardous. One mother of a five-year-old son described what it was like for her:

> I was overprotected, so I don't know what good limits would be. The other day, I got scared watching my son climb a tree. I was anxious and wanted to stop him, but I knew I'd be doing the same thing as my mother. By the time I made him stop, I couldn't stand it. I shrieked at him and scared him. I know I sounded just like my mother, but I don't want him to grow up as cautious as me. I want him to grow up to be confident.

Child analysts Anna Freud and Dorothy Burlingham reported that children and toddlers trembled if their mothers trembled but not when their mothers behaved cheerfully during the German bombing raids on London during World War II.[26] Similarly, infants will explore their world when their mothers appear secure but will interrupt their activity when they are anxious.[27]

Unless psychologically damaged, mothers instinctively respond to their newborns with a heightened sensitivity, automatically providing their infants with the required balance of stimulation and soothing.[28] Rhythms and movements choreograph to harmony as a mother adapts to her infant and her infant matches her breathing, mood, sleep, and emotions, feeling every emotional nuance.[29] In the process, the mother modulates the infant's basic physiological rhythms, autonomic function, and patterns of organized behavior.

After his basic needs are met, an infant is usually serene when the mother holding him is serene; when a mother is tense, her body is tense, and the baby in her arms responds to the tension. Stressful or threatening situations that impinge on the mother also impinge on her newborn. If a mother is afraid, her breathing is rapid and shallow; her eyes dart about, watching for danger; the odor of her sweat changes; her muscles are tense, twitchy, and ready for action. Her child cannot help but respond. Biologically, survival in the world is enhanced when offspring can be left with an impression of their parents' fears and feelings. Each generation can then be impressed by the emotions learned the generation before—without having to repeat the traumatic experience themselves.

The emotional interactions between parents and young children are so finely attuned that the emotional harmonics of one make the other vibrate. For example, Frieda, a woman of thirty, was thin, quick, and nervous. She sought help because over the last several months she had lost weight and had trouble sleeping. A friend had come along to baby-sit Frieda's five-year-old daughter, Rachel. After a round of introductions, Frieda bent down to Rachel and begged her to be good. Rachel, in turn, was whining, defiant, and seemed quite capable of wreaking havoc in my waiting room. The friend held Rachel's shoulder and tried to be reassuring to both of them. Before going into my office, Frieda and her daughter looked anxiously at one another. Holding back her tears, Frieda said:

> I've always been high-strung. I have a quick temper. Growing up, I was the one my father beat the worst, and my mother never did one thing to stop him. The one time she ever spoke up for me was after he broke my collarbone. But I've never lost my temper with Rachel. I'd rather die first. But I've been losing my temper with my husband. I love him, and he's pulling away from me. He's a good father. I'm afraid of losing him. We're fighting more and more now, though never in front of Rachel. She doesn't know what's going on. We don't want to upset her. She's upset enough already. She's had tantrums even before we started having problems.

After the session, Rachel was happily playing with Frieda's friend. On seeing her mother, she tensed before running over to her.

Frieda had the hyperalert, hyperreactive nervous system of an abused child, and Rachel might have spent her entire childhood resonating with it had her mother not sought help. As her husband became distant, Frieda became even more reactive, intensifying a destructive, circular dynamic that Rachel expressed directly in tantrums. The restraint Frieda imposed on her own emotional expressions both protected her daughter and left her insecure. Frieda did not know how to set limits for Rachel. The only limits that Frieda had learned growing up had been enforced with violence. Rachel was more sensitive to her parents' stress than they were; and Rachel, reacting badly to their high level of stress, knew she was adding to it.

Frieda decided to take medication to settle herself,[30] enrolled in parenting classes, and persuaded her husband to join her in couples therapy. Rachel became calm as her mother did, and an air of goodwill returned to the home.

EMPATHIC SENSITIVITIES AND DEPRESSED PARENTS

When we are adults, the moods of others still affect us: We are moved to tears seeing others cry; being around anxious people makes us nervous; one person yawning induces others to do the same; we can sense it when someone is staring at us; we get more energized in a crowd watching a sporting event than if we watch it alone on television; it takes just one person in a mob to induce others to panic. Without saying a word, we pick up on each other's feelings. Our emotions affect those nearby. How much more sensitive, then, are children, who are not yet distanced from emotions by the damping modulatory effects of the adult cortex? Psychologist Geraldine Dawson found that depressed mothers and their infants have similarly diminished brain wave activity in their left frontal lobes.[31] If we can imagine an almost telepathic, emotional permeability in children under five, we will also understand the enormity of their sensitivity to their parents' feelings.

Psychiatrist Myrna Weissman interviewed children growing up in homes where one or both parents had suffered from a major depression. Ten years later, she evaluated these same children again. They were, at the

adult
depression
↓
Children

time of the second interview, between the ages of seventeen and thirty-six; and she found that two-thirds (67 percent) had suffered from depression, 40 percent had an anxiety disorder, a third had problems with substance abuse (this adds up to more than 100 percent because of concurrent psychiatric diagnosis). Only 20 percent of the children had not had an overt psychiatric problem. According to this study, which has been supported by many other studies in the literature, children of depressed parents are three times more likely to have problems with depression, three times more likely to have problems with panic disorders, and five times more likely to be alcohol dependent than those whose parents are not depressed.[32]

We seldom appreciate the pain that continues long after a death that occurred in a parent or grandparents' early life. As we will discuss further in the following chapter, unwitnessed grief lingers[33] and looks like depression after the acute phase is past—depressed mood, sadness, loss of interest and pleasure in ordinary activities, loss of energy, insomnia, disturbed appetite. We usually don't dwell on their ramifications, but losses barely mentioned in the telling of a family's history may have been central in molding a parent's character, and central to a melancholy strain that may have been passed on to our own lives.

There is now considerable evidence, from both animal and human research, demonstrating that neuroendocrine function—the operations of and interaction between the pituitary gland (which regulates the other endocrine glands such as the reproductive, adrenal, and thyroid glands) and the hypothalamus (which regulates basic body functions)—is permanently affected by a parent's stress and the early deprivation of empathic care.[34]

THE DENENBERG EXPERIMENTS

The stress response originates in a phylogenetically old part of the brain that is common to all vertebrates. Although researchers and theoreticians must be careful not to directly impose phenomena that they observe from other animal species onto human beings, we should not ignore them either. What is stressful, and how that stress is expressed, may vary with the animal, but there is a strong likelihood that the basic biological reactions are similar—if not the same—in all. The form and function of the autonomic nervous system of all vertebrates are remarkably similar.[35]

In 1969, research scientist Victor Denenberg, investigating stress in infant rats, discovered that early trauma has profound biological and behavioral consequences for the rest of the animal's life.[36] Furthermore, traumatic events occurring during the mother's infancy also permanently alter neuroendocrine function and the behavior of the offspring.[37] Summing up his findings, Denenberg wrote:

> We have recently demonstrated that the experience which female rats underwent during their infancy significantly affected the behavior of their grandpups.
>
> These data are particularly fascinating because we have demonstrated . . . a nongenetic method of communication across generations. My frustration arises from the fact that I do not know for how many generations this effect will extend.[38]

Rats are traumatized when handled by humans. Their survival depends on their ability to flee from danger, but when the possibility of flight has been cut off, traumatized and defeated animals will not react as strongly to danger in the future. Blood samples taken from handled rats show hormone patterns that are different from those of nonhandled rats. The rats also show changed responses in the pituitary gland and the hypothalamus. In his research, Denenberg found that when rats are handled in infancy, their hormonal and behavioral response to stress is altered throughout life. Though less pronounced, these alterations carry over to the nonhandled offspring of the next two generations, at least.

We intuitively acknowledge the accuracy of Denenberg's findings as we try to protect our children from our own childhood pain. Every generation of parents wants to do right by their children, to do as good a job or better than their parents before them. We take note of and try to avoid our parents' mistakes in the hope that we will set things right for our own children. We want to provide an atmosphere of love and serenity for our newborns. We want to be our best so our children can follow our best example. We want to nurture our children, not cripple them. We want that, our parents wanted that, their parents wanted the same, and our children will feel the same way when they have children. But life has a way of thwarting good intentions.

LEARNED HELPLESSNESS AND DEPRESSION

In 1967, the research psychologist Martin Seligman noticed that dogs given inescapable shocks stopped trying to escape the stress of being shocked even when they later had control over the situation.[39] His work led to a theoretical model for the development of depression. Rats that have previously been unable to escape unwanted human handling will drown in a bucket of water, whereas nonstressed rats can endure there for hours. Resignation typifies the learned helplessness of depression. Initially helpless to escape the unknown human giants' control, the rat learns that any response is futile.[40] The rat has *learned* to be helpless. Among vertebrates and invertebrates alike, we find examples of learned helplessness throughout the animal kingdom.[41] From infancy to senescence, individuals who are unable to exert control over their environment often simply give up.

As newborns, we only have the power of the scream. The distress cry of an infant, for all primates, is compelling and disturbing throughout life.[42] More than any other species, a human infant must compel care. Since he cannot cling to mother's fur or go seek out his parents, the survival of our species requires that an infant's cry, in particular, disturbs the person caring for him. Adults who batter or kill their infants often later describe their desperation to stop the baby's crying. The infant who cannot summon the world to the bidding of his cry learns that he is helpless to command what he needs from life. He reacts to his world with the entirety of his being. If his mother does not respond to his cries, his whole world shatters and then is made whole again when she comforts him.

Normally, an intense bond forms when infants lock wide-open eyes with their mother's in a gesture that is forever understood to be one of love and trust.[43] If a mother does not reciprocate her baby's eye lock, the infant begins to struggle, trying to make contact with her.[44] The baby will extend its arms trying to reach for its mother's face. After that period of struggle, the baby slumps, becoming flaccid and, to all external appearances, depressed. After a period of rest, the baby begins to struggle for attention again, but this does not last as long as the first period of struggle. The period of slumping lasts longer. The third attempt at contact is of even shorter duration and the slump again longer.[45] The baby learns that struggle is futile and appears depressed.

THE TRAUMA OF INTERRUPTED LOVE

Having an emotionally unresponsive mother or enduring an early separation results in the disorganization of the child's biology and behavior.[46] We can see this clearly among our close cousins in the animal kingdom. Primates react to separation from social attachments in the same way they react to a threat. Disruption of any primate mother-and-infant relationship causes an intense physiological response in the hypothalamic brain, the pituitary and adrenal glands.[47] A mother with a postpartum depression cannot provide adequate emotional contact or the sensitive empathic responsiveness her baby needs. Her depression defeats the struggles of her infant to maintain their emotional connection. In the failure of that struggle, even tiny infants experience isolation, learn futility, and may experience the first inkling of depression.

The urgency of an infant's hunger may be relieved with the warm, sweet comfort of mother's milk, but fulfilling this one basic need is not enough. Communication and the softness of a mother's touch are necessary for normal physical and psychological development and, sometimes, for survival as well.[48]

Trust and our ability to form social bonds develop from the fulfillment of our needs when we are dependent in early life. Infants require a constancy of touch, holding, and the intimacy of locking eyes with a particular caretaker while nursing or feeding. The familiar touch and smell of one person provides necessary comfort, stability, and security in a bewildering world of sights and sounds still undifferentiated by experience.

In the past, orphanages did not provide a constant source of nurturing care for their infants. It was not understood why so many of these infants suffered what they called "hospitalism"—a syndrome in which infants separated from their mothers and without consistent loving nurturing ate poorly and stopped responding to the world around them. With such extreme emotional deprivation, many infants died.

In the thirteenth century, King Frederick II, founder of the University of Naples, hoped to determine whether infants taken from their parents would spontaneously speak the original language of mankind by taking a number of infants away from their parents and putting them in the care of nurses prohibited from talking to them. The report to the king said that the experiment failed: "All the children died because they could not live without the caresses, joyful faces, and loving words of their nurses."[49]

In 1920, a pediatrician, Arthur Schlossman, studied a major orphanage in Germany where infant mortality approached 75 percent in the first year of life.[50] Attributing the high death rate to infection, he instituted strict protocols of nutrition, hygiene, and quarantine. Though death rates dropped dramatically when these reforms were instituted, a third of institutionalized infants continued to die.

The connection between a baby's emotional needs and his physical health was again recognized in 1946, when psychoanalyst René Spitz concluded that institutionalized infants who were raised under sanitary conditions but with minimal stimulation became apathetic and unresponsive. Infants six to eighteen months of age became depressed when separated from their mothers in prison. Infant mortality approached 37 percent when caregivers held children only when feeding them or when infants had rotating caregivers.[51] Astonishing as it is, many people still cannot believe that what happens in infancy has that much of an effect on a person's adult life.

Meeting someone today who survived an experience such as those described in the above studies is very rare. In all my years of practice, I've only met one such person. It took a while to unearth the history. Linda was married for eight years and worked part-time in a flower shop despite suffering recurrent depression. Her problems with depression worsened when she turned to alcohol after medical treatments did not help. I was asked to see her in the hope that something more could be done for her depression:

> An attractive woman who looked like a model, Linda fell into a reverie after briefly answering each of my questions. Without questions to prod her, she was silent and distant. She seemed unable to concentrate or capture her own thoughts long enough to describe them. I had to question gently and suggest words for her so she could pick out the ones that seemed to fit. Her husband was sick of her drinking; he wanted children and had been threatening to leave her.
>
> Linda said she had always had a hollow, lonely feeling inside her, but after leaving home to go to college ten years before, the emptiness grew into bouts of depression that lasted from hours to days despite therapy and state-of-the-art medications. Without energy or

interests, she felt dead inside at those times; her life seemed meaningless and she withdrew from others.

Linda had been raised by loving parents from the Midwest. They
had adopted her at six months and provided a good home. Neither
Linda nor her parents suffered any childhood trauma or loss, and
the troubles the family did have seemed insufficient to account for
the extremity of Linda's symptoms. Linda's parents knew nothing
about her biological inheritance or the first months of her life in an
orphanage.

One of the staff members at the residential alcohol and drug
rehabilitation facility where I worked at the time had, however,
worked as an aide in that orphanage some time after Linda was
born. She described the staff at the orphanage as small while the
number of infants was large. The infants were only picked up during
feeding.

In the light of this history, Linda's symptoms made sense; she had been
traumatized like the infants that René Spitz described. Imagining her feelings of desolation during the first months of life unlocked the mystery of
Linda's depression as an adult. As an infant, her life had been threatened
by the emotionally unresponsive world around her. As an adult, Linda's
depression had the features of an infant's apathetic depression returning. I
suspected that preverbal emotional flashbacks to a life-threatening time
added to her depression. The biological aspect of her depression may have
been successfully treated by antidepressant medications; but medication
would not help when, suddenly and seemingly without reason, she became
withdrawn, bewildered, unable to concentrate, and unresponsive—like
flashbacks to the torpor and depression of her deprived infancy. During
those times, she walked around as if in a dream, preoccupied with intrusive
feelings that interrupted her emotional response to the world around her.
I tried to imagine how Linda would be as a mother. Given her history, it was
amazing that she could function as well as she did. If she had children,
would they ever understand this?

Linda missed a crucial time of nurturing. Her parents had been unable
to fill the hollow emptiness from her early infancy completely, and she had
not been able to heal. And after moving from her adopted home as an
adult, the separation from the parents who had rescued her brought back
feelings for which she had no words: the trauma was preverbal.

In time, Linda would learn to identify and name the feelings that were indescribable to the infant she had been, and summon others to comfort her when these feelings returned, thereby impinging upon the trance state induced by replayed memories. Then she would not be as helpless as she had once been.

Linda appeared to be doing well when she left treatment, but I did not find out what happened to her till years later when I saw her on the streets. She had stopped drinking and continued therapy until her husband left her. Then her life fell apart. At the time I saw her, she was homeless but had gone back to attending AA meetings. Such severe and early damage is hard to overcome.

SEPARATIONS

Though few children in America suffer as Linda did, as a society, we do not give adequate weight to separations that children endure. Infants and young children separated from their parents have the same immediate reactions whether their parents are gone for a week or a lifetime. They only understand that the parents they depend on for their secure and loving universe are gone.

A friend recalled how he had felt when separated from his father while emigrating to America on a cattle boat at the age of three:

> I was afraid of the boat, the strangers and the confusion. During the fire drills, we all had to go on deck. I was terrified I would fall and roll under the railing into the sea, but those were the times I got to see my dad; they had separated the men and the women. One time I went looking for my father and got lost. I was terrified but kept looking anyway. I remember the ache of missing him, a desperate kind of longing. I missed him so much.

The man narrating this story was in his fifties. To find his father, the three-year-old had gone looking for him despite his terror of falling into the ocean and of leaving his mother. Yearning for reunion with his father overrode the fear. He was still able to call up the sights, sounds, and smells of the experience with a child's clarity of perception.

Often, unexplained feelings or moods associated with unappreciated separations from early childhood return to confuse us in adulthood.

Two generations ago, two weeks in the hospital was the standard period of time for recovery following most surgery. Hospitals did not routinely instruct parents to prepare children for their hospitalization, and children seldom knew what to expect. Nor did hospitals allow parents to stay with their children or to visit them extensively. Because children cried when their parents came and were more difficult to manage afterwards, doctors believed that the visiting parents upset the children and kept them from adapting. Thus, they discouraged parents' visits. In fact, children whose parents did not visit behaved "better" because they were depressed, defeated, and easier to manage. When their parents visited, children expressed themselves; when they left again, the children wept.

A man in his forties described his hospitalization for a hernia as a seven-year-old:

> I remember it so clearly. The images are still with me, the feeling of the enema going in me, the sense of outrage, being wheeled to the operating room, the taste of the ether, counting backwards from one hundred, the black and white dreams. So clear.
>
> It seemed like forever being in the hospital. I couldn't understand why my mother wasn't with me, why my parents didn't take me home. Every day there was a new kid in the bed next to me, eating ice cream after having his tonsils out. Then his parents would take him home. After a while, I got depressed. I gave up. It was such a lonely feeling. I thought I was never going home again. I think it was my first experience with depression.
>
> I had a book about a boy, without parents, who lived on his own with his dog. He did everything for himself. I read it over and over. It was my favorite book. The night before the hospital let me go, my mother brought soup. She was happy and loving and told me I was coming home the next day. It was the best soup I ever tasted. It was even better the next day. I can still taste the tang of it.

This man's hospitalization was his first experience with depression. By the time his parents had come to take him home, he had already given up. The joy of reunion filled his emptiness more than the soup. It gave him back his taste for life.

CHILD TIME

Suffer the little children to come unto me,
and forbid them not: for of such is the kingdom of God.
Mark 10:14[52]

As adults, the sheer length of our personal history makes us experience an hour as short. We sleepwalk through our daily routine, partially numbed by the repetition of our days and our (illusory) certainty of outcome. As children, by contrast, we swim in a vast ocean of time. Every experience is fresh and new; what lurks around the corner is mysterious and frightening. The length and breadth of a single day are vast. Adulthood seems a foreign province too far away to imagine. Children absorb the moment, and in that never ending present, time can be magical.

As we age, each day rushes by faster and each departing day moves to the denominator of the past. As one elderly woman said, "I feel like I'm eating breakfast every fifteen minutes." A realtor in his seventies suggested that trees planted alongside a house would ensure privacy: "When you're my age, trees seem to grow fast." One day, we wake up to find we have more past than future.

In trying to understand our parents, ourselves, or our children, we should not forget the disparity of subjective time and impressionability between adults and children. Adults can spend a lifetime trying to fill the loneliness of their childhood years. For an adult, it may take a death or the separation of years to produce loneliness; for an infant, it may take only hours.

LONELINESS

We all become lonely from time to time, but loneliness is a louder background hum to parents who grew up with it. Those who grew up surrounded by loneliness flash back to it often; even consciously seeking solitude can trigger it. The hum grows loud in silence. In company, unexpressed feelings amplify it.

Solitary communion, on the other hand, is necessary and often welcome; without it we cannot sustain ourselves. But loneliness is not the same thing as solitary communion, and in its throes, we find it hard to be motivated to do anything: pursue a goal, clean a house, get dressed, or care well for children. Lonely people need company; but if their loneliness persists to become depression, they find company hard to bear.

Loneliness transforms easily into depression. Depression *is* lonely. During periods of loneliness, as with depression, health and life are threatened.[53] Alcohol, drug use, and rates of suicide increase;[54] hearts break and heart attacks are more frequent;[55] immune function becomes depressed, causing an increased risk for infection and cancer.[56] One study examining the difference between 842 women with and without breast cancer found that women who had breast cancer were lonelier and had more often lost their intimate partner within the past three years.[57] In all cultures studied, the death rate is consistently lowest among the married, higher among the widowed, higher still among the single, and highest for the divorced.[58]

Biologist Lars Wilsson, while observing yearling beavers, noted, "If they do not get companionship, [they] may simply sit where they are put down until they die."[59] Elizabeth Thomas, in her book *The Hidden Life of Dogs,* describes the reaction of a female husky whose mate was given away:

> She stayed in the window for weeks ... with her face to the window, watching and waiting for Misha. At last she must have realized that he wasn't going to come home.... She lost her radiance and became depressed. She moved more slowly, was less responsive, and got angry rather easily.... [She] never recovered from her loss ... she showed no interest in forming a permanent bond with another male.... She also showed less interest in her children....[60]

A depressed, alcoholic man in his fifties described living with his grandmother and waiting by the side of the road for his mother after she left him there when he was five. For six years, for hours each day, he waited. He waited till love turned to bitterness and bitterness required the anesthetic of alcohol. He still had the face of a hurt little boy when I met him.

A person's first experience of depression as an infant whose needs are unmet or as a young child who suffers a prolonged separation is often forgotten. Like the infant whose experience of the world is global, undifferentiated, and all-encompassing, depression is similarly global and all-encompassing in adults. The gloom of empty feelings envelops a person's entire world. The depressed person feels unloved and unlovable. He magnifies his faults, finds justification for self-loathing, is hypersensitive to rejection, and believes that others will see through his facade to the shameful person within. He withdraws from others and into himself. His world is dark. In severe depression, despair and hopelessness take precedence. Regardless of the support and accolades of others, a severely depressed person may be too withdrawn for the external world to nurture him.[61] Not surprisingly, as we have seen, depressed parents often pass their loneliness on to their children.

Becoming depressed permits people to stop reacting to the unbearable. Depression allowed Korean "comfort women" to endure years of repeated rapes, mercifully dulling the intensity of each repeated episode. The initial violence is branded in memory with norepinephrine's fire. But as we become depressed, we are more likely to forget later injuries. Under such continued stress, the days blur into each other.

Children who are contemptuous of their battered mothers' passivity make judgments on their mothers' character but do not take their neurobiology into account. One woman described the growing despair that she felt while living with her abusive former husband:

> He started out so kind and loving. When he first hit me, I was shocked. I couldn't stop crying. He begged me to forgive him. Then, every time he hit me he was so remorseful and loving afterwards. I'd forgive him, make excuses for him, and believe that he loved me passionately. I blamed myself, too. I'd try to do better, but he beat me no matter how hard I tried. I was too ashamed to tell anybody. I pretended like everything was fine and blamed my bruises on my clumsiness. After I miscarried, he got out of control. By that time, I felt so awful I thought I couldn't do without him. He told me no one else would want a pig like me. I believed him. If he was away at night, I'd panic. It was so dark outside, I'd close the curtains. I imagined someone breaking into the house, raping and killing me. I'd actually be relieved when he came home. But I felt so bad, I was so depressed, half the time I'd walk around numb. I just gave up. I knew he was going to kill me one day.

Janet was fortunate not to have had children with him and to have a friend help her move out. It's a common story: children in abusive homes or adults in abusive relationships feel helpless and trapped. The combination of chronic high levels of stress and helplessness is a common pathway to depression.

THE PROTECTION OF DEPRESSION

. . . by the sorrow of the heart the spirit is broken.
Proverbs 15:13

Professor Hans Selye, the "grandfather of stress research," defined stress as "essentially the rate of all the wear and tear caused by life," whether illness, overwork, or loss.[62] When stress is severe and inescapable, we adapt by dulling all physiologic response. All stimuli and response become muted. The resulting state is known as depression.[63]

Depression protects against damaging physiological effects of trauma when continued arousal is futile so that adrenaline does not flow to the point where the body no longer responds to it or where the supply is depleted.[64] Biologically, it makes sense to conserve energy when efficacious action is impossible.[65] Neither the brain nor the body can tolerate intense stimulation or chronic high levels of stress for too long without sustaining long-term damage. Research has shown that experienced combat veterans with full-blown posttraumatic stress disorder will, over time, lose brain cells in the area of the brain associated with emotions and long-term memory.[66] The loss of brain cells is accompanied by impairments of memory and increased difficulty in making sense of contemporary information presented to them.[67] In other words, when intense stress becomes chronic, we shut down in self-protection and become depressed.

People with symptoms of posttraumatic stress who are frequently aroused are likely, after time, to become depressed,[68] tune out, become less sensitive, feel hopeless. The brain stimulates the outer layer of the adrenal gland to secrete cortisol, allowing the body to adapt to the unfavorable circumstance.[69]

Adults with severe symptoms of PTSD do not have increased cortisol to protect them.[70] In situations of chronic stress and depression, however, the body's cortisol level rises and remains high in order to deactivate the stress response.[71] But high levels of cortisol can themselves cause damage if they remain elevated for too long: emotional response is blunted, healing of physical injury is delayed, resistance to infection and the body's protective inflammatory response diminishes.[72] During the time we are depressed, all fight is gone. Without energy, we are left feeling confused, uncertain, and ineffectual. We blame ourselves for our failures, and our supply of self-esteem diminishes. The body accepts its helplessness and actively depresses itself, gives up for the time, surrenders, stores energy, and waits for a day of future release.

LOSS AS TRAUMA

The death and loss of those we love is a cataclysm that rocks the foundations of our lives, a catastrophic stress that is harder still for children. The trauma leaves images of last moments. Intrusive images and recurring dreams punctuate grief. Following the death of a parent, spouse, sibling, or child, symptoms of posttraumatic stress combine with grief.[73] The grief that captures us seems unendurable and endless. We are helpless. We cannot restore life.

After the death of his beloved wife, C. S. Lewis began his journal entry, "I never knew how much grief felt like fear."[74] We respond physiologically to the loss of someone we love as we do to other major traumatic events in life. There is an initial outpouring of norepinephrine and adrenaline,[75] a burst of fear. However, when faced with the death of a loved one, energy and readiness for action are useless. There is nothing to be done. Emotions that impel us to action are futile, and we cocoon ourselves in cortisol.

In the confused, frightening aftermath of a loved one's death, the impotent torrent of emotions must diminish or it will cause bodily harm. The fullness of mourning wearies us with a pervading emptiness as our bodies, minds, and spirits adapt to the unrelenting stress of loss.[76] George Eliot writes:

> There is something sustaining in the very agitation that accompanies the first shocks of trouble. Just as an acute pain is often a stimulus, and produces an excitement which is transient strength. It is in the slow, changed life that follows—in the time when sorrow has become stale, and has no longer any emotive intensity that counteracts its pain—in the time when day follows day in dull unexpectant sameness, and trial is dreary;—it is then that despair threatens.[77]

MOURNING
The Emotion

The mourning of infants separated from their mothers appears the same as the mourning of adults following a death.[78] Manifestations of grief change with maturity, and cultures fashion expression, but the core emotions of mourning remain unchanged throughout life. Mourning a loss strips us down to the cry of an infant, though the wail may constrict in our adult throats.

Psychiatrist Louis Linn, also describing mourning during infancy, writes:

> Infants . . . deprived of the attentions of a suitable mothering figure . . . [are in] a state of mourning. Some of these infants fail to thrive. They may stop eating and then waste away and die. . . . Most survive but lapse into a phase of detachment in which the infants withdraw from human relationships and become preoccupied with inanimate objects or their own body parts, engaging in masturbation, fecal smearing, head banging or rocking.[79]

Each day in the psychiatric prison where I once worked, I saw inmates regressed to the level of infants in mourning: grown men rocking, banging their heads, smearing feces on the walls, publicly masturbating. These inmates were not necessarily psychotic. But as men they were devastatingly lonely in their isolation from family and friends, even though they were surrounded by people.

Yet many of them had been even lonelier outside of prison. Prisons are filled with men and women who were hurt and denied as children, who have overridden their resulting depression with anger, violence, and expressions of impulses they never learned to control. Too wary to trust, they take what they need and control what they can, but they are unable to receive the love they most desperately need—love they can trust to be freely given. That is why so many are afraid of returning to the world outside, where they can only compensate for their loneliness with the high of a drug, for their inner emptiness with the adrenaline rush of crime.

We regress toward infancy when we are deprived of love. During those times, prison becomes a metaphor we all experience. Without the love and attention to nurture and console us, we do not grow and may not heal. We languish or regress to an earlier developmental stage when we had what we needed. Unless we have sufficient support, witness and consolation, the slide from mourning to depression is biologically seamless.

For all of us, at any age, the fundamentals of love and loss are the same. We need witness and consolation to comfort our grief and end our cries. The chapters that follow examine the effects of particular traumas with multi-generational effects that we, our parents, or our grandparents might have faced. We will examine in greater depth how grief and trauma pass on to the next generation, and then discuss life's natural opportunities to heal the wounds of the past. But first we must look at the role of having a witness to provide consolation for the damaging effects of loss and trauma.

CHAPTER 4

MOVING ON AFTER BAD THINGS HAPPEN

The Need for Consolation and Witness

Attend unto my cry; for I am brought very low.

Psalm 141:1

Having a witness for emotional pain is essential for its healing. The impact of our most painful experiences can neither be defined nor endured without the presence of another to bear witness: someone who is present, who can see, hear, care about, and so give validity to an emotionally significant event in another person's life.

We must cry and share grief to know its magnitude. How often have we been surprised at the strength of our own sudden outburst of feeling? How often have we been startled by the intensity of feelings we did not know we had? One man who had been speaking matter-of-factly about his father's death burst into tears as he described his father saying goodbye to him for the last time:

> After the divorce, when I was three, my father used to visit me on weekends, or so my mother tells me. I don't really remember it. I do remember him smiling at me as he walked out the door the last time I saw him. He said, "See you later, partner." But I never did see him again. They phoned my mom to tell her that he was killed in a car accident.

Recomposing himself he said, "I didn't know all that grief was still in me."

Witnesses give the events of our lives a resonance and fullness of perspective that we cannot supply for ourselves. The friends we trust and consider wise understand us. As bystanders to our lives, they add to our understanding of ourselves as they reflect our experience back to us.

Those who love us give witness to our lives. Unless we make our pain visible to others, we wall ourselves in and others out. On the other hand, when we allow our feelings to be known, we are strengthened enough to endure any trial.

OUR NEED FOR CONSOLATION

When family members don't talk to one another about their lives, each member must endure alone. What is a child to do when his healthier parent refuses to acknowledge an alcoholic father's behavior or a mother's mental illness? How is the child supposed to make sense of his feelings or find perspective? Events muffled in family silence are confusing to children. We need someone to be there to receive the feelings we express and to give validity and meaning to our experience. Without another to know about or share an experience with us, we cannot appreciate its full dimension, because we measure our pain against another's compassion and our joy against another's delight.

One patient, who felt herself to be friendless, wept, saying, "When good things happen, I have no one to tell." We all need someone else to share our victories, to make them complete. Achievement without a witness is still hollow, as hurt is still bitter when no one offers solace.

A hurt child runs to his parents for comfort and to "make everything all right." But hurt adults often hesitate to express their needs, for fear of being rejected, considered weak, or judged infantile. This hesitation can be crippling. Unexpressed hurt does not elicit compassion.

As adults, we can live in emotional isolation, but we will not thrive. We may comfort ourselves with food, give ourselves rewards, or release emotional pressures by crying alone, but tears in isolation are pitiless or self-pitying. Whatever our age, we need someone else to receive our grief if we are to unburden ourselves of it. Even when grief is old, compassion for its expression comforts the loss.

We instinctively turn to our intimates when we are upset. In marriage, one partner expresses pain to the other in the hope of receiving understanding and comfort. Even when we are angry and accusation distorts our expression of hurt, we want our partners to comfort us rather than condemn us for our means of expression.

When our intimates express their hurt feelings in the angry terms of attack and accusation, if we can muster enough compassion to attend directly to the underlying hurt, going against the grain of natural defensiveness to really listen to the complaint, we can often mitigate the argument. Adults who have been traumatized or suffered emotional deprivation as children are often needy, angry, distrustful, and rejecting when they most need love and consolation.

We often have the childish expectation that those who love us should notice when we are troubled, without our having to say so. But this is unrealistic and unfair. It is the honest and raw expression of pain that moves others to respond. We need to allow others to see our feelings in order to get an honest response back; if we receive a compassionate response, we are consoled by the caring.

PARENTS AS WITNESSES FOR THEIR CHILDREN

We are tribal animals and our spirits wither in isolation. Unlike reptiles, who are able from birth to go without parental care, we humans are born needing both love and comforting attention if we are to survive. A baby needs someone to hold him and watch over him, to respond to his cries and delight in his company. A toddler needs his parents' expressions of admiration over the proud accomplishment of his first steps. When the toddler falls, he often picks himself up; and with a thundercloud of tears gathering on his face, he toddles over to his parents and starts to wail only as he nears the source of his comfort. He instinctively knows that he needs his parents' reaction to his cry in order to acknowledge his pain and make it better.

A young child exhorts his parents to "Watch me! Watch me!" as he shows his mastery of physical, spiritual, and intellectual feats. If the parents watch, they see him proudly pushing himself to new levels of achievement. Feeling parental praise, the child learns to persist, or to keep his temper, or to share. If the parents do not watch, however, the face of the child falls, all life and expression drain out of him, and his interest in achievement wanes. His proud accomplishment has been rendered meaningless.

Despite their push toward independence, adolescents need their parents to be witnesses to their lives as much as younger children do. An adolescent who talks of his life as he explores what is acceptable and unacceptable presents his parents with the precious opportunity to observe a life unfolding in all its uncertainty. The parent can, in turn, offer comfort, guidance, and understanding discipline.

Even when the adolescent goes on to disregard his parents' advice entirely, he is still communicating. Adolescents who anticipate disapproval typically lapse into silence, losing the parents' direction and often losing their way. The act of a parent listening patiently to seemingly endless teenage chatter is the same loving act as that of the parent who makes the effort to look up after his child yells "Watch me."

When parents are absent, ill, addicted, or preoccupied with problems of their own, their children, particularly adolescents, try and make do without them and are often unaware of the joy they are losing or how much unconsoled grief lingers. Without their parents' witness, adolescents only trust themselves and trust others reluctantly—a habit that jeopardizes intimacy in future relationships.

Les, an apparently successful man in middle age who had worked hard to achieve his success, regarded his wife as a remarkable woman and his best friend; and his children, too, seemed to be doing well. Everything was fine, yet Les felt "kind of trapped," and lonely:

> I had a happy childhood and loving parents. There were no huge traumas in my life or my parents'. My father was stoic and unemotional, but I've always been able to talk to my Mom. The only bad thing that ever happened to me was in my senior year in high school. I damaged my shoulder. I'd already won an athletic scholarship to college; I hoped to be a professional athlete some day. At the time, I was devastated, but so what? There are a lot of people who have it a lot worse than I do. My parents were divorcing each other at the time, and they were having enough of their own troubles, so I sucked it up, went to college, worked hard, and I've done well. But somehow, after high school, I was never really that happy again.

Les believed nothing terrible had ever happened to him, but it would be more accurate to say that nothing unusual had ever happened to him. When Les injured his shoulder, a dream of the future died at the same time his family was being destroyed. With his mother so distraught, he could grieve with no one. He pushed grief aside, made his adjustments, and moved on. Without having had a real witness for his grief, Les was unable to appreciate the depths of his own feelings, nor could he receive consolation for his losses. Years later, he continued to minimize the feelings that he had, keeping all those old feelings walled off. Les said his children were fine, but how well did he know them? And how well did they know him? With his inherited habits of stoic self-reliance, Les, for one, felt alone until he learned to express his feelings rather than minimizing them.

An unanswered cry for comfort may ultimately be more traumatic than the initial wound itself. Hurt is even more bitter when no one is there to offer comfort. When a person believes others have failed him, he learns to harden his own heart rather than rely on others to be there for him.

Many adults complain that their parents ignored them as they were growing up, or had ignored them at the most crucial times. They portray their parents' negative character traits without having consideration for the pressures their parents had been under at the time or had suffered in the past. Parents push children away when they are preoccupied and stressed. The stress may be external, as when there is illness in the family, an IRS audit, problems with the immigration authorities, or a civil suit; or the problems may be internal, as is the case for a parent dealing with the aftermath of a traumatized childhood.

Parents who are too preoccupied to give witness to their children's lives are preoccupied for reasons that children must someday grow up to understand. One child of Holocaust survivors who had resented his mother's absences during his childhood said, "When my mother was elderly and sick and I was taking care of her, it dawned on me that if she had been home more when I was a kid, her bitterness and grief would have crushed my spirit." Nonetheless, when we are hurt, we need someone to comfort us, to hear our story of woe, to find us worthy, and to sit beside us patiently. Without this, our lives are difficult at best.

One ferocious-appearing man, tonelessly describing a long criminal history, his eyes flat with anger, spoke of the lectures his father had given him as he was growing up. Describing his childhood and adolescence, he said, "My father never once asked, 'What's going on with you?' " Seeing him, I imagined him as a boy and said, "You wanted your father to talk with you." He broke into sobs to reply, "I wanted my father to *listen* to me." He needed his father to witness his life.

At some point in their lives, fathers and mothers need others to show them how to relate well to their children. Fathers who have grown up without fathers, and mothers who have grown up without mothers may not know how to *be* with their children. Their children may not know how to be appropriately intimate with their children either. Whether it be a parent, grandparent, aunt, teacher, or friend, we need others to teach us how to sort out and express our feelings. Like Spanish, French, or English, the ability to express feelings is a language we must learn and become familiar with if we want others to understand us. But many people have difficulty mastering the language of feelings.

ALEXITHYMIA

As with any language, with practice we can become fluent in the language of emotions, but we must first learn the vocabulary before we can express its nuance. People who suffer from varying degrees of *alexithymia* never learned the vocabulary, or at least never learned to use it well. Broken into its three parts—*a,* "without"; *lex,* "words"; *thymia,* "feelings"—*alexithymia* literally means "without words for feelings."

An infant's cry signals his distress, and he remains distressed until his mother responds correctly. But before she can respond appropriately, she must first determine whether the infant is hungry, lonely, cold, wet, or in pain. Like a toddler who is crying and doesn't know whether he is tired, cold, or has hurt feelings, many people with eating disorders eat because they are tired, lonely, depressed, anxious, or thirsty; and they must be trained to first recognize their feelings before eating to make themselves feel better.

Feelings often remain amorphous unless given clarity in expression to others. Children who grow up with parents who express and inquire about feelings don't need to learn "feelings" as a second language, but learn to recognize and express their feelings as a matter of course: "What's wrong, Johnny? You're looking pretty upset." Other people help us hone and clarify our feelings as we talk about our lives. Parents who are abusive, neglectful, depressed, mentally ill, or empathically unable to relate to their children typically have trouble making sense of their own feelings, let alone helping their children identify and differentiate theirs. One of the results of therapy, intended or not, is that people often learn to distinguish and express their feelings.[1] When we can speak from the heart, we can confront our own misperceptions and mistaken beliefs rather than allow them to take root; destructive thoughts can be exposed and then countered.

The inability to express feelings leads to frustration and tension that is, at first, unrecognized and then may become overwhelming. Before they learn to "talk it out," children will hit one another, and unless adults learn how to talk out their feelings, they may do the same. For example, after a stroke damages the language center of their brains, people with *aphasia,* the inability to find the correct words that they need to make themselves understood, are frustrated, angry, and may also hit. Parents who are even moderately alexithymic may explode in rage at their children rather than explain themselves to them. And the bigger the person and the denser the alexithymia, the more explosive it becomes. Unless we learn to recognize and express our feelings, we are likely to act them out—much to our own and everyone else's detriment.

When we are able to speak fluently from the heart, we confront our own misperceptions and mistaken beliefs rather than allow them to take root. Otherwise, these distortions remain pent up and may accumulate danger-ously. Those who cannot express their feelings may end up hurting them-selves or others. The more we can express in words, the less we need to express in action.[2]

In a study conducted in Finland,[3] half the people who had attempted suicide were found to have significant degrees of alexithymia. People who attend clinics for chronic pain tend to have a significant degree of alex-ithymia.[4] Anger-management courses and prisons are filled with pained, lost, and often violent souls who have no words for their feelings. They are alexithymic. Without words for feelings, they cannot recognize or differ-entiate emotions. This was the case with Jack, a prisoner I interviewed after an incident of violence:

BG:	Why did you stab him?
JACK:	I don't know.
BG:	Were you angry with him?
JACK:	No.
BG:	What were you feeling?
JACK:	I don't know.
BG:	Were you taking revenge on the system?
JACK:	No.
BG:	How long were you planning this?

JACK: I wasn't.

BG: What were you thinking while you were sharpening that toothbrush?

JACK: I wasn't thinking anything.

Jack may have been able to recognize excitement or tension once it became intense enough, but he was unable to differentiate his feelings beyond that. Unable to recognize his other feelings, Jack unconsciously anticipated violence and was indifferent to its consequences. He could only express himself in destructive impulsive acts that often made no sense, eluded his control, but also relieved the tension of his unacknowledged anger.

Abandoned by both his parents, Jack had been passed from relative to relative and foster home to foster home as a child and then barely survived on the streets. He grew up without anyone to talk to about his feelings, so he never learned to sort them out or identify them. This did not mean that Jack was without feelings. On the contrary, Jack carried with him an immensity of hurt, anger, emptiness—and consequently great tension—that he could only deal with by numbing himself to the extent that he felt nothing. He did not have a clue about the feelings and events that had led up to his act of violence.

I placed Jack on mood stabilizers and antidepressants to safeguard him from the feelings that would otherwise overwhelm him as he thawed. After twelve months of medication and therapy that tried to convey the grammar and vocabulary of emotion that he'd missed as a child, Jack began to communicate feelings that he confessed made no sense to him. He asked to be locked up when he felt "stressed," fearing he would lose control. It was a start. Gradually, he got better. He may do well after he is released from prison—*if* he finds someone who continues to teach and guide him, something he has needed since childhood.

Fortunately, most of us are better able to recognize our feelings and express them enough to have sustaining emotional relationships. Commonly, after a bad day at work or at home, many people unleash their undifferentiated feelings of stress on their partners or children, only to later say, "I'm sorry. I had a lousy day at work. It's not you." After explaining and expressing (and thereby clarifying) the feelings about what happened to an *attentive* partner, much of the intensity is drained from the emotions, and life can resume normally. On the other hand, those who say "I don't want to talk about it" isolate themselves and continue to fume and ruminate. It is the same bad day, same bad feelings, but one person has been witnessed and the other has not.

We would do well to become fluent in the expression of our feelings. There are varying degrees of alexithymia. Even if they are not severely alexithymic, people who have trouble expressing their feelings tend to suffer from more stress, depression, loneliness, and social anxiety.[5] People who have PTSD already suffer from the effects of emotional numbing and dissociation, but they suffer more if they remain unable to identify or otherwise express their feelings.[6] They cannot receive support, comfort, or consolation. They are hurt people who only get more hurt, and they become hurtful parents who can be extrapunitive toward their children[7] and unable to offer support to them.

CULTURAL BARRIERS TO EXPRESSION

How is it that so many people have difficulty expressing themselves emotionally? Both culture and circumstance can mitigate the expression of feelings. For instance, during the Great Depression, many people hid their pain and uncertainty to keep from adding another burden to their families already struggling to survive. People who lived through those years learned to contain their feelings, and society respected those who did a good job of it. Likewise, American soldiers who returned from the bloody battlefields of World War II turned their energies to making a good life and rarely talked of their difficult experiences. Therefore, the generation of Americans raised in the fifties and sixties had parents who served as models of emotional forbearance. Their goals of finding the "good life" of material solidity addressed the feelings left over from the frightening economic insecurity of previous decades. This change in circumstances set up both generations with barriers to witnessing each other's pain.

Not expressing one's distress in times of crises, when everyone is overburdened, is altruistic. But not expressing one's distress during secure times is alienating. The sixties' and seventies' "generation gap" pitted parents who had been traumatized in childhood by financial instability against children who had never been concerned about basic survival. The children found their parents' emotional restraint to be stifling, and they challenged their parents' conventions with a freedom of expression that their parents regarded as degenerate. The conflict intensified with the Vietnam War— parents who had fought against threatening, predatory nations clashed with children who were afraid of their own government. The generations shared no common vocabulary and so could not give witness to one another. Even though the youth at the time believed themselves to be emotionally free, it was a time when it was "cool" to be "laid back." Painful intimate expression was still unfashionable.

Additionally, a cultural gender barrier inhibited masculine expressions in asking for or giving comfort. Even today, boys are taught that "big boys don't cry" and quickly learn not to be "crybabies" or "sissies." Although women have historically been permitted a greater range of emotional expression, men have often demeaned them for it. In 1963, Jacqueline Kennedy's tearless stoicism at her husband's funeral was universally admired. The macho code, adopted by both sexes, portrays silent forbearance as strong and heroic, but it also demands an emotional isolation that shuts out the love of another person's caring.

The prevailing fashion of masculinity still leaves little room for vulnerable expression. Most men remain hidden behind emotional walls they are too frightened to breach. When a display of tears is considered shameful, the corollary is that too much of an empathic display is likewise embarrassing. When crying is equated with "breaking down," shame interferes with both expressing and witnessing. The macho code that demands an appearance of strength cripples the already wounded. The prisons are full of ferocious-appearing men with flat eyes and a chilling swagger. That silent armor makes relationships lonely, leads to anger, and causes the spirit to wither.

Our jails would be emptier and our lives fuller if we all opposed our inhibitions and respectfully expressed more of our feelings to our intimates—our parents, partners, and friends—and taught our children to do likewise. Then we could see ourselves through the eyes of a compassionate witness and not through the shades of dark, solitary experience.

WHAT THE HEALING OF A WOUNDED PAST MEANS

The Fellowship of those who bear the Mark of Pain . . .
belong together . . . united by a secret bond . . .
and they all know the longing to be free from pain.
Albert Schweitzer, *On the Edge of the Primeval Forest*

What has not been comforted at the time of original injury is less likely to be understood later. Twelve-step programs such as Alcoholics Anonymous and Narcotics Anonymous are gatherings of the wounded who come together to face their grief and pain in the strength of each other's company, giving and receiving witness from those around them.

Support groups provide a safe place to risk openness because members have experiences in common. They can understand each other's experiences, compare and contrast them, and make sense of their feelings in each other's company, thereby breaking free from the bonds of their former isolation. They become each other's healers as each member gives comfort to the others, and to the extent he is open, allows comfort from the others. The very act of joining such a group is a return from isolation to the fold of mankind.

Those who are scornful of therapy, or support groups, or the necessity of having witnesses to the healing process may not understand what healing entails. *Healing grief does not mean making it disappear, but rather making peace with it, incorporating it into one's life and expression.* The pain of the past never goes completely away; the past cannot be erased. But grief or trauma that is expressed to others loses its painful edge, and after a time the pain neither dominates nor directs life. Buried grief, however, never heals, but continues to influence and threaten.

Acute pain diminishes when we can express it and when another person understands and cares enough to receive it. In his book *The Illness Narratives,* Arthur Kleinman describes a poignant encounter when he was a medical student working on a burn unit with a seven-year-old girl who had sustained burns over most of her body. To protect her from infection, her dead skin had to be removed each day; and each day, the girl screamed and begged the surgical resident to stop hurting her as he pulled away her dead skin with tweezers. Dr. Kleinman held her hand to reassure and comfort her:

> I tried talking to her about her home, her family, her school. . . . I could barely tolerate the daily horror. . . .
>
> Then one day, I made contact . . . I found myself asking her . . . how she tolerated . . . the surgical ritual day after day. . . . She stopped, quite surprised, and looked at me from a face so disfigured it was difficult to read the expression; then in terms direct and simple she told me. While she spoke, she grasped my hand harder and neither screamed nor fought off the surgeon or the nurse. Each day from then on . . . she tried to give me a feeling of what she was experiencing. By the time my training took me off this rehabilitation

unit, the little burned patient seemed noticeably better able to tolerate the debridement.[8]

Nothing had truly changed for the little girl. Her situation was the same. The people who saw her day after day were the same. But in sharing her inner experience, she was no longer alone and no longer just an object to be manipulated and talked at. In the telling of her pain, her doctor had become real to her and she to him. He could offer his witness as well as his hand. Because she no longer felt alone, her situation was no longer intolerable.

Regardless of theoretical orientation, what is common to all therapy is the occurrence of one person turning to another and telling his story in order to get help. If the therapist or friend truly listens, he is already helping.

CREATIVITY, CONSOLATION, AND WITNESS

People today are often urged to use creative means—art, journal writing, etc.—to express themselves. Private meditation and journal writing allows us to reflect on our experience, connect with our feelings, and make sense of our turmoil. We can transform pain into art or use it to heal others. When the pain of the past continues to overwhelm the present, and efforts to surmount anguish have failed, we need the consolation of human contact to heal our wounded spirits. Otherwise we become depressed. True consolation requires another person to do the consoling.[9]

The powerfully written expression of painful experience offers clarity, not comfort. Painful emotions arise in the process of writing, but without another person's physical presence to react to them, we lose the healing force of human contact. Memories surface and wound again. When we are alone, flashbacks of emotions in the recollection of past injury are a retraumatization, not a relief. Relief requires a witness. Anne Sexton, Sylvia Plath, John Berryman, Randall Jarrell, Virginia Woolf, Heinrich von Kleist, Ernest Hemingway, Yukio Mishima, Stefan Zweig, Sara Vogan, Jean Amery (Hans Meyer)—how long is the list of writers who have written from the depths of their hearts and gone on to commit suicide? There is joy in creation, relief in sublimation, but in the lonely silence of writing, the telling of pain is met with no answer from another. In their darkest moments, they were alone.

Saul Bellow, describing the tragic life of the poet John Berryman, writes,

"His poems said everything. He himself said remarkably little."[10] Berryman was twelve when his father shot himself in the heart; his mother remarried within weeks; and the parents' own feelings must have been so explosive that neither of them gave adequate consideration of their actions' effects on the children. Berryman was given no opportunity to grieve; instead, his unwitnessed grief pervaded his life, directed his experience, and ultimately led to his own suicide. In his biography, *The Life of John Berryman,* John Haffenden writes, "Berryman believed he had gone through an agony of grief after his father's death, but ... his mother ... [may have] confused his natural feelings. Berryman could never actually recall his immediate sensations about his father's death."[11]

In his book *Recovery,* Berryman names himself Severance. Severed from memory and his grief, he was severed from those who would have consoled him. Alcohol removed him further. In a psychiatric alcohol treatment community where he could not escape his pain but only express it, a counselor-in-training's act of generosity[12] cracked a glacier of tears that Berryman had frozen forty-five years before. Berryman wept with friends for two hours while they comforted him. Healing began with his mourning. He had years of grief to heal, and sometimes it can seem endless. He was on the road to recovery when he lost faith—in himself and the process of healing. Despair can also return as a flashback. Two and a half years later he, too, committed suicide. Had he only continued ...

When an experience is overwhelming, the mind shuts down in response and memory itself is sealed from consciousness. The experience is initially too much for the person to apprehend, and then later becomes too much for the consciousness to contain. Repressed memories of painful experiences typically reemerge only later to filter into consciousness in flashbacks and nightmares. Whether it is our own or our parents', unexpressed pain is preserved within. Unless it is uncovered and witnessed with compassion, it dominates life, affects our intimacies, and harms the next generation. But many people who are aware of having repressed painful feelings are afraid to tap into them for fear of going crazy or because they fear that once they start crying they will never stop.

Although the fears dissipate when others are present to provide consolation, the need to protect oneself from the pain of the traumatic experience conflicts with the need to receive comfort for it. The fear of feeling may be precariously balanced against the pressure of the unexpressed feelings, leaving the person locked in an airless stasis where growth, intimacy, and inner freedom are all blocked by constricted memory. Unless the balance shifts, it is possible to spend one's days in emotional stasis, losing the joys of everyday life to an event that took place many years before.[13]

Lacking the language necessary to explain themselves and requiring adults to offer witness to put their experience in perspective, younger children are at a great disadvantage when they have been hurt. If a young child cannot speak about a devastating experience, he stops thinking about it. In time, the memory may be forgotten and so deeply buried it becomes repressed, unmodified by later experience, other associations, or other people's perspectives.

abreaction

Whether forgotten or not, the emotions tied to a particular experience are still raw when we first speak of it, no matter how much time has passed. Speaking triggers unwanted emotions that flash back with the telling. The moment when a person first speaks of a traumatic event may be a dramatic *abreaction*—the living expression of feelings frozen in time and preserved from long ago. When this happens, the listener feels as though he is actually witnessing a recording of an event from the past that had been branded into the speaker's brain. The person acts as though he were reliving the injury, and looks at the listener as if he has come from the future to comfort him. It's an eerie experience, even for a therapist:

> Cheryl, a sweet-hearted, pretty woman with innocent eyes, a little girl's manner, and a four-year-old daughter, had recently been hospitalized for a psychotic depression—she had become progressively more withdrawn, stopped eating and sleeping, and described feeling an evil presence within herself that had hurt her stomach. For most of her life, Cheryl had felt a desperate kind of loneliness and did not know why. In our fourth session, she confessed that she was nervous about coming to an office so near to a seedy part of town. That morning the newspaper headline was about a particularly gruesome murder that had taken place the day before. As she examined her fear, she settled into what appeared to be a trance, then suddenly gave a wail so heartrending that I began to weep (I later found that the people in the waiting room and in the next office also wept). Cheryl's posture folded to that of a little child, she held her stomach, and in the voice of a three-year-old moaned, "Oh, it hurts! It hurts!" She held herself still, frozen. I felt I was watching the rape of a little girl, as if time had stood still for thirty years and I was looking

through a window to the past. Then, wailing, she said, "He took the color from the flowers." Later she recalled that an uncle was once arrested for child molestation.

During that session, Cheryl experienced only physical sensations—the memory of her rape was inscribed in her body, in her voice, and in her movements. The moment had been frozen in time, unwitnessed, uncomforted. Cheryl had only a young child's inadequate vocabulary to communicate what happened. Alone with her pain, she had long felt isolated from everyone she loved.

The return of Cheryl's memory brought her a world of pain—wave after wave of grief, fragment after fragment of returning memory. I became the witness to an event that had happened thirty years before, and comforted her in the simple language that a child could understand. But one reliving of the experience was not enough: too much of her life had been built around the event to allow a single cathartic moment to heal it. She needed to grieve the loss of wasted years and wasted possibilities. But Cheryl finally understood the pain that had unconsciously affected her for so long. In time, she could respond to feelings rather than the absence of feelings. The day Cheryl recaptured her memory was the beginning of her healing. She could face her depression knowing what it was that she was dealing with; and when her children grew up, she could explain it to them.[14]

SPEAKING THE UNSPEAKABLE

Many people remain silent for years. One such man was Gustav, who had survived four years of Auschwitz. I met him in synagogue, a bent, stooped man with a sad face marked by resignation. He stuttered and was desperately shy, but he was also kind and giving to others. He rarely exposed the numbers tattooed on his arm. He never spoke of his experience, but he did not conceal the fact that he was a survivor.

I first heard him talk in 1984 at a Holocaust Memorial before five hundred people. When he spoke, his voice carried such an agony of pain that it was painful to hear. When he spoke again the second year, he appeared ferocious, his voice now carrying the strength of rage. I last heard him speak a year later to the liberators of Auschwitz. I was startled to see him standing straight, speaking strongly without a stutter. He had a full smile and a vigor I had not seen before, appearing ten years younger than when

I first met him. Years later, he is younger still. His movements are lighter. He laughs and jokes. He has an aura of welcoming warmth about him.

Speaking of his pain before hundreds of rapt witnesses released Gustav from its stranglehold. In sharing his rage with so many, he unburdened himself. Expressing his gratitude to the liberators of the camps, he thanked those who had saved his life. But to free himself from the painful prison of his past so he could live again, he had to speak before the witness of others. To heal, it was necessary for Gustav to have others feel and acknowledge his experience. Expressing his feelings to so many others at one time liberated the man he had always been at his core—kindhearted, humorous, and loving.

People who are grieving a loss or suffering from the sequelae of trauma are often told to "get over it, the past is over and done with; it's time to go on with life." In the face of the neurobiology of grief and trauma, such advice is naive and selfish because it is impossible to do. A young child who runs to a parent to make a bruised knee feel better only feels worse if the parent offers no comfort, or worse, gives him such "character-building" advice as "Toughen up. Life is hard." The parent conveys to the child that he is not tough enough, and that he will have to toughen himself to compensate for a character flaw he does not have. On the other hand, should the parent simply kiss the knee to make it better, the parent acknowledges the child's feelings, makes the hurt better, and restores the child to balance.

Thirty years after the war, in a speech before a college audience,[15] Elie Wiesel talked of his previous inability to speak of the war. For ten years he had been silent. He told no one of his experience. He let no one know that he was a survivor of the concentration camps that had taken away and killed his mother. He was unable to speak of his life in the camps or his father's death.[16] Then years later, Elie Wiesel, looking at all the innocent, shining faces before him, sighed and said, "I have to do this over and over and over." Elie Wiesel, like the rest of us, finds healing in speaking.

Though most of us have lives less filled with tragedy than Wiesel's, we all suffer trauma, we all suffer loss, and we must all ask for and give witness so we and those we love can overcome life's tragedies and live full lives.

CHAPTER 5

HOW THE WARS OF OUR FOREBEARS RELATE TO OUR LIVES TODAY

The majority of the people living throughout the world realize that war has either directly affected their own lives or profoundly affected the life of a parent or grandparent. But Americans who have not directly fought in wars, or suffered the death of a parent, child, or brother in battle have been relatively protected from the experience, and seem unaware that their parents' or grandparents' wartime experiences are directly relevant to their own lives. In particular, the children and grandchildren of immigrants, especially those who fled from war or political repression, need to understand what their forebears endured if they are to make sense of their lives.

The knowledge that a grandfather had fought in a war may seem to have nothing to do with one's own life. A boy may grow up loving the sweet grandfather who has always adored him, and never connect his grandfather's wartime history to his own father's tense volatility. He may feel contempt for his father's angry outbursts without imagining what it must have been like for him to grow up with a father who was fresh from the trauma of war.

Those who have survived war rarely, if ever, speak of it in the detail necessary to convey the depth and totality of the experience. The details are often too upsetting for them either to remember or to express. The depression and anger that suffuses the home may be an expression of their silent grief; the loneliness that pervades the home may be the shell protecting them against their unexpressed and unwitnessed memories from a time of horror long ago. Their children may be harmed by the aftermath of experiences they know little about.

MAINTAINING THE SILENCE

In keeping quiet about the past, survivors of war may be desperately trying to avoid bringing to consciousness a grief that is too great for them to bear, and which is still freshly preserved in the memories they seek to avoid. As parents, they often mistake silence for protection, trying to shield their children from the injuries of the past as well as the incomprehensible pain they themselves continue to endure.

Reacting to feelings they can't understand in homes suffused with their parents' unhappiness, children of war survivors want to keep their parents' misery from staining their lives. They want to avoid emulating the distortions and flaws of character they perceive to be at the root of their parents' problems. Their parents' unhappiness is obvious to them, but the triumph represented by the mere fact of the parents' survival may not be. Without understanding the effects of war on their parents' lives, children may see their parents as failures—"irrational," "unloving," "self-absorbed"—an entire litany of negative characterization, based on ignorance.

Such had once been the case with N.C.'s children, who grew up watching their father dull his grief and terrifying memories in a blue cloud of opium smoke. The children could only see N.C. throwing away his life and money to stare into space and do nothing; though he was physically present, he was empty and silent in their company. Too young to imagine details of a story they had never heard, how could N.C.'s children know the depth of pain that had hollowed him out—or the dangerous, battle-trained reactions he had to control?

Twenty years after being forced into fighting a war, N.C. had developed chest pain. But his doctor said the real problem was in his emotional heart. Finally, through an interpreter, N.C. spoke of a time he had rarely spoken about and, certainly, never with his children. Long since addicted to opium, N.C. could still hear the screams from the decades before:

> N.C. had grown up in a large house in a small Laotian village with parents, grandparents, aunts, uncles, brothers, sisters, and cousins all living and farming together. At thirteen, N.C., the oldest child in the extended family, had been taken from his home and forced to fight

with the Laotian army. He had survived five years of combat, frightened and homesick throughout. He started smoking opium at fifteen. Three years later, with the Laotian army defeated and the Communists victorious, N.C. knew he would be executed if he did not flee. It took him a year to walk and fight his way to Thailand. Though alone, starving, and continually sick, with no one helping him, N.C. never gave up; and he never stopped worrying about his family.

N.C. met his wife in a refugee camp, where they comforted one another; they then tried to make a new life in America. After fifteen years of sending unanswered letters to Laos, N.C. finally received a reply: his mother and a sister were alive, but few other family members had survived. The country's new policy permitted correspondence and return, but N.C. should be aware that because he had been in the army, his grandparents, uncle, father, and brothers had been executed as "enemies of the people." Nevertheless, N.C. felt he had to go back. Upon arriving in Asia, N.C. learned that his mother had died two weeks before.

During the entire interview, N.C. kept his eyes down and spoke in a monotone, until he asked, "For what was I taken?"

N.C. was only a child of thirteen when he left his family for good. At that point, he left behind, also, the future he had assumed would be his. Having the familiar life of childhood truncated and access to his family prohibited, something basic was missing in the new life N.C. had started in America, something too painful for him to talk about.

As adolescents, N.C.'s children thought they'd understood his history— "My father was a kid when he had to fight in the army and he lost his family." But that sentence couldn't begin to encompass the pain of their father's experience. Even the details that they could imagine—the day the army had taken him away; that first night and second day with the army; the first death he had witnessed, the first friend he had lost, and the first person he had had to kill; the accumulation of homesickness, fear, and grief—did not convey enough of his experience. Too much was unspeakable, and too much was unimaginable. Had their father been able to speak more fully of his experience, they might have learned aspects that would have made their father's suffering comprehensible to them.

War experiences can be so savage that parents omit the worst details and children respectfully do not probe. Inquiring about a parent's war experience may be a family's best hope for closeness—and what the parents do not say, children must try to imagine.

Shortly before she died, my mother described an incident in her flight to Russia from Poland that she had never before mentioned.

> As we came to the village that first morning, I saw stacks of wood in the distance, but as I got closer, I saw arms and legs of people piled high on top of each other. I had heard rumors of such things. But I had never seen anything like it before. I knew then that I would never see my father or mother again.

In those specific details, I could feel what it was like for my mother at nineteen, the morning after her mother had urged her to flee. I wanted to embrace and comfort her. In that moment of revelation, she cracked another brick in a wall of silence that had isolated her, separated us, and had kept us both in pain. The broken silence became a tender moment of reconciliation between us.

HEARING THE UNSPEAKABLE

Children of war survivors can expect that their parents will always shroud some experiences in silence, preserving distance and an unshared and therefore unwitnessed pain that does not heal. The people that war brings closer together are those who have shared the experience, depended upon one another, and trusted each other with their lives—friends and comrades, who are often lost during war.

For instance, Boris was for years unable to talk to his family about his painful experiences of the Second World War. In fact, decades passed before he could even start to appreciate those experiences himself:

> I'm married, I have made money, and have successful children. I've done well in business and I don't need the money, but I want the German government to acknowledge my suffering. They denied me war reparations because they say nothing indicates I suffered permanent damage in Auschwitz. But I live with the effects every day. I love my family more than my own life, but I am isolated from them. There is a wall between us. My wife and children are American-

born, and they cannot understand my experience; and if they did, it would only hurt them. I can't talk about the family I lost. How can I talk about it?

I was a child when the Nazis came to power. Suddenly, my friends wouldn't talk to me. People I had known my whole life made fun of me: "Jew! Jew!" Friends I had my whole life. I remember walking down the street one day. Maybe I was eight. An adult spit in my face. I ran home crying. I can still feel the spittle on my face. I was thirteen when they took me to Auschwitz. I remember the long lines at the bathroom. I'd stand in line for hours, and when I was through, I'd go to the back of the line again. At the time, it seemed even worse than watching people being murdered. I felt nothing. Now, fifty years later, scenes of the camp keep haunting me. One memory in particular, I can't shake: a child ran up to a van that was taking his father away. The father pulled his son's fingers off him and yelled at his son to go back. I knew then that the boy would never see his father again. Now I look at my own children and I know exactly how hard it was for the father as well as the son. And I can't look my own children in the eyes.

We can only absorb overwhelming experiences in gradual, painful portions; our minds and bodies keep us protectively numb until we can cope with them. Then, over time, we make sense of details we hadn't noticed before.

As a child, Boris had to die emotionally in order to keep living physically. Once living became easier, he still felt dead emotionally. He kept the nightmares and the flashbacks that were the emotional resurrections of a tortured past to himself. He did not want to inflict such memories on anyone and so didn't share them. He was afraid that if his children understood his pain, it would hurt them too much; if they didn't understand, it would hurt him too much.

A therapist finally encouraged him to open up to his family. After speaking with them, it was clear how much they had longed to be closer to him. But they had not wanted to hurt him by asking too many questions and felt they had to wait until he brought it up first.

Speaking of their experience is especially hard for those who survived war as young children. Psychiatrist Robert Krell, describing two patients who had survived the Japanese prison camps for three years in Indonesia, said they had not previously spoken of their experience because of their difficulty in verifying their memories. One child was six; the other, two and a half. Their parents believed that young children forget. In fact, however, rather than fading in time, the memories of their experiences had intensified over the years.[1] Without witness, children neither make meaning nor sense of their experience; feelings without witness seem to lack validity and context. We all need someone to affirm what we feel; otherwise, how can we be certain what our feelings mean or even if what we feel is right?

FEELINGS WITHOUT WITNESS

Parents who have endured conditions of prolonged horror are likely to be unable to minister to the pains of their children's normal childhood. How can a child talk about such everyday mishaps as the teasing of an insensitive friend or an unfair teacher, to parents who were once starving or tortured? No matter how intense their feelings may be, children know they mean little next to the experiences of parents who have endured so much to survive. The ordinary concerns of a child raised in secure circumstances are trivial in comparison. Children of survivors have parents who cannot relate to their lives; their less burdened friends cannot relate to them either.

Those who suffer an injury directly are more likely to receive comfort than those who suffer indirectly. A child of eight suddenly swept into war with the rest of his family may be able to speak and have witness for the experience. Furthermore, that child will have had eight good and secure years growing up with undamaged parents, while a younger sibling, born after the war, may have had none. As an adult, the older child may remember the experiences that damaged him, while the younger sibling, born after the war, will have to deal with the puzzling experience of having been raised under relatively secure circumstances by the parents who had been damaged by it. His indirect, empathically derived injury that was impressed on his emotional core in infancy will not be easily defined. As a consequence, he will neither have witness nor healing for it.

Jonah, a child of Holocaust survivors who was also born after the war, described his parents' war experience as the dominant event of his life:

> To me, as a child of survivors, the Holocaust was everywhere. During college football games, I'd look around the stadium and try to imagine twice as many people being put to the ovens in Auschwitz in a single day. Walking down the street, I'd imagine the city desolate

of all people—an empty New York City, or twelve Seattles—trying to grasp the meaning of six million deaths. I found myself evaluating everyone I met with the question "If it came to it, would he hide me?" It's as if I'm living in 1945, but there are no Nazis here. I want to live now, but I keep getting dragged back there.

Since he had been secondarily traumatized by his parents' experience, the Holocaust remained the dominant theme of Jonah's life. To the detriment of his own children, the reality of a past he himself had never endured held more currency than the present life he was trying to live. Fortunately, Jonah was emotionally open and communicated well with his children, so they understood him and forgave him for his lapses, moods, and erratic behavior.

The damage sustained in war takes generations to heal. We can see, for instance, that the anger for the injustice and harm done to their forebears continues to smolder among the grandchildren of the Japanese-Americans who were interned by their own government during World War II. One young man, even while denying that his grandparents' experiences at the camps at Tule Lake in California had affected him in any way, spoke about it with a bitter edge to his voice: "Economics had a lot to do with it. It was harvest time when the government liquidated their property and sold it to Caucasians—at bargain basement prices." A physician whose grandparents suffered similarly said, "It can happen again. There's still a lot of anti-Asian prejudice." Another said: "My uncle served in the 442nd Division—the Japanese division—the most highly decorated division in World War II. They were used as shock troops, and they sustained the most casualties of any division during World War II. He was wounded and his best friend got killed, and when the war was over, he couldn't get a job."

The adult children remember, as do the grandchildren: the legacy of pain, the humiliations of bigotry, the outrage of injustice and betrayal, all affect them. Reparations cannot heal the insecurity of subsequent generations. There is always the question "What if it happens again?"

THE LEGACY OF PAIN
Unconscious Reenactments

Psychoanalyst Yolanda Gampel noted that children reenact painful traumatic scenarios of their family's history even when they have no direct knowledge of the events they act out. She describes a seven-year-old girl who began having problems with her memory, suffering amnesia and fugue states—absences from which she suddenly awakened as from a "lost state." In answer to a child analyst's question, the girl said:

> "[I] would not want to be an electric fence in the Warsaw Ghetto; they put soldiers there, and if they touch the fence and electrocute themselves, they will die." The analyst then . . . asked [the girl's] mother for help in understanding it. The mother turned pale, appeared shocked, and said, "My husband was in the Warsaw ghetto as a child and later in a concentration camp. But we have never spoken about this with the children. How does she know?"

The child's symptoms resolved after her mother told the father's story.[2]

As explored in depth in Chapter 9, "Mastery and Reenactment," we find, in hindsight, that our lives have been dominated by the unconscious reenactments of the traumas that have affected us—our own as well as our parents'. In an attempt to heal the painful injuries of the past, we replay these minidramas in the families we create, in the small moments of our day, and in the broad sweep of decisions that change the landscape of our lives.

Psychoanalyst Marion Oliner writes:

> To many people's surprise and pain, children who were often conceived in order to reaffirm life have shown signs that the past suffering of their parents plays an important part in their own existence, and that their concern with the horrible events preceding their own birth is expressed by a tendency to repeat the suffering themselves.[3]

During the Persian Gulf War, for instance, an adult child of Holocaust survivors described having come to a startling revelation:

> My son is nineteen, there is talk of resurrecting the draft, and he's struggling with the same situation with the Persian Gulf War as I myself did during Vietnam. I've heard my old fears coming from my son's mouth.
>
> When I first registered for the draft, thirty years ago, I was immobilized for hours when I came to the box that asked, "Do you object

to any and all war?" I finally checked "No." I knew that if I had been alive then, I would have wanted to fight Hitler, but I thought the U.S. had no business in Vietnam. Six years later when I was in graduate school, I fought to get my status changed to conscientious objector. I was scared the whole time. When my appeals fell through and I received my induction notice, I fled to Canada. I realize now that I had been reliving my parents' story of having been fugitives and fleeing war to safety. I had lived in fear for almost two years; my parents had lived in terror for four years. They were hunted people.

During Vietnam, I ran as my parents had run, and I came to understand what it means to be an outlaw and a fugitive. I can now understand how my parents' fear seeped into my bones, and I can deal with it better for knowing this. My fear was a paler reflection of theirs. And my son's fear was a paler reflection of mine.

This was also the case in Germany during the 1930s. Whether or not the adult children of that generation had known their parents' and grandparents' individual stories after Germany's defeat in World War I, they still responded to their parents' emotions. Hitler's rise and the aggressive foreign policy stance he inaugurated and helped legitimize also helped redress the wounds of the generation before: the children achieved mastery over their parents' former helplessness in reenactments that triumphed over their parents' defeat.

FAMILIES OF SILENCE

After the Second World War, the rest of the world looked upon Germany as a pariah nation waking up from a blood frenzy. Those who had embraced the Nazi cause could not admit their guilt, and those who had been terrified into complicity were sickened by the recollection of their actions. The men and women who had participated in the cause rightly feared retribution: the trials for those crimes against humanity continued through the 1990s. Presuming that anyone whose sympathies had not been with them during the war would be against them once it had ended, a generation of parents began to hide, closing the doors to the past and simultaneously shutting out their children. A generation of parents interposed a wall between themselves and their children, who subsequently longed to be closer to their parents. Describing his relationship to his father, one man said:

My father had been a Nazi. He kept his old uniform in a closet in his study. I wasn't supposed to go in there, but he had all this memorabilia that fascinated me. I once asked him about it, and he got furious. He refused to talk about the war, and I knew better than to ask again. I spent a lot of time in therapy dealing with the distance between us. I had always wanted to be closer to him. It hurt me, especially when his army buddies came over. They'd go into his study and close the door, and I'd hear them laughing and singing.

Behind closed doors, the son heard the voice of his father sharing an intimacy with others that he had never granted to his own son.

It does not have to be this way. In the Bible, God offered Cain a chance to redeem himself for the murder of his brother by mitigating his misdeeds with honesty and accepting the consequences of the truth. With penance, regret, and reformation, forgiveness can come even to murderers. But without complete honesty, reformation cannot be complete, nor can forgiveness be whole. True reconciliation, and healing between the generations, requires painful honesty.

Unfortunately, however, there are likely to be some stories and particular details that are too hard for parents to tell, and the children of parents who survived wars do not have the experience to appreciate the impact of the events that parents describe. This was the case with Audrey, who was intelligent and pretty, but also painfully shy. She was afraid to leave the house and used alcohol and marijuana to get up her courage. Hyperactive and inattentive in school, her problems seemed unconnected to what she knew of her family's history. Her mother, however, had been depressed, rarely went out of the house, and became anxious when her children did so. Audrey could not imagine that her mother's childhood experiences could have anything to do with her problems, and she was annoyed when I persisted in asking about her mother's childhood. When pressed, however, Audrey had mentioned this incident:

My mother was a little girl when she came to this country. Maybe she had some rough times. I know that when she lived in Germany, her family lived on a farm and everyone had enough to eat all through the war. Nothing bad ever happened to her or her family; but once, when she was little, she saw some children being shot in a field. But I don't think anyone in our family got killed.

Audrey never considered herself a victim of war because she wasn't alive then and her mother never talked about it. But what Audrey's mother had witnessed was something that would be deeply disturbing and inexplicable to a little girl. She must have wondered what the children had done and why they had been shot. What could parents say to a young child to reassure her and explain it? I could imagine Audrey's mother having flashbacks for years, and perhaps continuing to suffer.

Had Audrey grown up in Europe, however, where the effects of the Second World War continue to be recognized and discussed, perhaps she would have understood the ramifications of her mother's story as she talked about it with others. Audrey herself had no personal history that would have made her mother's story immediately come alive for her. Faced with her mother's silence about the past, Audrey was unable to understand herself in the present.

Audrey had been nurtured and raised by a mother whose faith in life and in her fellow man had been shattered when she was a little girl. Having witnessed the sanctioned murder of children her own age, Audrey's mother had grown up in a world she understood to be violent and arbitrary. She felt helpless and threatened all her life. No wonder she rarely left the house and was so depressed and overprotective of her children. No wonder Audrey herself was frightened, shy with others, hyperactive, and involved with alcohol and drugs. She had been medicating the fear and depression she had absorbed from her mother—maternal emotions that had altered Audrey's neurochemistry and responsiveness—with self-prescribed doses of alcohol and marijuana. Later, Audrey came to function better on antidepressants, but sadly, she was unable to get her mother to do the same.

War's damage affects families everywhere, even among those who feel far removed from it. Soldiers, often teenagers when sent to battle, return home with symptoms of PTSD that they, perhaps unknowingly, express in their families. Children all over the world meet fathers who had left them years before and are raised by fathers who return bearing hidden wounds from events they cannot discuss.

Wars displace masses of traumatized people who have lost family members and friends, their homes and communities, and their faith and sense of security. Families all over the world have been marked with death, horror, and too often, silence. It is likely that some war somewhere has had significant personal ramifications in the life of a parent or grandparent—and the stories we are least likely to hear are the very ones that have had the greatest effects.

Not talking to a parent about their war experiences, however, or about the friends and family members who died, estranges both parent and child. Without sharing the pain, neither one can truly know the other; and in that breach of loneliness and misunderstanding, a parent who survived a bitter experience may, perhaps, feel more bitter still.

Wounds of nature we can accept. But the injuries that people deliberately cause one another stick in our throats. The bitterness of human betrayal cannot easily be comforted. What comfort is there for the murder of a mother or father, sister or brother, a child, or an entire family? The pain that war brings the generations is almost beyond comprehension.

Talking to a parent about his wartime experience may very well evoke ugly, painful memories; but the child who makes an effort to do so becomes a witness to the parent's life, offers consolation, and builds a bridge of love and understanding between them. The human spirit is strong and resilient; in the process of communication, parent and child are both strengthened.

CHAPTER 6

NEEDING TO LET OTHERS KNOW

Healing from Childhood Sexual Abuse

I felt like he was injecting me with Evil.
Donna, a woman raped by her father

Trauma begins to heal when it is spoken. Hiding the secret of sexual abuse can cause as much damage as the abuse itself. A wounded child's silence separates him from others and walls him off from those who love or would support him. Sexually abused children suffer more pathological symptoms than other abused children[1] and grow up to be parents who have to overcome the scars of abuse.

PRISONERS OF HIDING

Children being sexually abused remain silent because an abusive adult can easily intimidate and manipulate their vulnerability. The abuser exploits the child's innocence—threatening, shaming, and making him feel responsible for unacceptable acts. The abuser may say, "I'll kill you and your parents if you ever tell them," or "If your parents ever find out, they won't love you," or even "I know you enjoy it." Once abused and terrified into silence, the child no longer feels safe; his world is no longer a protected one. Soon keeping secrets becomes a way of life. Worse still, the child may become the abuser's possession.

Because only the child and the abuser know the truth, the child begins to think the abuser is the only one who truly knows him; his self-image derives from what the abuser tells him. If a parent picks him up and hugs him, saying "I love you," the child wonders if that would still be the case if the parent knew his secret. The voice of a molester saying "You bad thing" speaks louder and more convincingly.

Living in the grip of unwanted sexual stimulation, some children dissociate from the experience and become numb; others, confused by the pleasurable sensations nature hard-wires into everyone's body, feel guilty for responses they cannot help. Though they may grow up to realize rationally that they were not responsible for the abuse, they must tell others what happened in order to emotionally free themselves from their childhood guilt. One victim of sexual abuse I counseled wept through his sessions week after week as he spoke of his confusion[2] for continuing the relationship with his abuser over a period of a year.

> I'm so ashamed, but I thought he cared about me when everyone else was too busy. It took me a long time to realize just how much I had been used and exploited. I was thirteen then, and now twelve years later I'm just beginning to get over my confusion over my sexual orientation. I'm just beginning to realize that I'm not gay. All these years, I've felt so ashamed and guilty over this. I was so vulnerable then, I was a sitting duck.

Those who have been sexually abused as children do not like their feelings and usually do not think much of themselves. Many also dislike their bodies. As children, they defended themselves from the violation of both body and spirit by minimizing what happened to them physically. The trauma had been so overwhelming and their struggles so futile that they had to shut down their sensations and emotions. Adults describing how they dissociated to cope with the experience often speak in the vocabulary and intonation of a child, saying, "I'd just go away." Later, therapists working with adult survivors can often tell their patients' age at the time of the molestation by the tone of their voices and gestures.[3] As adults, when overwhelmed by flashbacks or stress, they become numb once again as they did as children. They "go away" to preserve themselves, and put the feelings on ice for another day.

People who have been sexually abused as children have flashbacks to feelings that are so terrible that many describe relief when seeing their blood well up after having cut or mutilated themselves. Physically cutting through the protective but deadening psychic numbness that both contains and preserves overwhelming feelings from the past momentarily releases them from the terrible underlying emotions. The scars that are left give testimony to the pain a person can't express in words.

Fearing what others would think, molested children are afraid of losing what love they have and feel guilty for wearing a mask to get the love they receive. Pretending to a normal daily life while concealing the truth from everyone, these children feel counterfeit, ashamed, alone, emotionally tied in knots, and angry that their parents seem not to notice. No longer sure of their parents' love, these children grow up feeling empty and worthless inside. As adults, they have difficulty in their intimate relationships; and as parents, they need their children to understand the origin of their worst failings.

INCEST
The Ultimate Betrayal

Incest is the ultimate betrayal. A basic trust is defiled as parents breach sexual boundaries to violate a son or daughter's body. Children of incest are left confused. Their emotions, thoughts, and physical sensations are scrambled with complexities as fathers[4] satisfy their momentary desires and rob their children (and perhaps their children's children) of an easier future.

Yet children (most commonly, daughters)[5] who grow up with incest often feel more betrayed by a nonabusing mother than by the father who abuses them. Abusive fathers may, to an extent, be forgiven because "they are sick" and "can't help themselves." But what of the other parent? The child, who believes that parents are all-powerful, cannot understand why a mother would tolerate the abuse when the child's welfare was at stake.

When incest is hidden in the home, sexually abused children often believe that their mothers knew but did nothing, and feel fundamentally betrayed by both parents. Children believe that their mothers must have known even if they never spoke of it. How can a mother not know when something so huge is happening right under her nose? Yet the idea that sexual abuse might be occurring within the home may be unthinkable to parents who have never been abused. Sometimes the mother does know, or at least suspects, what is going on and sacrifices her daughter in fear of her husband hitting her or leaving her, or to spare herself from a sexual relationship that is repugnant to her.

For the child, the abuse constitutes the basic, underlying reality of the home. When their mothers do not believe them initially, daughters have difficulty forgiving them even if they do later file for divorce. In any case, the long, arduous process of healing accelerates when their mothers finally acknowledge that the abuse occurred and was harmful.

HEALING WITNESS, GRANTED AND DENIED

Children who gather their courage to talk of the abuse are devastated when their parents do not believe them. The injury of the parents' disbelief may be worse than the molester's injury. But parents who accept the molester's more articulate and often polished explanation of an incident abandon their children to a hostile world. What can a child do to counteract the accusation of the parents' disbelief? The bitterness of the parents' betrayal leaves children alone in families that no longer shelter them, and they live with the bitter belief that they are unseen and unloved.

If children do not feel close to their parents, they grow up feeling empty inside. Children who have been sexually abused almost inevitably feel alone, and bad feelings define their life. Until they break their silence, the uncountered fears, anxieties, and false beliefs about themselves continue to dominate their lives. A delay in talking about the abuse allows false, negative beliefs to worm deeply into their self-regard. When such children become adults, speaking of the abuse triggers pain; but further efforts to bury the truth repeat the injury, and defensive maneuvers to avoid triggering pain prevent healing. Therapy, counseling, and support groups all provide the long-awaited release that helps heal adults who were sexually abused as children and were silent or not believed.

ABUSED CHILDREN AS ADULTS

When children who are sexually abused grow up and become parents, they need their children to forgive the injuries they may cause them as a consequence. The psychic numbing that once protected these parents from the shock of sexual trauma leaves them partially dead to new experience and adds to their sense of emptiness. Having been condemned to silence while growing up, they became preoccupied with finding relief and security in something they themselves could control. Many grew up to become alcoholics or drug, sex, or food addicts; many hurt themselves or attempted suicide, believing that when they die they will go to a better place. Residential programs treating alcohol and drug addiction report 20 to 25 percent of men and 40 to 68 percent of women were sexually abused as children.[6] The majority were parents,[7] but unfortunately, in many families, the parent's history of childhood sexual abuse remains hidden as a deep, dark secret because of the parent's shame or desire to protect the children. Yet for all their sakes, they need their adult children to know, understand, and witness their pain rather than condemn them for the consequences of it.

SEXUAL ABUSE AND FLASHBACKS

People who have been sexually abused as children often flash back to it all through their adult lives. The flashbacks can be directly imposed on tender moments and interfere with intimacy, or they may appear in subtle fragments of moods, fears, and feelings that interfere with individuals' ability to use their emotions to help make sense of the world.

One woman who had been sexually abused by her father as she was growing up wept while describing the flashbacks she had the first time she tried to make love with someone she truly cared for. Her previous sexual encounters had been with strangers and men with whom she shared no emotional intimacy, and she had not had a problem with flashbacks then. But with someone she cared for, she felt only the weight of her father on her. She did not tell her partner, and so missed an opportunity for a caring person to witness and give comfort to her when her emotions were raw. She had felt alone and desolate for years. Had she told him, she may have had a moment of true intimacy. Instead what was supposed to have been an intimate moment only wounded her more.[8] Like so many women who were sexually abused as children, she went on to spend years avoiding the feelings that came up for her with intercourse before she was able to successfully reintroduce sexuality into her life.[9]

In addition to the direct trauma of their abuse, the isolation of their hiding, and the loss of love and trust in their parents, sexually abused children also suffer from the intense exposure to the raw force of their molesters' emotions. Molesters' actions are illegal. They would be ruined if they were caught. Fear, excitement, sex, anger, and resentment toward adults who would condemn and punish them—all mix together. The children pick up on the molesters' queasy mash of illicit emotions, and it permeates their experience of the molestation.

Children, whose psychic boundaries are still permeable, come to believe the perpetrator's feelings are their own, and unwittingly take them in as a part of their own being. The empathically derived feelings are traumatic enough to return as emotional flashbacks. As adults, these abused children feel there is something evil inside them. They often choose silence because they believe that if anyone else knew the truth, or were to be exposed to it, the people they loved and respected would retreat from them.

RECOVERING FROM SEXUAL ABUSE
Two Cases

When I first met Ronda, she had just left the hospital against medical advice after a six-month stay. In her thirties, Ronda wore baggy layers of clothes, barely made eye contact, and spoke as if she were four years old one minute and a world-weary adult the next. Terrified and feeling suicidal when she went into the hospital, she felt no better when she left and was still overwhelmed by waves of panic, with horrific images and sensations of half-remembered events that uncontrollably intruded on her reality. For Ronda, a sense of the passage of time disappeared into a fog of anxiety; at other times, she had only the vaguest memories of what had happened to her. Given a diagnosis of multiple personality disorder, her psychiatrist urged her to give up her children to their father or to foster care to devote herself to her recovery. Knowing that her children needed her, she chose to leave the hospital instead. I agreed to work with Ronda, with the understanding that a suicide threat would end therapy; Ronda agreed and has never violated her word.[10]

Over the next ten years, I witnessed Ronda's grief as her painful memories boiled over. Ronda's symptoms had begun after she left her husband the year before:

I was eighteen when I married, and when my husband beat me, I thought it was normal. But when he beat our son, I realized it was wrong to beat anyone and I left him. The flashbacks started soon after I left him. I didn't know what was happening to me. I thought I was going crazy.

The ending of her marriage triggered flashbacks to a previous time when she was alone in the world. From the ages of three to five she lived with and had been sexually tortured by her grandmother and her uncle. She had been mute for years afterward. In the voice of a four-year-old, she said:

> I'm bad. I'm no good for anything. Everything I do is wrong. There is no place I belong. Not on earth I don't. No! No! No! I can't talk or something bad will happen. Grandma made me do things. And she got mad at me if it wasn't right. Uncle Dennis made me do things too. Momma made me stay with them cause I'm bad so she threw me away.

Later Ronda continued in a more adult voice:

> Grandma said I won't remember. I never forgot. When Momma came to take me back, I told her what happened. She said it was not true. Then I stopped speaking and I can't remember when I started again. I do remember talking in high school.

In the trance of her flashbacks, she gave voice to distortions, beliefs, and fears that had gone unexpressed, unwitnessed, and unchallenged for thirty years. I felt like an adult coming from the future, traveling into the past to bring comfort to a distressed child. In time, as she revealed her secrets one by one, her memories lost their terrible power.

Unlike so many people who had been sexually abused as children, Ronda never drank or used drugs. She was all too painfully aware that her children had been hurt when they were young. Throughout her hospitalization, Ronda was also aware that her children were being hurt by her absence, and had she believed that her children would have done better without her, she might have given them up and remained in the hospital. But that was not the case. Despite all the hardships Ronda's children had to endure—her physical and emotional absences, her panic attacks, and her withdrawal—Ronda knew that her love for her children was the foundation of their strength, and she knew if she stayed in the hospital, custody of her children might be returned to their father, who would beat them.

Ronda felt that her children had been hurt enough already. Her own suicide threats had been particularly hard on them. Parents who threaten suicide leave children insecure for a long time.

Ronda never wanted to let her children down like that again. Her children endured hardships, and were comforted knowing that their mother loved them more than she loved herself. She was honest and open with them about her problems, so they understood when her reactions had to do with the past and not with them. They witnessed her grief, understood it, and knew that their needs would pull her back to the present—any threat to their welfare marshaled her mature strength as a survivor. Even in difficult times, they were secure knowing that she was determined to be there for them. For Ronda, healing the past had to take second place to her children's present need. And knowing that, they loved her. Her strength, bolstered by their compassion, gave them the strength they needed to do well in their lives.

Donna was another young woman I treated who was dealing with the aftermath of sexual abuse. When I first met her, she seemed like a tough, refreshingly honest, engaging kid who could take care of herself, but it soon became clear that at nineteen she had already experienced a world of hurt that she needed to express. She had jumped from a freeway overpass several months before and miraculously survived. Despite the ready smile on her face, Donna vibrated with dark energy that she could barely contain; anxious, agitated, and angry, she literally could not sit still, and there were no medicines that helped her. Donna was filled with turbulence that threatened to overwhelm her. She felt exhilarated in situations of danger or when thinking of killing herself. She would enter the hospital whenever alcohol, drugs, the support of friends, and therapy failed to relieve these unbearable feelings.

> My father first raped me when I was seven. He drank every night and came after me stinking of booze. He liked it when I tried to fight him. He'd buy me presents and give me money. When I was in the seventh grade, I told my mom and a teacher about Dad. Nothing happened. Nobody cared. I went wild drinking, drugging, and causing all kinds of trouble. I finally stopped him myself when I was fifteen. I stabbed him in the chest with a pair of scissors. They didn't go in deep, but I warned him that I'd kill him the next time. He knew I meant it. He'd still try grabbing me, and try forcing me, but I was able to fight him off after that.

Despite the advice and support of many friends, Donna never cut her parents off. She knew that the tenuous threads that held her to life were tied to home. Despite the many friends who cared for her, she felt too lonely to leave and too empty to live.

Over time, some of the staff at the hospital where she was frequently admitted became hostile and regarded Donna's multiple admissions as counterproductive, labeling her as a dependent, staff-splitting "borderline personality disorder" who was consciously abusing the hospital and getting nowhere. Others saw her fighting to survive and in need of intermittent shelter.

One night, Donna called me long-distance, sober, suicidal, and gently rational. I was frightened; she was not. She was at a moment of decision, a crisis I had sensed would come one day. Death or life—it was for her to choose. I was relieved to hear her voice the next day.

> I was sober when I drove into the mountains. I had no idea whether I was coming back or not. I only knew I had to decide for myself one way or another—whether life was worth the pain—I thought of all the people who love me and wondered if that was enough.

From that moment on, Donna gave up drugs, alcohol, and suicide attempts—her previous means of escaping her pain. She stopped running, began accepting her pain, and continued to express it to the people she trusted to stand by her. It took years, great commitment, AA, and the help of many good, caring people before Donna was able to free herself from the tyranny of her pain. Her life eventually became full and stable. She now works to salvage others in trouble and has a child. Donna and her son both seem to glow.

While she was growing up, Donna's father deprived her of the right to control her own body. He took her body as his possession, denying her singularity, her will, the meaning of her own humanity. The adults who were supposed to protect her failed her. Once Donna realized no one was going to stop her father, she gave up trying. She preserved herself by ceding her body to her father and making it insignificant to herself; she repeatedly attempted suicide because the way she saw it, if she died, it would be more her father's loss than her own.

Donna's relationship to her father was so intense that every other relationship paled beside it. The mixture of a daughter's love and the hatred of a child toward her rapist became explosive when detonated by the hormonal surges of adolescent sexuality. At times, Donna's feelings were too much to control and so she needed the hospital to contain her.

Suicide beckoned Donna to put an end to the feelings she could not tolerate. Part of her wanted to live, but was terrified—not of her father, but of a wildness within her that could easily cause her to kill herself on impulse. The knowledge that she could choose to die reassured Donna that her life was hers to control, but it also added a dimension of terror to already intolerable feelings.

Donna's exuberant, charming directness drew people to her, and her openness allowed others to comfort her. Her unconcealed torment stirred compassion, and that compassion became the love that sustained her. Some hospital staff members believed she was crying wolf; they doubted her fundamental honesty and dismissed her, but Donna did not despair. Instead, she turned to those who believed in her. To them, the very real possibility of her death evoked the passionate caring she needed to match the explosive intensity of her incestuous relationship to the father. Alone, with her life in the balance, Donna weighed the love that others gave her against the weight of her torment, then gave herself to life.

Through the years, Donna worked with a caring nurse she called "Mother Janie." During Donna's worst times, Jane spent hours on the phone with her—comforting her, guiding her, bearing witness to Donna's tormenting pain. When Jane was tired, unavailable, or unable to listen without resentment, Donna called me. Such help has to be compassionate and uncontaminated with resentment to be healing. For the therapeutic relationship to work, Donna and her therapists needed to be exceptionally honest with one another about their feelings.

With time, the intensity of Donna's neurophysiological response diminished. Her pain abated enough for her to free herself from it; and after more time still, in the honest self-evaluation of her stability and inner clarity, Donna realized she was ready to become a mother. Her exuberant, joyous son will attest that she was right.

Donna's and Ronda's children were fortunate. They have mothers who spent years in therapy struggling to overcome their injuries; they faced themselves honestly and denied themselves the escapes of alcohol, drugs, and suicide; in addition, they had support to help them get through the many years before they were stable enough to work. Until then, they had to rely on the help that others were willing to provide out of compassion.

But many children of sexually abused parents are not so fortunate, and grow up with parents who are still emotionally frozen, wounded, and child-like. Their parents have gone without the help they needed because therapy was unavailable or they were too afraid, despairing, or distrustful. Furthermore, many children of sexually abused parents may never hear their parents' story of abuse, because their parents are still hiding, and using alcohol and drugs to dampen their overreactive nervous systems and emotional flashbacks.

Children of such hurt parents have to forgive the pain their parents have passed on to them in order to heal themselves and protect their own children. They must mature beyond the stage of complaint, beyond blaming the parents who hurt them. They must grieve not only for the care their parents were not able to give them, but also for the pain and sadness that their parents had to endure as children. Though forgiving parents who were absent or unavailable may be difficult, the knowledge that those same parents were so badly hurt as children may make the effort easier. We heal ourselves even for the attempt to understand and forgive hurtful parents.

CHAPTER 7

GIVING GRIEF ITS DUE

With the death of a husband [or wife]
you lose your present; with the death of a parent
you lose your past, and with the death of a child
you lose your future.

Norman Linzer, *Understanding Bereavement and Grief*

We love at our peril: love always risks certain loss. No matter what our age, one day too soon death arrives in our lives. No longer an abstraction or a stranger, death becomes all too familiar. We grieve what we lose. In the end, the love that we need to sustain us breaks our hearts.

If we are fortunate, our lives are filled with love. Son. Husband. Father. Mother. Wife. Daughter. Sister. Brother. Friend. The very words have power. At any time, however, someone can say, "I'm sorry to tell you but your ——— is dead." No matter how we fill in the blank, life shatters. For a time, our hearts flood with grief. After the first numbing shock of grief subsides, we feel the loved one's absence so keenly that it is hard to feel anything else. Cut off from a part of our hearts, we are cut off, too, from any illusions we may have of either our importance in life or our ultimate security.

To be able to function in our daily lives, we count on continuity. We take our families for granted because we need to presume that we will see those we love a next time; otherwise, we are too afraid to give our attention to anything else. Unless we believe that those we love are safe, we cannot rest. If those we love are threatened, nothing else matters.

Our worst fear is that death will come prematurely, out of proper sequence. We believe that no one should die "before his time," that children should grow up with parents, that we and our brothers and sisters should live till old age. We hope our marriages stay intact to flourish into our seniority. We expect our parents to die only when they are old, and we hope to die before our children. To each of us, any alternative to the ideal world is a tragic one.

We need to know what to expect in order to manage in times of loss, so that we can promote and not oppose our own or anyone else's recovery. If we cut our time of grieving short, we reject our natural feelings, curtail our expression, lose a dimension of ourselves, and forfeit the ability to be compassionate toward others. Understanding the long aftermath of various losses allows us to sympathize, and not judge others negatively for the residual grief they carry. Unless we learn to accept and express our grief, the suppressed emotions become part of the background to our future experience and that of future generations. We can only heal from loss if we take enough time to mourn.

RITUALS OF MOURNING

Though I would take comfort against sorrow,
My heart is faint within.
Jeremiah 8:18

Every human culture provides mourning rituals to acknowledge the mourner's grief.[1] Mourners in Europe wear black; those in China, white. Off the Bengal Bay of India, Andaman Islanders, remote and isolated survivors of an ancient race of tiny forest dwellers, weep over the body, cover themselves with clay for weeks, mourn for months, and leave shredded palm fronds at the entrance of the village to signal that there has been a death there.[2] The Inca mourned up to a year, wore black, and shaved their heads.[3] Mourners among African and Australian aboriginal tribes may amputate one or more finger joints[4] to show that something has been cut out of them; observant Jews rend their garments or a symbolic black cloth to show that someone they love has been torn from them: "flesh of my flesh." (Genesis 2:21)

After a death, among the Trobriand Islanders, spouse, children, and nonmatrilineal family shave their heads, cover their bodies with soot, and wail. After the funeral, the widow enters a small cage in her house and lives in the dark, forbidden to speak. She accepts food and drink only as they are placed in her mouth by kinfolk who remain with her. Mourning lasts six months to two years.

The way Trobriand Islanders grieve physically expresses what happens to us emotionally. For a period of time after the death of a loved one, we express our grief and make it visible to others. Then, it is as if we have entered into a dark and confining zone that separates us from life. The love that nurtured us is gone, and so we need other people to nurture us through our grief. We do ourselves harm if we rush our natural rhythms in order to conform to external pressures.

Customs such as formalized mourning for a year, withdrawing from others and from ordinary activities, and periods of abnegation and self-denial are common to various cultures[5] and in harmony with our human nature. For a time, so much changes inside that the outside world is more difficult to engage.

Individual cultures decide when mourning becomes pathologic. For instance, the traditions of the ancient Hebrews structured a year for grieving the death of a father, mother, or spouse; the formal mourning time for a child was a month. If mourning were to last a year for each child who died back then, people would have spent their entire lives in mourning. In ancient Hebrew society, grief had both its limits and its time. Emotionally, the community "carries" the bereaved for a year. The intensity of communal support diminishes as the mourners recover with time.

In the Jewish mourning ritual, the mourner "sits shiva." For a week, he remains in the home with mirrors covered and all vanity put away. Friends and family come to offer solace, to listen and follow the cues of the mourner. For a month, the mourner neither shaves nor wears new clothes. For the entire year following the death, he recites the mourner's prayer when praying with others. After a year, the gravestone is unveiled and the mourner is encouraged to participate in life again. Each year, on the anniversary week of the death, the Yahrzeit, the "time of year," he stands before others and again recites the mourner's prayer. The congregation answers, witnessing his grief.

We need memorials, funerals, anniversaries, and keepsakes to help us remember so that those we love do not just evaporate into the mist, taking part of us with them. In the living moment of memory, we resurrect the dead to comfort us. Revisiting our memories of those we love fills our hearts, and in their memory we preserve ourselves.

The price for not expressing grief is high. Like the painful emotions evoked by other traumas, grief cannot be assuaged unless it is consoled. Unexpressed sorrow dominates life, surging in a constant river beneath the surface of other emotions. Feelings stored without being mourned return, unbidden and unrecognizable, to trouble future times. A child may bury grief for a parent and not notice its presence, but when he becomes a parent, his children will feel the outlines of that sorrow. If grief is buried, it can distance families, debilitate individuals, or transform into anger for being unconsoled.

American society has little patience with sorrow and little time for mourning. One neighbor was upset with his young son for refusing to go to school a day after the boy's uncle, the man's brother, had died of a sudden heart attack right in front of him; he felt that it was best for him and his son to return to "normal" as quickly as possible. Another friend did not attend his father's funeral because he was too pressed at work.

We demean ourselves when we fail to honor our grief. Grief ennobles life by reminding us of the magnitude of our sorrow. After losing someone we love, we feel the depths of the love we have carried; we appreciate life that we had taken for granted. Grief enriches us when we embrace it and shrivels us when we deny its existence.

A brother dies, and a mother and father weep. A mother dies, and a father and children grieve. It takes more than one generation for a family to heal from the death of a child, and more than one generation for a child to heal from the effects of a parent's early death. As long as grief is unconsoled, the legacy of sorrow passes on through the generations.

A DEFINING EVENT
A Parent's Death in Childhood

Losing a parent as a youth is a defining event. The sorrow lingers for life—for what never has been, for what never will be, for failed opportunity and failed possibility. The universe becomes darker, colder, and more frightening. When a child loses a parent, he retains an enduring sadness[6] and can never again recapture the same innocent trust in life's continuity. Adults who lost parents in childhood often use the words "hole in the heart" to describe the feelings. In his autobiography, *Growing Up,* newspaper columnist Russell Baker writes that his father's death "slid an icicle into my heart."[7]

After that [my father's death], I never cried again with any real con-
viction nor expected much of anyone's God except indifference, nor
loved deeply without fear that it would cost me dearly in pain.[8]

A child cannot adequately anticipate a parent's death. The parent may
be ill, wasting inexorably; death may be understood, a foregone conclusion—and still it comes as a surprise to the child. When a parent has been
the solid ground beneath the child's world of change and flux, he becomes
larger than life, and his death is unthinkable.

A parent's death redefines a child's life, and changes the definitions of
his character. The loss implodes the expanding world of a child or adolescent; the aftermath reshapes his emotional and physical world. For a time,
the entire family's emotional landscape is rubble, and everyone in the family struggles to pick up the pieces. From infancy through adolescence, the
consequences touch every aspect of a child's development. Later, new love
is built on old loss. A strain of sadness—born of the knowledge of
inevitable loss—infuses love. As an adult, the individual brings the grief of
having lost a beloved parent into the new family he makes.

Though it may be barely perceptible, a sense of sadness from the death
of a parent is undeniably present in a child's eventual marriage and as he
raises his own children. There are also subtle effects that are hard to define:
a nagging sense of absence, an emptiness, a sense of void, that something
is missing. Even when he is grown, the lost expression of the grieving child
does not fade, but remains present in a look, a gesture, or tone of voice.

Absorbed in play, a grieving young child "forgets" about a parent's death
and then "wakes up" to it as if it were a bad dream. The times of forgetting
become longer and more frequent, until the young child seems to forget
altogether, leaving the adult he becomes without conscious images or
memories, only feelings that return as emotional flashbacks. These unconnected sad flashback emotions are deceptive as they are played out in relationships with spouses and with children. As we will later see, until a person
can recognize and express these feelings as that of a grief-stricken child, he
will continue to respond to the reawakened emotions of the past as if the
causes were entirely in the present.

A family loss before maturity predisposes the adult to depression.[9] A loss
in early life can lead to physiological alterations of the brain that change a
person's response to life events.[10] New or symbolic loss can trigger old grief.
Even joy can invoke past sorrow. When a father or mother's witness to a

child's victories and life transitions is absent, room must be made for the sorrow that attends in the parent's place: learning to ride a bicycle or drive a car, the events of puberty, awards, graduations, marriage, the birth of a child. One woman who lost a mother as a child felt the emptiness on her wedding day. After acknowledging and expressing her grief for her mother's absence, however, she was able to go forward and enjoy the day.

Children have greater needs and fewer resources to cope with death than do adults. In the wake of one parent's death, a mother becomes a widow, a father becomes a widower. At the funeral, surrounded by friends and family, the sorrowful parent watches the rich years of shared history being buried in the earth. A bitter shovelful of dirt is thrown onto the lowered casket and the surviving parent and the children are reminded to trust in God and the order of the universe. But young children can have no understanding of death or of its permanence, and the friends and family supporting the surviving parent may overlook the reactions of a child numbed to passivity with grief and distracted by the attendant confusion. The person whose presence the child most wants at such a time has died; not even the remaining parent will do. The ability of the surviving parent to console the child rarely matches the child's need.

For the surviving parent to console a child in the midst of his own bereavement is a heroic feat of strength. Already overwhelmed with grief, he has to learn the tasks his spouse had once managed and is disconsolate just when a child needs him the most. But the loneliness is the hardest to bear, especially for the younger widow or widower. It may briefly subside in the company of others, but it continues for years until the survivor reattaches to someone else.[11] According to one study, within two years after the death of a spouse, the death rate for widowers—but not widows—increases significantly.[12] Women tend to have a community of friends to support them, whereas men often do not develop such a community for themselves, having relied instead on their wives' social involvements. Men have more trouble asking for help and allowing themselves to be vulnerable. As a consequence, widowers are lonelier, and we have seen what loneliness can do. Among survivors of both sexes, however, 20 to 40 percent never regain the previous level of healthy emotional adjustment.[13]

Meanwhile, the sad undercurrents of the household surround the child. He not only grieves for the parent he lost but at the same time empathically absorbs the grief of the parent who survives—and the experience all takes place in the endlessness of child time.

A grieving parent who is too devastated to care for a child adds yet further injury. Should the child be sent away, the child loses one parent to death, another to grief—and then loses the familiar support of friends as well. A child who is sent away at such a time feels betrayed and often becomes angry when the parent returns, especially if the child had become attached to those who cared for him during his time of need.

LOSING A ROLE MODEL

Children need their same-sex parent to learn how to be (or not to be) parents. Boys who grow up without fathers and girls who grow up without mothers need to follow the lead of someone else of their gender. If they do not find someone worthy, the vacancy dominates their lives. The child will be left with only a cultural ideal to emulate, rather than a specific, flesh-and-blood person to gauge feelings against. Although cultures define general masculine and feminine roles, children need real models for these roles in order to become good parents later.

Our parents temper the idealized cultural images of men and women with a more forgiving reality. Boys can father imperfectly like their fathers; girls can mother imperfectly like their mothers. Given reasonable examples, both can tinker with the cultural ideals without having to reinvent the role. But a nine-year-old girl whose mother dies may mother like someone emotionally frozen as a nine-year-old, and she will only be sure of her mothering until her child reaches that age. After that, she must explore new territory without the benefit of a map.

Studying the effects of primate maternal deprivation on the second generation, psychologists Stephen J. Suomi and Chris Ripp found that

> when a female monkey was separated in life from her mother, she herself had severely impaired mothering capacities. Motherless monkeys were prone to parental abuse including mutilation and killing of offspring. The younger the mother the greater was the likelihood of abuse. Peer socialization compensated for parental deprivation.[14]

Psychoanalyst Anna Freud noted that children who lose stable mother figures before age five have a harder time in adolescence than children who lose mothers later. Preadolescents who have lost mothers desperately search for a mother figure.[15]

Hope Edelman, in her book *Motherless Daughters,* writes:

Half of all motherless women surveyed said they either fear or once feared having children.[16] . . . Thousands of children in America develop characteristics of motherless children even though their mothers are still alive. Why? Because they've been raised by motherless daughters. Because motherless daughters, like all other daughters, often reproduce the parenting behaviors they received, their children can end up profiting or suffering from the loss of a grandmother they never knew. And these children, in turn, are likely to parent their children in similar fashion.[17]

. . . A daughter's early identity forms in large part from the experiences she has with her mother. . . . Losing a mother can bring this process to a premature halt, freezing a daughter's identifications at a very specific point and time . . . their identifications don't have a chance to mature.[18] . . . The mother is the primary female image a daughter internalizes and refers to for comparison throughout her life.[19]

But if she accepts a loving mother surrogate, the child can flourish and, in turn, mother well. The role model a surviving daughter selects, however, is rarely the stepmother.[20] In her survey of eighty-three families with motherless daughters, Edelman found that more than half of the fathers remarried within two years of the mother's death.[21] A Canadian survey found that unlike widows, widowers nearly all remarry and they remarry more quickly as well.[22] But remarrying too quickly after a mother's death is a sure formula for disaster, since without sufficient time to grieve, daughters reject the stepmother as a mother and a model. One woman said, "I ended up really resenting my stepmother. I picked her [to criticize] because she was the mother figure, the person I wanted most that I didn't have, and I blamed her for everything that went wrong in the family afterward."[23]

Boys especially need their fathers during adolescence. Teenage boys may rebel and act as if their families intrude on their lives, but they hunger for closer contact with their fathers; they need to observe them react as men. Generation after generation, adolescent sons who are separated from their living fathers often become unmanageable and behave obnoxiously to their mothers as the unconscious, instinctual need to be near their fathers reaches a peak. After a father's death, however, an adolescent son may become prematurely responsible, taking on tasks that constrict his freedom to explore; or he may rebel, finding his freedom and identification among peers.

Boys need to prove themselves men, and those raised without fathers often seem to hold themselves (and sometimes their sons) to an impossible standard that neither takes into account human frailties nor allows them to comfortably express their vulnerabilities. When they become parents, fatherless boys may be critical of their sons and emotionally guarded or withdrawn from their children as they resist or succumb to the effects of an underlying low-grade depression and of hiding "shameful" feelings of self-perceived weakness. A cultural icon like John Wayne may swallow manfully after a friend dies in battle, but he will not weep like a baby, nor will he betray fear except as a swaggering admission for the benefit of the younger rookie. By contrast, boys who know and respect their own fathers seem to comfortably accept a wider range of masculine emotional expression without feeling ashamed, because the living reality they know tempers the media images.

Today's inner-city gangs are, for the most part, gatherings of boys without fathers who derive their notions of masculinity solely from each other and the media. Any expression of weakness is derided. Grief is denied, expressed only as anger. The only loyalty is to one another. The ideal to emulate is all image: cool, nerveless, cold-blooded. Like the soldiers who braved No Man's Land in World War I, many gang members die proving themselves men. Prisons are filled with fatherless men; two-thirds of them have fathered children. But underneath the masks of men in prison and of every "gang-banger," beneath the cool and bitterness, are anxious, lost children desperate to find another world and to follow another image.

So it was with Jerome, an anxious, jittery, somewhat heavyset African-American man in his twenties I met at a residential alcohol and drug treatment facility where I once worked. Jerome would not fight to make a place for himself in the white world, but did fight for respect in his world. One day, when he came in for a therapy session, Jerome brought in a chart that he had made showing gang friends who had died of drugs or bullets. He was sure I wouldn't understand him unless he put real faces onto his heartbreak; otherwise, he felt his world could only be an abstraction to a white middle-class man. He pointed to each face, named each friend, and told me who he was, what he had been like, and what their relationship had been. Seeing Jerome's chart reminded me of something a patient in her nineties had said years before: "I feel like the last leaf on a tree." All her friends had died and she was alone. Though he was decades younger, there were only a few leaves left on Jerome's tree.

FILLING THE VOID

Adults who grow up with two living parents cannot comprehend the struggle for wholeness someone endures after losing a mother or father in childhood. After the death of a parent, any love a child receives plummets into vast emptiness. The child hungers for someone to fill the void, meanwhile immortalizing the dead parent as an ideal that no living person can match. Elyce Wakerman, author of *Father Loss,* was three years old when her father died; her mother never remarried. She writes:

> In my father's image, I created a god. He alone among adults remained wise and all-knowing even during that teenage time when no one over twenty-one could possibly understand anything of importance.
> . . . To my first serious boyfriend, I brought expectations nothing short of omnipotence . . . and being loved by a man meant total liberation from feelings of separateness. . . . I bestowed on Edward the power to see inside my being, to touch and anticipate my frailties and needs, and to love me for them.[24]

A three-year-old child peers out through the eyes of the person growing up—expectantly, waiting for a return that will not happen. No one living person can measure up. In searching for a perfect partner, he may leave behind a trail of discarded relationships and unhappy marriages, rejecting and wounding good people for the crime of not measuring up to the idealized lost parent.

In losing a parent of the opposite sex, a child loses an organic model for intimate relations. A living, breathing human can only disappoint when contrasted with an ideal. A girl growing up without a flesh-and-blood father cherishes fantasies that she hopes someone will fill, and grieves for the disappointing end of each relationship as if the grief were new to each goodbye.

The child deprived of love after a parent's death may later assume an air of bitterness that protects him from getting hurt again. In order to feel safer, he vows not to allow himself to depend on anyone so much again, and the proud self-reliance preserves the ache of unfulfilled childhood needs.

One man in his thirties spoke tearfully of his mother's death when he was seven:

> When I think about my mother, I feel an emptiness, like my heart's gone, like there's an empty space there, an intense longing. I didn't get to talk to her before she died. [He put his head down and wept.] This is what I go through every time I [talk about] this. [What] I always feel, every time I go to bed. I won't let anyone get that close to me.

The child's grief can heal, but the extent of that healing depends on how long he is allowed to grieve, the amount of comfort he receives, and how much a surviving parent can give. The surviving parent defines the emotional world of the child and must sustain him until there are others to love him as well.

The early remarriages that widowers with children tend to make are often emotional minefields. There are too many ways that a replacement mother can hurt a child when she steps in and lays claim to precious time the father would otherwise have spent with the child. While the father builds a new life, the child feels disloyal in abandoning the old one and attaching to another emotional world so quickly. In making a new attachment, the surviving parent seems to be asking the child to surrender the loving bath of memory of the lost parent, embrace the new life, and live happily once more. Meanwhile, the child, needing more time to grieve with the father, feels estranged and even more alone.

Unless a parent remarries, however, home often remains a very lonely place. The surviving parent is overburdened with tasks: going to work, cooking, cleaning, shopping, paying bills, caring for children, getting enough emotional sustenance for himself, and continuing to be loving and comforting to his children. Under such circumstances, children may learn to be overly responsible at a young age. One patient recalled going to the store down the block for milk and bread at the age of three after his mother died.

A mother is usually the emotional center of a family.[25] When she dies, the emotional heart of the family dies with her. The surviving father and children must somehow manage. In the aftermath of a mother's death, it is hard to give grief its due. The following two vignettes are about sons who lost their mothers and how they filled the holes in their emotional universes:

Harold was a well-respected man whose face reflected his integrity. With the help of his wife and AA, he had been sober for eight years. Harold consulted me after being offered a position that was financially tempting but required him to travel. His wife was afraid. After having attained sobriety, Harold became depressed whenever he was away from home too long. During the early years of marriage, however, Harold had enjoyed traveling and entertaining clients. His drinking never interfered with his work, but it strained the marriage and was all too apparent to their three sons. Harold had been distant and irritable when he was home until their oldest, eleven, began having trouble in school. After his wife's tearful confrontation, Harold agreed to stop drinking, travel less, and involve himself more at home.

In our first session, Harold startled himself with the intensity of his grief, and with the sudden, vivid, long-forgotten image of his mother lying in a casket at her funeral. Harold had been five. A year later, his father married a woman who seemed to care less for Harold than for his younger brother and half-sister. But Harold did well in school, took care of himself, and asked little of anyone until he met and married his wife.

In retrospect, Harold regretted the years he had missed with his children and the hardships his wife had suffered during the years she had raised the children alone. After considerable deliberation, Harold decided not to take the promotion or use antidepressants that might "help" him function but blunt his sensitivity to the rhythms of closeness and distance so important to his emotional balance.

As a little boy, Harold had not received the love he needed to console him for his mother's death, but he had managed. Later, as an adult, without the balm of alcohol to fill the emptiness inside him, he found that leaving his wife and family drained his spirit. When he was on the road, the loneliness of a five-year-old emerged until Harold again rejoined his family. Harold realized that his depression was in fact a sensitive barometer of his need for intimacy. He respected his feelings and chose not to overcome them pharmacologically. He decided not to leave his family again.

Achieving emotional intimacy is not easy for children who grow up without others to rely on. As adults, the doors to their hearts creak open slowly to reveal a painful vulnerability. Being in a position of dependence unlocks the distress of childhood's unmet needs that must be fulfilled over and over again. This is particularly difficult for men, who have to overcome the shame they learned, as boys, for needing to cry or for being vulnerable.

As a child, Harold inured himself to loneliness in order to endure it. But to have true intimacy as an adult, Harold had to open himself up to pain, then express it honestly. Until he could do that, however, Harold's wife and children had borne the loneliness that he defended himself against. When he could no longer ignore their suffering, he undertook to endure his own pain for them. When he did so, his wife could witness his pain and give him comfort for feelings that had needed consolation for years. Harold was able to give his own children the love that had been denied him as a child, rather than pass his emptiness on to them; and he also gave them the strength of his honest self-confrontation. In return, his children gave him love and respect. Facing himself and his problems honestly, and trusting the love his wife gave to him, Harold was able to grow beyond the loneliness of his bereaved youth.

RESILIENCE AFTER PARENTAL LOSS

Children are resilient creatures; they tend to bounce back from life's blows, and the love that is given to them later in life can compensate them for their early losses. Adults who lost parents during childhood can do well if they find solid emotional support as children or marry well as adults.[26] A loving community or parent surrogate can embrace a child when a mother or father no longer can. Although residual grief may emerge later in life, the child can grow up emotionally healthy and complete[27] despite undercurrents of sadness and a greater than average vulnerability to subsequent loss. A resourceful child may do well even without consistent emotional support at home:

> Craig, an only child, was two years old when his mother died. His father remarried within a year, and then spent his nights reading the paper and drinking quietly by himself. His stepmother was resentful

toward Craig and angry at his father; perhaps she felt she had been used.

Growing up, Craig spent as much time as possible away from home, with friends and with their parents, at school and with school activities. In high school when the other kids began experimenting with alcohol, Craig refused to drink because he ran track. Although it was difficult for him to concentrate on his studies, he managed a B average by working hard.

As an adult, Craig maintained his calmness with the aid of anti-depressants and a daily regimen of running and watching his diet. Intolerant of stress, he chose to work for himself, charging less than other electricians because he worked slowly. Craig married a loving, supportive woman and devoted himself to his family, but he had been depressed for most of his life; and though he was concerned about the long-term effects of antidepressants, he did not want to risk bringing gloom to his family.

Knowing of no long-term effects of antidepressants that required Craig to stop, I encouraged him to stay with his program and agreed to call if any bad long-term effects were reported.

Craig somehow survived his early loss and managed to raise himself to be a good, loving adult who was close to his family. Even though he had felt deprived of love as a child and his life was colored by sadness, he was able to avoid the lures of drugs and alcohol, and gradually, through years of trial and error, learned to structure his life to ward off debilitating depression.

Craig did not know enough of his father's history to understand why he had given up trying to make a full life, or why he avoided intimacy by hiding behind a newspaper and alcohol. Craig only knew he did not want to share his father's fate, that he did not want his children having to enter life's fray with depression tying one hand behind their back. Unlike his father, Craig did not retreat from life to avoid his grief. Instead, as a child, he had found surrogate parents among his friends' families. As an adult, he maintained a discipline of exercise and diet, established work conditions he could live with, and centered his life around his family. His ordinary healthy life was in fact a remarkable achievement.

An adult's befriending a child in difficult circumstances—respecting his feelings and not dismissing them with injunctions to "cheer up"—can rescue him. Attention from a loving adult may mean the difference between a life of love and one of bitterness. Children soak up whatever love and kindness seems true to them. Craig's friends' parents helped Craig and his future children more than they would ever know.

A child who has lost a mother or a father needs others to be kind. In Exodus 22:21–23, God decrees, "You shall not afflict any widow or orphan. If ever you afflict them and they cry out to me, I will surely hear their cry and my wrath will wax hot."

At a bereavement conference, I met Joanne, a slender woman who appeared younger than her forty-six years. Her eyes were striking in their clarity. She spoke of her longing, her search for something to help with a grief that never went away. Her mother had died of a heart attack at fifty-one, having never been sick before. Her father died six months later. An orphan at sixteen, she relied on the kindness of strangers and friends to give her support. I asked how she had made it. She said:

> I remember thinking, "I'm responsible for my own life now. I have to make it on my own." I became very focused and determined. My grandmother wanted me to stay with her. I loved her but knew I'd never make it with her. She was always complaining, always unhappy. I didn't want to hurt her, but I stayed with my girlfriend and her mother until I finished high school. I got straight A's. For a time, I smoked marijuana. I really liked it, but I made myself stop. I thought, "If I'm going to have a good life, I can't do this." In college, when I read *Children of the Holocaust*,[28] I realized there were words for what I felt. I never went through the Holocaust, but my parents' death was my Holocaust.
>
> My husband's a very good man and we have a good marriage. I've been married now for twenty-six years. At first, I didn't want children. I thought I was going to die young and I didn't want my children to grow up without a mother. Gradually, I realized that I wasn't automatically fated to die young, like my mother. Now we have two wonderful children. They're both sensitive in their own ways. My older one is artistic. My younger one cries when I talk about how much I miss my parents. I wanted to protect my children from my grief, but I knew that would be wrong. I have an especially hard time on the anniversary of my parents' death. My parents gave me such a solid foundation. We talked over everything. They let me make my own decisions and they were always there for me.

I was impressed with Joanne's openness, balance, and wisdom. She accepted her loss, embraced her grief, expressed it, and allowed others to witness it. She was grateful for the strength her parents had given her. She did not seek to relieve her grief with chemicals, run away from it, or hide it from her husband and children. She gave grief a place in her life, turned to those who could give her support, and found the strength to cope with her loss.

Children of divorce, however, find it hard to mourn adequately. The depth of lingering grief is often hard for children to appreciate: the grief may not be so easy to detect in children at the time, or even found by scientific studies years later. But the unmourned grief lingers.

DIVORCE

If a man divorces his first wife, the very altar weeps.
Babylonian Talmud

Before you marry, make sure you know
who you're going to divorce.
Yiddish proverb

With divorce, a family dies. Hearts break. A couple smashes their bond, discards their good memories, and then holds the shards of their hopes and dreams up to the grimy light of failure. Unlike the case of the death of an individual, there is no funeral to comfort the family, no societal ritual to make sense of it all, nothing to guide anyone through the next year. In civil divorce, the last rites are performed by attorneys who call the mourners "clients," and who, for the sake of "fairness" and the children, often hone their client's distrust for one another to lethal sharpness.

In Hebrew, the writ of divorcement is called a *Get*, which means, "to cut."[29] In divorce, sacred vows are cut, trust is betrayed, the soul of a couple is severed. Husband and wife each take back their half. People who have gone through a divorce often describe it as being more painful than having a parent die. After a divorce or the death of a beloved intimate, adults demonstrate all the phenomena associated with posttraumatic stress disorder (PTSD).[30]

The death of a family is harder to understand than other deaths. With divorce, what dies is home, security, belonging, a predictable future, and a more innocent, less complicated childhood. Regardless how much parents encourage their children to express their hurt and want to give witness to their pain, children generally do not receive support commensurate with the intensity of these losses.

Jeff, for example, was twenty-six and depressed. His wife, Betty, had left him after four years of marriage, and filed for divorce. His own parents had divorced when he was nine, and he had never wanted to go through anything like that again:

> Betty just left. She never explained why. We were great in bed; I did the housework; we rarely fought. She never even said she was that unhappy. She stayed only as long as I was the one doing the giving. Sure we had problems: I was at a dead-end job; I was depressed. I needed support. But when you're married, you work through the hard times, right? Nothing was wrong with our marriage that we couldn't fix. But what would Betty know? Her mom's been divorced three times and now lives in an ocean condo and drives a Mercedes. Betty was probably looking for a better deal.
>
> My parents didn't know how to have a relationship, either. Dad's mom also divorced three times, and Mom's parents were alcoholic. My parents were always arguing and then broke up when I was nine. Mom said they just didn't love each other anymore. When she said they'd always love me, I remember thinking, "They believed that they'd always love each other when they got married, too." I moved in with my dad to start high school. I really needed Dad then, but he was having a hard time, too, so I never complained. I hung out with friends, smoked pot, and kept up my grades without studying. I went to college for a few months and dropped out. Big mistake. I've worked at crummy jobs ever since. All I ever wanted was a good family. But all women care about is what you can provide for them. I feel like you can't trust any of them and it scares me to think this way.

Jeff was probably right on a number of accounts. Betty was probably looking for "a better deal," but she had also lost a chance to heal herself. Like Jeff, she had endured a broken home and like Jeff, had to rise above her unhappiness. Jeff's unhappiness had exposed the pain of Betty's childhood, and Jeff's prospects for making her happy again did not seem promising to her.

Divorce often occurs when partners' old childhood pain and their emotional needs are exposed. The crisis demands change and presents an opportunity for grappling with and healing childhood wounds. Divorce also occurs under the weight of continual, unrelieved stress as happens when one or both partners become depressed. Betty ran from the unhappiness inside her. When Jeff could no longer make her feel better, Betty abandoned the relationship without giving it a chance. Jeff had hoped they would work through their painful times together; fixing their relationship would have required each of them to face the unhappiness of their own childhood, and that Betty was unwilling to do.

Children tend to bury their grief. They cannot adequately mourn their parents' divorce at the time it takes place, and later, regardless of custody arrangements, the child is always missing someone. Depriving a child of either parent drains the child's spirit—overtly for a time, and then covertly, as a lingering emptiness emerges in times of quiet. Shared custody is often better than the prolonged absence of a parent with a diminished role. But even shared custody cannot overcome the child's loss of one parent or the other. Visiting a noncustodial parent on alternate weekends, holidays, and summers deprives a child of crucial day-to-day contact with both; the brief visits are all too fraught and pressured, and the "vacations" away from the "primary" parent may make a child homesick. Children may seem to accept the situation but still suffer from the long separations of parents who live far away from them. In time, they adapt and may seem to do well, but the cost to them may become apparent in later life.

Children of divorce need others to show them more successful styles of intimacy than those that failed their own parents. Jeff was a smart, good-hearted little boy who apparently did well as he was growing up, but he watched his home destroyed by his parents' arguments. He could not follow their example and instead tried to set his own. Rather than fight for the attention he needed from his struggling father, he grew up coping with depression. Friends and marijuana helped him rise above his depression in adolescence. But he sought to avoid the solitude of studying, since it would have evoked his loneliness. As a consequence, he dropped out of college and denied himself the possibilities of more satisfying work. The only thing that seemed important to Jeff was marrying and making a good family. He hoped to do that with Betty. When she left him, his already fragile trust in the possibility of having a good relationship was broken. He had risked his heart again and had lost. Jeff will not trust as easily the next time.

Relationships seem perilous for children of divorce. They feel that the future contains buried land mines, invisible to the naked eye but deadly nonetheless. Children of divorce, in particular, ask, "How do you know you're with the right person?" They continually scrutinize potential partners for the fatal incompatibility that will doom the relationship—and too often they find it.

Children of divorce become vigilant looking for flaws that can destroy love and family; they may fear committing themselves to any relationship. The disappointment they feel in their parents makes them distant from them.[31] Searching for flaws, the children find what they are looking for. As adolescents experimenting with expression and relationships, they may try to vanquish normal healthy expressions of emotions. For instance, years after his parents had divorced, one man suppressed his ordinary masculine assertion and invariably became hostile toward the women he dated whom he had initially allowed to dominate him. His mother had continued to disparage men after her divorce, and he was afraid to be anything like the men she disparaged.

Children of divorce often distrust the makeup of their own characters. The once adoring son who imitated his father now resembles the man his mother rejected. The daughter who tried to be like her mother now winces at the comparison. They cannot trust their parents to be good models for intimate partnerships, and they judge the good and bad qualities in their parents' characters without having the years of experience or perspective to do so reliably. All children go through a stage where they become disappointed with their parents, but children of divorce become disillusioned prematurely, and have difficulty seeing their parents from a less judgmental perspective later.

Parents going through a divorce are not at their best. They are crazed with fear, grief, and anger, not only for the ending of their own relationship, but also because they feel the lives of their children are at stake. Each parent is afraid the other will fight to take the children away, or somehow hurt their relationship to their children.

Genes urge parents to kill or die for their children. They know nothing of civil actions. When the relationship to a child is in danger, nothing else matters. The same genetic imperatives that instinctively rouse parents to action when children are physically threatened are the ones that drive their behavior when they are threatened in custody battles. Judgment clouds over with passions that have gone over the edge. It may take divorced parents years to understand the experience fully. But before they do, they usually blame each other.

One parent, seeing the other parent's failings as sick defects in character, wants to protect the children from them, wants friends to witness and the courts to recognize them. The other parent, sickened at the other's portrayal of him, feels unseen and maligned—and afraid, too, that others' opinions have been contaminated by the unfair characterization. Unspoken and unacknowledged, each parent also fears there may be some truth to the other parent's portrayal.

It is hard to be judicious in the face of the parental passions that children evoke, and custody rulings are often affected by a judge's personal preferences toward mothers or fathers. Parents who are denied custody of their children by the terms of divorce live with grief their children can feel and may later consider a part of their parent's character.

One man, talking about his parents' divorce when he was twelve, looked back at a time of bitter loneliness that had seemed exciting at the time:

> They were both so whacked out with each other that I just made my own way. I didn't rely on them for anything. I took care of myself. I became strong and independent. I'm not sure my parents noticed. I learned to scam. I looked older and I changed the date on my ID. By the time I was sixteen, I was tending bar and making good money. It felt pretty cool at the time. But I look back and realize that I was a pretty lonely kid. I'm finally getting close to my parents again, but I wonder whether I'll ever be able to settle down.

A mother and father at war with each other harm their children by the intensity of their conflict. One parent's victory damages a child's relationship to the other. Wounds to either parent become scars to the children. Both parents, present or absent, make up a child's emotional home. Even after the mayhem of the actual divorce, a child is surrounded by the feelings parents put into it.

The level of healing or injury the child brings to his own marriage later also depends on the honesty of his self-scrutiny. When parents are civil and caring, children and adolescents often deny that their parents' divorce has had an effect on them. At the time, the divorce seems to belong more to the parents. Children see their parents in pain and do not want to add their own to it. They need their parents to support their lives, but their parents are often too distraught to do so.

With parents reeling in the throes of divorce, the children see a frightening cataclysm in their future. They try to hold on to stability while their parents are in flux. Young children live in the moment; adolescents gird themselves with bravado and friends and pretend the divorce doesn't affect them much. But they do know its effects. No child of divorce ever wants to go through a divorce of his own. Divorce, the death of a family, is a defining event, radically dividing a childhood into a before and after.

The popular belief that divorce is better for the children than the extended misery of an unhappy marriage is often untrue. Adult children of divorced, nonabusive parents often date their difficulties to the divorce; and the upheaval is prolonged in child time. Divorce may come as a relief if parental conflicts had been intense, but most children of nonabusing divorced parents look back on the time before the divorce as a golden time of coherence.

A stepparent cannot replace the parent who is gone, and often displaces a parent the child prefers. Whatever their hopes or expectations, stepparents have no intrinsic authority with their stepchildren. Children easily see stepparents as interlopers and resent them for their influence, for their presence, for competing for the parent's attention, and for taking time away from the only parent who is near. Children may take advantage of newfound powers as parents compete for them, and are lonelier for doing so. The emotional life of the blended family is often tangled, and its fabric is apt to unravel under pressure. The abstract loss of a family cannot compare to the concrete absence of a mother or father, but adults looking back on their parents' divorce see the magnitude of the loss.

THE LEFT AND THE LEAVING
Abandoned Children, Abandoning Parents

My mother told me [my father] left because
he was disappointed I was a girl.
Elyce Wakerman, *Father Loss*

Losing a parent under any circumstances is difficult, but especially difficult is the loss of parents who abandon their children by leaving the home or killing themselves. Abandoning parents cause far more harm than those who die a natural death.[32] As they mature, children voluntarily abandoned by a parent trust again only cautiously, if at all. They grow up believing that they were not lovable, good, or important enough for the parent to stay. As adults, they may protect themselves from getting the love and intimacy they want and need. Instead, they keep themselves apart, believing that if they do not trust there can be no betrayal, that without love there will be no heartbreak. They have much to grieve and many problems to overcome, but if they avoid the pitfall of drugs and alcohol, their life stories are often heroic testimony to their resilience.

Abandoned children typically make up stories about the parent who left, and they readily believe the stories the remaining parent tells about the one who has gone. The stories that abandoned children and parents tell may or may not be true, but they are born of hurt, not understanding. The ones that children fabricate usually feature an abandoning parent who is happy without them. The stories are invariably wrong and the assumption hurts the children who make them.

PARENTS WHO RUN AWAY

Early in the child psychiatry portion of my training, I was assigned to work with two brothers who were continually getting into trouble. The boys, four and five years old, seemed like a couple of sweet kids who felt bad about being bad. I played with them and talked and listened to them while their mother spoke with the child psychiatrist. I had no idea how to be a child psychiatrist and the boys' mother didn't have a clue how to be a mom. I never knew much about her and did not know enough to ask. I only saw an overburdened, tense-looking woman on welfare struggling to raise her two children without any other support.

Her children were out of control and so was she; she seemed over-whelmed and ready to explode. Her breathing was rapid and her muscles tense. She tried to control her anger when disciplining them, but she was either ineffectual or enraged, and the children ran wild. She could not get anyone to baby-sit for her, so she was unable to develop a life outside the home. When she finally blew up and began screaming at them, everyone felt bad. Expressing their anxiety with hyperactivity and anger, the boys attempted to draw their mother close by behaving badly. At the same time, they hated themselves for hurting her: they told me so in words and in the stories they made up as they played with dolls.

In the weeks that I worked with the family, it was obvious that the mother was trying to keep a lid on her boiling emotions, while her children clung desperately to her and thrashed about. Still, I was unprepared for her decision to give the children up for adoption.

When I came to work one day, I watched three hearts break. Everything had already been arranged. The mother kneeled to her sons, looked them in the eye, and told them she would never see them again. She tried to explain why she had to give them up, how she loved them, how it wasn't their fault. The wailing children, clutching her, promised to be good; and I vainly hoped for some reprieve. I tried to imagine their future, and feared for them all.

Abandoning a child is an act of desperation, an urgent grabbing for life, a flight from pain, or an expression of a parent's terrible fear of harming his child. Some parents, tormented because of their own unfulfilled needs, may leave their children to grab compulsively at other relationships. Other parents, unable to endure the relegation of their parenting to alternating weekends, abandon their children after court-imposed custody arrangements legally deny them their biological imperatives. But no matter what the reason, there is no solace in losing or putting aside a child.

After giving birth, unmarried teenagers face heartbreaking choices that only they should decide: keep the child and give up youth's dreams or put the child up for adoption and then live with a hollowness that will haunt them? Under difficult circumstances, a young girl must decide two futures—her own and that of her baby, and they must both live with the consequences. No formulaic "right" decision can help her, and the parent who pressures a new mother at such a time can leave a lifelong legacy of pain and resentment.

Regardless of the reason, parents who "give up" children suffer a decline of spirit[33] just as the children suffer a decline of spirit in losing a parent. New intimacies cannot fill the vacuum of having lost a child. In my professional career, I have met only two women who were able to say casually, "I don't miss my children." Both were chronically psychotic and addicted; I had the sense that their psychosis helped them avoid regret. Fathers may be less attached to infants than mothers, but they are just as attached to children they raise. A parent who abandons a child may build a new family later or attempt to seal grief away, but there is, always, a dangling connection, with something missing at the other end.

If parents are not honest about their actions, their children are left with a distorted reality that becomes a part of their identity. Whether a child decides "I'm not good enough" or "My father (or mother) is no good," his parenting skills later will be damaged not only because of his own parent's abandonment, but by a character that has been additionally distorted by his false beliefs.

Men who abandon their children often had fathers who abandoned *them.* Having grown up without a father's love and having relied on others for support, these men often say they don't want to "mess up" their children by reentering their lives. But in underestimating their importance, they harm the children they are trying to protect by leaving them to grieve and misunderstand, and they hurt themselves even more.

Hugh was one such man. Hugh's father had committed suicide, and he himself had not seen his own children in the years since he had stopped drinking:

> Hugh was the father of three adult sons he was reluctant to contact. He felt he had failed them. They had rejected him, he thought, and they now had families of their own to think about. Hugh had been depressed, off and on, from the time he had been a teenager, ever since his father's suicide; and despite counseling and antidepressants, his depression had deepened during the years of his sobriety. Now sober, middle-aged, and feeling the profound emptiness of his life, Hugh only clung to life to protect his children from having to deal with the consequences of his own suicide. Finally, after much struggle and soul-searching, Hugh wrote his sons letters of apology. Afterward, Hugh and his adult sons reconnected, and over the next several months they reconciled. Their restored relationship was a joyous discovery that made all their lives fuller. And knowing their father and understanding his life story corrected their negative impressions of him from the earlier years.

Hugh had attributed his depression to his father's suicide, but in fact his depression had deepened despite antidepressants, therapy, and sobriety because of the absence of his children. Hugh had heroically stood guard, enduring tormenting isolation for years, in order to protect them from the ravages of his suicide. Not attempting suicide was an act of strength, not a non-action. Hugh spared his children the anguish he had endured.

Abandoned children, like children of suicides, have much to grieve and try to understand. Most of them believe a parent abandoned them because that parent had chosen another life in a calculation of self-interest. They do best to find the truth—to understand their parents' lives enough to find compassion for both of them, grieving, then accepting rather than resenting the painful circumstance of their childhoods.

The remaining parent, however, is not usually sympathetic to the spouse who abandoned the family. The abandoned child's anger intrudes on his grief and opposes it; and without understanding the parent who left him, he has no capacity to temper the betrayal with compassion. He cannot grieve sufficiently, and more turbulent emotional undercurrents linger.

Abandoned children can, however, imagine a future day of reckoning or reconciliation. Unlike suicides' children, they do not fear a lethal trap-door within.

THE LEGACY OF SUICIDE

When a parent kills himself, a child must come to terms with an event that never should have occurred. In order to love, this child must learn to trust the future despite the enormity of his parent's betrayal. To enjoy peace and intimacy, he must overcome the dread of what may lie in wait in some unknown chamber of feeling by facing and expressing his feelings. To forgive, he must learn to understand a life the dead parent found too painful to endure.

The reason for a parent's disappearance affects a child for a lifetime. While all abandonment calls into question the love of the parent, suicide is an abandonment that accuses survivors of culpability—the last straw in an excruciating history. People commit suicide to end physical or emotional pain or to punish those they blame for hurting them—not necessarily to die. As the child grows up, he must come to terms with painful, haunting questions.

To begin his memoir *A Hole in the World,* Richard Rhodes writes:

When I was thirteen months old, my mother killed herself. . . . (And good lord, writing these words now, all these years afterward, for the first time in memory my eyes have filled with tears of mourning for her. What impenetrable vessel preserved them?) I didn't know my mother, except as infants know. At the beginning of my life the world acquired a hole. That's what I knew, that there was a hole in the world. For me there still is. It's a singularity. In and out of a hole like that, anything goes.[34]

Then later:

If she hadn't killed herself she'd probably still be alive. Her older sisters are. Fifty years of her. I can't imagine. I'm sorry for her pain, but what pain she inflicted on us all with her selfish suicide.[35]

Parents who die leave children with "a hole in the heart." Parents who kill themselves leave children to understand and overcome, or be defeated by, pain that they themselves cannot bear.

REENACTING A PARENT'S SUICIDE TO MAKE SENSE OF IT

When a grandparent had committed suicide in a parent's childhood, the traumatized parent must bury dark emotions—emotions that can linger as an undercurrent, or return as flashbacks, and be overwhelming. Afraid of becoming depressed, they become anxious as well if their children feel too blue. But skirting their own or their children's bad feelings interferes with intimacy between the generations.

Children of suicides may also unconsciously re-create a parent's anguish in order to answer the question "What could make life so unendurable for my father (or mother) that he would do such a thing to me?" In the hope of understanding their parents, they may unconsciously create painful situations in their own lives to make their parent's act comprehensible to them. To live a life beyond bitterness, children of suicides need to understand their parents enough to temper their harsh judgments with forgiveness, grieve for their parents, and go on with life again. A child survivor needs to find out all he can about his absent parent in order to love and trust again. Following a parent's suicide, the effects can usually be traced for four generations; to understand a parent, a child must try to imagine what the emotional climate had been like for the children of each generation sequentially.

Those who do not express their pain in words commonly express it in their actions. Swimming in the perilous waters of reenacting a parent's pain allows the child of a suicide to have enough empathy to forgive his parent, grieve his loss, and begin to breathe again—but he also risks drowning in such dangerous waters. This was the case with Eric, a tall, powerful, thirty-year-old man who was separated from his wife and three children. He desperately wanted to stop drinking and win back his family:

> Eric had been twenty when his father killed himself ten years before. He married and had three children by the time he was twenty-four. His father had been raised in an abusive home, and he began drinking heavily after he crippled a neighbor's child in a car accident. Drunk, despairing, and unable to work, his father had talked of suicide for weeks. Eric awoke at 4 A.M. one morning with a terrible sense of dread. He found his father by the side of the house: "He blew half his head off. He made sure I was home. He knew I could take it better than any of the others. He muffled the sound of the gun with his face. He stuck the gun in his eyeball.[36] I thought he was alive when I got to him. It was December 10; steam was rolling off of his head."
>
> In the years that followed, Eric both worked and drank in a fury until his wife left with the children. "I had a nervous breakdown," he admits. "It just got worse and worse." Eric then got a bottle of liquor, went home and sat with a shotgun in his mouth for about an hour. "After this I was a wreck. I couldn't see my kids. I didn't want them to see me like this. I want help. I hope my wife will take me back. I don't want to live without my family, but I don't want to do my kids the way Dad did me."

Eric extracted what consolation he could from a moment of indelible horror that was traumatically imprinted into his brain, forever warning him to be alert to some future circumstance that would prove lethal to him and endanger his family. Believing that his father trusted his strength and had entrusted him with the family, Eric was left with a heavy burden, a bleeding wound, and an image of necessary masculine toughness that disallowed the expressions of vulnerability that would have allowed his wife to comfort him.

We do not usually move to comfort the strong, even when they are ready to crack and fall over. The alcohol that helped him appear strong relieved Eric of having to express the vulnerability he felt when sober. It also took away the possibility of receiving the consolation that would have genuinely strengthened him. Eric needed his wife to comfort him, but she needed to witness his pain when he was sober in order to give Eric the support he needed to work through his father's premature death. Eric, however, did not allow his wife to help. Instead, seeking to avoid the pain that threatened to debilitate him, Eric submerged himself in work and drink, abandoning the potential intimacy that would lay him open to raw grief and then to its healing. Eric's wife and children were left with the pain of his absence; the pain that Eric avoided and had hoped not to inflict on them was transmitted to them nonetheless.

In leaving him, Eric's wife violently stripped him of his armor, revealing his overwhelming grief and his sick horror, and leaving him to face the full burden of his pain. It was her only hope. Had she remained, she would have continued to be helpless in the face of Eric's distance. Her only hope was that, left on his own, Eric would face his feelings. If he was unwilling to do it with her, she reasoned, perhaps he would have to do it without her.

With a shotgun planted in his mouth, Eric finally understood what his father had felt: a moment of wild, insane pain, terror, and self-loathing, an expression to his family of everything that was inside him. It was the moment of truth; and in that moment Eric chose another path, sparing his children the worst of his father's legacy.

A MOTHER'S SUICIDE

In the hospital psychiatric unit, on the top of a pile of pink message slips, I found a note stating "Maureen killed herself." The date and place of the funeral followed.

We had worked together years before and I had not seen her since. Maureen. So gentle, airy-light and wispy-delicate. I loved the beauty of her spirit. Her patients had been graced by it.

But Maureen carried a secret: her mother had killed herself. She was fourteen years old and alone when she found her mother's body; her mother had been twenty-nine. She had once shyly spoken to me about the day of her mother's suicide. Her mother had said something cryptic that had left Maureen feeling uneasy all day. Leaving for school on the bus, she had felt a sense of dread that almost made her turn back. Upon returning from school, Maureen found her mother hanging in the closet.

In hearing her story, I wept; in telling it, Maureen wept. Afterward, for weeks, Maureen began to weep whenever she passed me in the hall. She then bashfully ran into a room so no one would see her. After a time, she seemed more embarrassed than grieving; it seemed like an affectionate confidence the two of us shared, almost humorous. But in responding more to her embarrassment than her grief, I misunderstood.

Maureen was also twenty-nine when she killed herself. In the last months of her life, she had become increasingly withdrawn, but no one had understood what it meant. The atmosphere at the funeral was thick with grief, guilt, and anger. Her husband, friends, and everyone else in the room were stunned.

We could only imagine what those last months were like for her. I worried for her husband and was glad she had had no children. Maureen's mother's suicide had left her with horror, grief, and a gaping emptiness within her, which she had for years successfully assuaged with good friends, compassionate and meaningful work, and a love that seemed to pour out of her. But whatever had triggered her depression, I cannot help but wonder if Maureen, like Eric, had been drawn to the dark waters of despair by a need to understand why her mother had killed herself. Like Eric, she had not let others witness her pain. Unlike Eric, she could not find her own way out.

A SUICIDE IN THE FAMILY

Following his release from the hospital after a psychotic episode, Michael, twenty-three, was brought to my office by his parents. They were afraid for his future; and Michael's faith in his own judgment, feelings, and perceptions had been badly shaken:

> While in church, earnestly praying for some answer to his restless soul, Michael had suddenly felt an oceanic love envelop him. Everything was made clear: in the cosmic web that sustains us all, everything is connected; life and death are just different parts of the weave. Michael sang his ecstasy in the middle of the sermon and was placed in the hospital for a brief stay.

Michael's grandmother had killed herself six weeks before his mother, Margaret, had given birth to him. Michael's father had wanted to console Margaret after the suicide; but Margaret said she hadn't been surprised at her mother's act and denied having been close to the unhappy, bitter woman. Margaret had been six when her mother had run off with a boyfriend and eight when she returned. Margaret considered herself blessed because she had a loving father. He had remarried a wonderful woman who had stepped in and had taught her what it was to have and be a good mother. Her mother had hurt her while she was alive, and Margaret was determined that her mother was not going to inflict still more damage with her death. Michael's birth was a joy, she had a newborn to nurse, and she staunchly maintained that her mother's death did not affect her much.

For all Margaret's protests to the contrary, however, the suicide of her mother did have the potential to damage the crucial early years of Michael's life. Margaret was so resolute in her determination to provide a tranquil shelter for her newborn and so angry at her mother that she did not allow herself to mourn. But despite Margaret's heroic attempts to defend herself and her baby from the aftermath of her mother's suicide, they were caught in its web.

Lost in the early romance between mother and child, Margaret could gaze into the eyes of her baby and give her son a love that filled the hurt, lonely spaces inside herself. In order to protect the calm she needed to respond empathically to her newborn, however, Margaret had to disconnect from her grief, hurt, and anger. Her sensitive son grew up relating to the hurt and absence that remained buried in his mother.

Michael grew up with neither the words to describe nor knowledge of the history to explain the unaccountable sadness and emptiness that he felt inside—that unidentifiable void that he needed to fill. It made him lonely. The spiritual ecstasy that filled Michael may have returned him to unremembered feelings that he had experienced before, as an infant in complete rapport with his mother. Words cannot describe the loving, oceanic feelings of an infant's universe. The feelings overwhelmed his rationality.

Margaret, denying the pain of her mother's death, had not given grief its due, and the denied feelings had affected her infant son. But she did not mask her feelings about her son's illness. With her support and his father's,

Michael assembled a community of friends, established a routine of meaningful work, and gradually tapered his medication. From what I have heard, he has married and done well.

GRIEF IN ADULT LIFE

The world becomes a scarier and lonelier place when death resides in it. A grandparent is most often our first close relative to die.[37] From a grandparent, a child receives love with fewer conditions than his parents' and learns of life with its wisdom distilled and the consequences of its lessons visible. In a grandparent's company, a child sees his roots extend back in time, anchoring him to the family and its history. He can look to the past to see what he is made of and to see what it was that made his parent. With death anticipated, in the proper sequence, and without the complexities of a parent-child relationship, mourning a grandparent is usually straightforward.

This is ordinary life, simple grief—expected, understood, and straightforward. But grief is not so simple when death is unexpected or out of sequence. Nor is grief simple for children raised by grandparents who then pass away. They lost their parents first, and then the grandparents who raised them after. These children and young adults can become bitter and afraid to accept a love they desperately need.

Grieving the loss of a parent, too, is filled with complexity when the relationship between parent and child had been fraught with hurt and unresolved anger. When children judge rather than understand the parents who disappointed them, grief is not simple, and cannot be simply expressed. Complex feelings linger until the child understands enough to have compassion for the parent.

Even when it is anticipated, death is traumatic for the survivors. The division between life and death is terrifyingly abrupt: in an instant, a person's existence just vanishes. When there has been a long illness, we may believe we are prepared for a loved one's death, but the suddenness of that transformation leaves us in shock. Try as we might, we are still unprepared for the silence left after love's last goodbye.

The death of someone we love leaves us with an altered reality we cannot comprehend, so we ask unanswerable questions about the very nature of death: Can a life whose spirit had once shined so brightly be extinguished? Just like that? Is there not even a trace after memory passes? What happens when we die? Do we have a soul that lives on? Where does the spirit go? Is there a reason for our existence or do we exist for no other reasons than the ones we make? The death of a loved one calls into question the very nature and reality of the universe. The reality of that death can only hammer into us over time.

If it is unexpected, the death of a loved one is overwhelming. After the shock, our lives are in disarray, our minds are confused, our hearts broken. Frightened and angry, our bodies rouse to electric intensity, and yet there is nothing to do. Then time passes, shock wears off. Fear settles. Anger grinds down. We mourn. Emptiness fills. In time, our bodies and lives reorganize to establish a new equilibrium. But for a long time, a startle of lucid memory will pierce consciousness with the edge of grief still keen. We do not get over grief so much as we learn to embrace it along with life.

If we are fortunate to live so long, we all lose someone we love, and if we are very fortunate, we have a lot to lose. The lessons from catastrophic trauma are not meant to be easily forgotten. We grieve as nature's way of slowly healing from life's inevitable catastrophes.[38] The grieving our parents do spares us their sorrow. The grieving we fail to do becomes a challenge for our children. The scars we bear are signs of heroic endurance. So it was for our parents and so it will be for our children—each generation grieves the passing of the one before in a continuous chain stretching back to the dawn of humanity.

CHAPTER 8

PROTECTING AGAINST DANGERS THAT ARE NO LONGER THERE

Passing On Survival Reactions

The fathers have eaten a sour grape,
and the children's teeth are set on edge.
Jeremiah 31:29

ACTIVATING THE NERVOUS SYSTEM AND THE BODY

As we have seen, after a trauma, once we have learned to react, we do not forget. As adults, after a grave threat, our brain becomes hypersensitive to even vaguely similar confrontations. As children, it takes comparatively little to cause a similarly deep impression. Furthermore, our former sense of helplessness amplifies our future response, so we can be better prepared the next time: norepinephrine floods the brain, and adrenaline readies the body to full alert. If we meet the challenge, we return to balance. But if we can do nothing in the face of unceasing threat, we shut down physically and emotionally. To protect ourselves from the damaging intensity of our own response, we become depressed.

Evolution decrees that learned dangers are not to be forgotten, and successful reactions in meeting dangers are repeated. When parents react to threat, children react to their parents' stress. The parents' stress activates the child's nervous system to forewarn the child of a danger he has never encountered before. A child can learn to fear a hot stove without having to be injured by it first. Consciously and unconsciously, with words, tone of voice, and physical reactions, parents "light up" the child's nervous system with an awareness of the dangers that they themselves had endured. In later adult life, children often stumble on these lessons as impediments after conditions have changed. Such was the legacy for the children of the survivors of the Great Depression.

The survivors of the Great Depression had been traumatized by years of desperate economic uncertainty. They had been among or had witnessed those who were unemployed—the helpless, hungry, and homeless. Their lives had been indelibly marked by the frightening insecurity of the times, and they could never again be assured of tomorrow's provision of basic necessities. They went on to raise children who were largely unacquainted with economic insecurity, many of whom later criticized their parents' emphasis on work and money.

Many adult children whose parents lived through the Depression feel alienated from them. They feel devalued or unloved because their parents were so stingy with them. Others denigrate their parents for having led suffocatingly constricted lives, going to their oppressive jobs day after day and coming home exhausted, with little expression of joy.

For those who survived the traumatic conditions of the Depression, however, money represented food and security and was not to be spent on the unnecessary or the frivolous. Not surprisingly, then, when children of Depression survivors spend money, they do not do so casually. When they were children, their Depression-trained parents had anxiously watched every penny and showed anger at any sign of waste. Even when the children of Depression survivors do spend freely, they likely do so as a small act of defiance, consciously or unconsciously made in opposition to their parents' anxiety.

Similarly, a woman who has been raped and threatened with death is affected for years, and her children are affected by her insecurity, anxieties, and quickened startle reactions. Even though she may tell her daughter nothing of the rape, the daughter is nonetheless still likely to grow up to be hypervigilant for danger.

On the other hand, a timid mother may have a daughter who ventures out fearlessly and is, at times, reckless in her behavior.[1] Refusing to be imprisoned by her mother's limitations, the daughter may attempt to cast off her mother's anxiety (and her own) by responding sarcastically to her mother's realistic fears as well as those that are exaggerated.

LEARNING A PARENT'S OUTMODED RESPONSES

As we have seen, a single sufficiently traumatic event can cause irreversible emotional reactions throughout life, reactions that can become superfluous,[2] annoying, and even dangerous when circumstances change. Children imprinted with the outmoded responses of a parent are limited in their ability to adapt to a changed world:

> At age twenty, with a one-year-old son at home, Lena was brutally raped at gunpoint. Before the rape, Lena's marriage had been a romance and motherhood a joy. Afterward, she became quite fearful, quick to anger, and easily upset. She winced at being touched but had a daughter the following year. The children were fifteen and seventeen when their parents' marriage ended. Thirty years after the rape, Lena's fearfulness had only muted, not gone away. Lena was never really comfortable socially again and her children picked up on her reaction.
>
> Both of Lena's children attribute their fearfulness to their mother's rape. Lena's son prefers staying home with his wife; leaving the house makes him anxious. Lena's daughter considers herself to be an overly protective mother who is more alert to the possibility of danger than her friends.

Nontraumatized animals show responses similar to those of their traumatized mothers.[3] It is not necessary to experience trauma directly to behave as if traumatized.

ABSORBING PARENTAL EMOTIONS

Besides overriding trauma, children are affected by the unique day-after-day emotional atmosphere of their family home—its warmth or coldness, degree of tension or ease, humor, idiosyncratic practices, etc. We consider the happiness passed on to us to be normal, so we don't comment on it. We tend to notice more when something is not right.

As adults, we are all affected by any pall of depression in the home; how much more so then are children who live in that home? Younger children and infants absorb their parents' feelings through their pores. Infants absorbing their parents' long-forgotten sorrow will not know the sorrow's origin when they become adults.

When a child dies, for example, the parents' grief never really goes away; it only dulls with the passing of time. Children born after the death of a sibling are affected by a lingering sorrow that their parents may never express. The grief without a name becomes part of them. People who lose a sibling in early childhood are, as adults, often out of touch with how much they have been affected, because they were too young to remember the days of grief and horror that surrounded the death.

The parents' grief continues for years, and the effects on the surviving children are profound.[4] Children who grow up with a parent's unexpressed grief breathe sorrow daily; then, as adults, they must deal with amorphous feelings of hurt that are without any basis in their own personal history. The feelings can make no sense to them because the injury was invisible.

In an old Bavarian custom, after the death of a child parents named the next-born child *Erdemüde*, which, translated literally, means "earth-weary." The name offered recognition that the child was born to a grief-stricken mother who measured her new child against the child who was lost. The child may be the joy that fills the emptiness left behind, or a bitter reminder of loss. Though some may regard the custom as cruel, the child so named at least knew he was born to sorrow. He did not have to wonder about the air of melancholy that pervaded his life.[5]

PASSING ON UNEXPRESSED GRIEF

Children may grow up with a background hum of grief that is constant and over time may be tuned out. If the reason for grief is not discussed within the family, the children will have no words for an inchoate sense of unhappiness they may or may not overtly express. They may appear happy and content, but when they start their own families, their children grow up with a grief twice removed. Grief's grandchildren squirm with feelings that detract from life, make no obvious sense, and make them feel there is something fundamentally wrong with their characters.

Empathically derived feelings can alter genetically inherited temperament.[6] Uncomfortable feelings that extend to earliest memory, with no "apparent" historical justification, can often be traced to events endured by parents or grandparents. The key word here is "apparent." For instance, Eliot, a man in his late sixties, finally emerged from his cocoon of isolation late in life. Always a loner, he was painfully shy, and he seemed to be continually apologizing for himself. But after Eliot had a realization that changed how he thought of himself, he belatedly began developing friendships:

> I always thought there was something wrong with me. I could see that my mom loved my two older brothers, but she was distant with me, pulled back. I thought it was my fault. No matter what I did, I could never make her happy. I was in my twenties when my dad died. He was buried right next to this little grave with our family name on it. I asked my mother who the baby was, and she said, "That's your sister. She was only four months old when she died." I was shocked. And suddenly I knew why I had this sad, empty feeling in me all the time. It wasn't until a few years ago that I had another epiphany. I realized that my mother was probably afraid to love me too much. She never knew why my sister died. When I realized that, I realized that there wasn't anything wrong with me.

We would be wise to consider our parents' stories and lives imaginatively, immersing ourselves occasionally in daydreams of their experience. Emotional problems our parents don't resolve remain in the family until someone resolves them. Consider what happens to a young widow with a new baby. Regardless of how much witness and consolation she receives, she must grieve and nurture her infant simultaneously. Looking at her child with both love and sorrow, she either expresses her tears or holds them in. Holding her baby in arms that feel heavy with defeat, she knows what her child is too young, too innocent to realize: the child will never know its father. The sunny future she had imagined with her husband and children is lost, and may never be as happily replaced.

The newborn is nurtured with sorrow, grows up with melancholy, and unconsciously adapts to it. The effects may be invisible. Yet a child in the following generation may absorb the feelings and be confused by them.

The source of his melancholy may become clearer to that young widow's grandchild if he imagines living her life. Typically, a young bride and groom are steeped in the romance of marriage; they are in love and are armed with innocence, faith, and hope for an idealized future. Then the groom disappears suddenly, taking the bride's dreams with him. For her, the romance of youth did not come to a natural end, but instead remained idealized in her imagination. This always happens when people die young. In posters and our imagination, we still see images of the young James Dean and Marilyn Monroe. They never age, while the romantic image of a young Marlon Brando has given way to the ravages of time. John Kennedy remains forever young in our minds, while we see his younger brother Ted as a paunchy older man.

The grandchild of a young widow can imagine his grandmother, young, grieving, and making the best of her life; he can imagine his father as a boy too young to remember his own biological father. He can imagine his grandmother still quietly grieving for the man her son would never know. I have seen this pattern repeatedly: when one spouse dies in a young marriage, the other's relationship to a subsequent partner suffers in comparison, falling short of memories of a romance that had not yet given way to years of ordinary life.

Like a variant of Erdemüde, children born to a widow or widower's second marriage may grow up reacting to sadness without appreciating its source. But with grief unstated, the remarriage is, at best, a compromise and at worst, a factory reject, a second. Without understanding a parent's relationship to a lost, early love, children born to a parent's unhappy second marriage may misattribute causes of family unhappiness. They only know that something is wrong with the fabric of the parent's marriage, and that someone or everyone in the family stands accused for the failure to make it right.

We would like to wave a magic wand so the young, grieving widow would accept her loss, grieve, get over it, and go on. But there are no magic remedies for her. The best she can do is freely express her loss throughout the years and, in those moments, allow the second husband to accept and witness her grief, and console her for the bride she had been. He must accept that he may suffer in comparison. An aging, heavy Marlon Brando can never romantically compete with a young, shining James Dean. Although we would wish it to be otherwise, in real life there may not be a happy-forever-after story. But if we can accept and understand the truth of our feelings, we can put them in perspective rather than letting them direct and damage our lives.

MAKING SENSE OF FEELINGS

The grief that comes to us out of the blue may originate in our parents' lives and not our own; it may be hard to differentiate between unhappiness that arises from the past and that which is caused by present events. We may mistakenly blame our partners or circumstances for feelings originating in remembered or unremembered events from our childhood.

Children do the unfinished grieving that parents pass over. Parents who lock their feelings in, emotionally lock their children out. As a consequence, the children are left with feelings they cannot understand, respond to, or explain. The parent's intimacy that emotionally sustains the child thins, and the child may feel rejected. The child harbors the feelings his parent avoids. In the immediacy of a child's world, feelings absorbed from parents are unquestioningly accepted, quickly forgotten, and buried, only to return later, out of time, out of place, and out of context.

Generation after generation of parents and children become distant from one another because parents keep their pain to themselves. How many tight-lipped fathers deny the pain and anger contained in their chests? How many mothers, outwardly cheerful, feel pained and hollow within? How many parents cannot sit still long enough to enter the immediate world of their children and just be with them? Parents may wish to, but they cannot entirely shield their children from their own unhappiness.

Researchers have long noted that depression seems to run in families. A genetic predisposition is likely; but genetically predisposed or not, an individual's depression[7] can almost always be traced to roots in earlier development: a loss in childhood or adolescence, or to the emotions absorbed from a parent. Although there is literature that denies this is so, in over twenty years of psychiatric practice, I have not observed otherwise. Exploring the life and childhood history of the parents and grandparents as well as the events of the individual patient's early life usually illuminates the origin of puzzling emotional reactions.

Who has not been struck by a hollow mood when, out of nowhere, a sense of emptiness suddenly cracks through to consciousness, when the security of ordinary reality wavers for a moment? That moment may be a flashback to a time long past and not consciously remembered, a time before we had learned words to express ourselves.

Feelings that come "out of nowhere" are hard to recognize, difficult to express, and harder to sort out. But until we learn the meaning of our emotions, they can play havoc with our lives. When we cannot recognize the origin of a feeling, we stumble around blind and lost in life, attempting unsuccessful experiments in healing that can occupy decades: seeking happiness in a bottle, parties and good times; moving to new places to outrun the feelings, never stopping long enough to feel them; ending relationships and making new ones. Attributing old unhappy feelings arising from the past to a partner's deficits has broken many relationships.

Because we cannot understand them, empathically derived emotions that we pick up from our parents stand out with special intensity. At the same time, the feelings can be so old and familiar that they seem like part of our very temperamental makeup, our identity, a defect deep within ourselves. Left to puzzle over the confusion, we ponder our misunderstood feelings. We try to make sense of the message hidden inside the emotion.

Whether they are expressed in words or in silence, the feelings we take in from our parents can guide us if we understand them, or haunt us if we don't. For instance, if a person can recognize his sudden, lonely, empty feelings of depression as having arisen from the past, an emotional flashback, he can say to his partner, "I don't know what it is. I just felt this terrible wave of loneliness. I was looking at you and I suddenly felt empty and it scared me." As hard as it may be to say such a thing, such words are likely to evoke a partner's concern, heightened emotional involvement, witness, and comfort, or even a fight that clears the air. We will discuss this further in the chapter on marriage, but unless we recognize these emotional flashbacks for what they truly are, we may begin to suspect wrongly that we are unhappily trapped in life with the wrong person.

If we understand the origins of our emotions, we can express them appropriately. We can use the anxieties we absorb from our parents as additional information to help us evaluate the dangers of a situation. Furthermore, those we love can become witnesses to our painful emotions after we stop acting as though they had caused them.

Consider the story told by Richard, a talented musician with classic good looks who sought help after his second suicide attempt:

> Though outwardly he seemed to have everything, Richard described his inner world as desolate and barren, and he blamed his parents for passing on their cold formality. An only child, his feelings of emptiness extended to his earliest memories. Years of therapy and a sophisticated antidepressant regimen had failed to stop his depressions. He only felt alive when drunk or playing music. He knew something was wrong with his feelings so he pretended to be content and concealed his disappointment when his relationships did not measure up to his hopes. He first felt relieved and then despairing when the relationships ended.
>
> Richard described his father as passive and removed. His mother was poised and emotionally controlled. Family dinners were quiet, with little speaking and much attention to etiquette. Richard knew little about his parents' lives before he was born. Richard's grandmother had died when his mother was very young, so his mother had been raised by an aunt until she was old enough to be sent to boarding school. His father had grown up in an alcoholic family and was wounded in Korea, but he never talked about either experience.

Seemingly unaffected by the atmosphere in the home, a child may play unselfconsciously during the day but will return to his parents' feelings at night. This was the case for Richard, who experienced the feelings of his parents as an emptiness within himself. He absorbed their feelings as part of the love they gave him while shielding their painful, unwitnessed emotions behind convention. Richard's experience was that of being outside a wall that allowed him no emotional contact with the parents he needed.

Richard blamed his parents for their coldness because he had no sympathetic comprehension of their experiences in childhood and youth. Although he knew a few facts about his parents' history, their meaning was hidden from him, and his cold, angry lack of compassion for them added to the chill of his inner being. Richard's parents had to shut down emotionally to protect themselves. They both had grown up without parents they could turn to for solace, and neither had homes that could serve as healthy models. We can only imagine the feelings locked inside Richard's mother as a little girl: she had lost her mother, her home, and the company of her father, and then had been reared by an aunt, only to be sent away to boarding school later. And what of Richard's father? A child of alcoholics, he was also a graduate of combat; pain is in the details. Richard experienced the inner desolation his parents had experienced but had hidden from themselves and from him as a little boy, and it came back to him as an adult in emotional flashbacks.

Adults may deny their feelings, but infants and young children experience and absorb what the adults around them deny. Richard's emptiness had a name and a history; he just didn't know what it was: *The injuries had occurred before he was born.* Veiled trauma dominated his life. The dark and low feelings that came out of the blue made him wonder "What is wrong with me?" and also made him question his intimate relationships. The lack of accessible answers made him despair.

Antidepressants usually help with depression, but as with Linda, the woman who spent the first six months of her life in an orphanage, the feelings of emptiness that Richard was fighting were empathically absorbed from his parents as well as from the lack of nurturing that their emptiness denied him. Either is traumatic to infants and young children whose physical and emotional well-being depends on feeling loved. For Richard, the feelings came back as unacknowledged emotional flashbacks that needed to be expressed, witnessed, and comforted. His therapist did not recognize the traumatic origin of that inner emptiness because therapists rarely apply their knowledge of trauma to categories of grief and loss. Richard and his therapist had been trying to fight something neither understood, and each return of the depressed feelings indicated to Richard that his pathology was beyond redemption.

With encouragement, Richard learned his parents' stories, and was able to imagine his parents as young children. He began to feel compassion for their sorrows. Paying attention to his feelings of emptiness rather than simply reacting despairingly to them, Richard gradually realized his feelings were emotional flashbacks to childhood feelings. Consciously naming his feelings allowed him to master them. Richard learned to express the feelings that once puzzled him and no longer had to pretend to be normal until he couldn't stand it anymore. It took a while, but he learned to express his lonely feelings so he was no longer so alone with them; and he learned to use his sensitivity to pick up on and comfort unexpressed emotional subtleties in others. Even before he attained fluency in the language of his own emotions, Richard felt less alone and more optimistic.

RESPECTING OUR SENSITIVITIES
Vulnerability's Hidden Strength

Adult sensitivities are born of hurt; they are vulnerabilities that derive from a painful past, our own and our parents'. A person who felt rejected as a child may feel hurt at the merest hint of another person's negative regard. Such heightened sensitivities are emotional flashbacks to childhood that are easily triggered in adult life. When we understand the origin of our sensitivities, we can learn how to work with them, master them, and allow them to become strengths. On the other hand, if we do not understand our feelings or master our reactions to them, the same sensitivities can become liabilities that defeat us, that trip us up again and again. When we do not master them, we feel helpless as we replay old emotional scenarios; or we learn defensive maneuvers to avoid the triggers. In doing so, we blunt our responses to the nuances of intimacy. But like Richard, we too can learn to recognize our feelings, master our automatic responses to them, and use them to become more sensitive to other people.

We can spend years destructively reacting to injuries that become the recurrent themes of our lives, and all the while remain unaware of how the suffering of our parents and grandparents has determined the themes we live out. Consciously or unconsciously, questions about situations that hurt or overwhelmed us as children may become life quests that can drive us to replay old scenarios in an attempt to answer or master them. Those who are born to families mired in pain may endure lives restricted by their parents' injuries, or may enlarge themselves in the process of healing.

CHAPTER 9

MASTERY AND REENACTMENT

Overcoming Our Limitations, Growing Beyond Our Families

*Those who cannot remember the past
are condemned to repeat it.*

George Santayana, *Reason in Common Sense*

*. . . in 1944 [George Bush] was shot down . . . over
the Pacific. . . . His two fellow crew members were killed,
and Bush sustained serious cuts and bruises when
he pulled his rip cord prematurely and banged his head
on the burning plane's fuselage. This time the old soldier
was determined to jump without glitches.*

Newsweek, April 7, 1997

The drive to achieve mastery over life's difficulties is essential to species and personal survival. Evolution discards species that cannot overcome their challenges and renders them extinct. Achieving mastery can be more compelling than hunger or thirst for both animals and humans.[1] The first impulse of a newly trapped animal, no matter how hungry, is to escape to freedom rather than eat. A woman who is attacked but is able to beat off the attacker will continue to be able to live her life undaunted. A woman who is raped and beaten, however, may subsequently be afraid to go out by herself; until she faces her fears, she will remain a victim, a prisoner to her fear, depressed and confined to her home. She can, however, free herself by mastering her fear, repeatedly going outside anyway; or by taking a course in self-defense, so that she feels better prepared to face the situation again. We only move on with our lives after we face our limitations.

In evolutionary terms, an individual's or a species' helplessness or a defeat in a time of crisis constitutes a desperate situation, and the pressure of such a failure may never go away. Even a simple, meaningless defeat, such as a minor humiliation or a social slight, can rumble around in our heads with an intensity beyond reason.

Our lives constrict when we allow our fears to rule us; we resign ourselves to failure when we are capable of doing better. A child's first step in learning to walk is a triumph. Should the child not master that first step, he will be crippled. Once we give up in a situation, we learn to be helpless in it.

By increasing the levels of the neurotransmitters norepinephrine and/or serotonin in the brain, antidepressant medications reverse the biological effects of learned helplessness in animals[2] in the same way that they reverse depression in the majority of people. Normalizing a person's neurochemistry may allow him to face the situations that had defeated him before so he can move on to achieve mastery. As a consequence, the stress he faces diminishes and the previous lessons of learned helplessness can be undone. The process also works in reverse: achieving mastery can undo the neurochemistry of depression. One woman overcame the depression that had plagued the first fifty-six years of her life when she began painting, and her life continued to be personally and professionally rewarding over the next thirty years.

OVERCOMING HARMFUL ASSUMPTIONS

We learn to hope and we learn to despair. *Learned helplessness can be undone by facing the situation of former helplessness.*[3] Our belief in what we are able to do determines what we are willing to try. The assumptions we make as children steer the direction of our later life experience. They shape who we become, determine the kind of intimate relationships we develop, the interpretations we make in life, and the attitudes we embrace. But we are often not consciously aware of these assumptions.

Years ago, when I was the psychiatrist for a project providing care for people who had previously been unresponsive to treatment, a patient of mine was committed to the state hospital. After visiting him there, I spoke to his psychiatrist, Dr. A., a weary-looking man with a German accent.

Looking at me from across a wide expanse of desk, Dr. A. seemed overwhelmed with the hopelessness of his task, as well as wary of dealing with another impatient young doctor.

Much to the detriment of my patient, Dr. A. had me sized up pretty well. Back then, like many newly trained psychiatrists, I considered myself more up-to-date than my older counterparts, whom I suspected of not having kept up with the newer developments in the field. Dr. A.'s therapeutic defeatism aggravated me; I wanted him to treat my patient aggressively. In the meantime, however, Dr. A. was becoming defensive and my presence and attitude were alienating him.

Looking for an emotional point of contact, I asked when he had come to this country. He said he had come in 1938, when he was ten, with his brother. The rest of the family was to have followed, but World War II broke out and the doors to emigration closed. Everyone else in the family was killed.

We learn attitudes of hope and optimism as children. In childhood, Dr. A. had been helpless to save his family; his hope had been betrayed. Now, forty years later, again and again, he worked with people he felt were helpless and had little hope. I worked with the same population, but my patients got better. I rarely thought anyone hopeless.

Unlike Dr. A.'s parents, mine had escaped the concentration camps and, by their active efforts, survived. My mother put all her heart and time into working for a better future. Her faith in that future rarely seemed to waver. In retrospect, I realize that my mother transmitted an attitude that became a fundamental assumption in my life and in my work: my therapeutic optimism derived from a family attitude.

THE IMPORTANCE OF ADOLESCENCE

Youth is the only season for enjoyment, and the
first twenty-five years of one's life are worth all the rest . . .
even though those five-and-twenty be spent in penury
and contempt, and the rest in possession of wealth,
honors, respectability.

George Borrow, *The Romany Rye*

If learning is the work of childhood and youth, mastery and growth are at their most intense and deliberate in adolescence. At puberty, a child awakens to hormone-triggered changes in consciousness and is suddenly forced to reevaluate his feelings in order to understand them. The body changes. Physical and psychological desires and needs shift. Adolescents undergo flights of independence, retreats to dependence, explosions of energy, and dramatic challenges to self and family. In adolescence, the child has to reinterpret his entire emotional world in order to live successfully in it; he looks at his parents with a new, more critical objectivity as he tries to have fun and re-create himself without suffering from his parents' now apparent limitations. In a hormone-propelled fury, he begins to explore both the outer world of society and the inner world of feelings, desperately wanting to know who he is, what his feelings mean, and who he can be.

Adults may look on with amusement as teenagers agonize over their appearance and every detail of their lives, but the regard of others during this time defines the limits of possibility of an adult's self-image later. Appearance is important for acceptance, inclusion, and self-regard. As teenagers begin to see themselves through the eyes of peers, they get another perspective on life, expand on the worldview of their parents, and start to take their measure from the adolescent world around them. Buffeted by sexual urges for which there are, as yet, no referents, they explore new relationships and cram in as much experience as possible, taking on identities, friendships, and enthusiasms with a rapidity that seems callow to adults.

ADOLESCENT MASTERY
Moving Beyond the Limitation of Our Parents

As adolescents, we are blessed and cursed with a torrent of energy that can scarcely be contained. The surge of energy helps us to move into adulthood, to grow beyond a dependence on the family, beyond the limitations of our parents and the accumulation of traumas that may have defined our family's history. In adolescence, our task is to discover what brings us happiness. As adolescents, we try on behaviors for size, necessitating a bewildering array of behavioral shifts. As teenagers, we fight parental constraints as if our very lives depended on it. In breaking away from our parents, we begin to define ourselves as adults. Though we may be absorbed in extracurricular interests and friends, rather than in responsibilities and homework, we are in fact engaged in serious business.

The "acting out" that teenagers do is the exploration of children seeking to push beyond the limits of their parents. *Adolescent experimentation provides a significant opportunity to heal the emotional wounds that parents transfer to their children.* As adolescents, we grow past our parents' limitations by exploring the unfamiliar. We cannot accept parental decisions or beliefs without challenge: if we do not learn to judge for ourselves, we will be circumscribed by our parents' fears and will duplicate their solutions and failures despite hoping to do better.

By the mid-teen years, a child has long since passed judgment on a parent's strengths and weaknesses. Adolescents adopt styles of coping that attempt to improve upon parental traits they judge to be faulty. Unacquainted with adult responsibilities, however, adolescents are typically determined to correct perceived parental flaws they are too inexperienced to evaluate properly. In the strength of newfound perspectives gained from going outside the family, adolescents feel themselves superior to the parents, who have fallen from the grace accorded them by the child's earlier view.

An adolescent may try to overcome his parents' "flaws," while failing to appreciate how much of a triumph those "flaws" represent. Adolescents who regard their teetotaling parents as stifling and boring may drink to overcome their family's unhappiness, only to later reenact the suffering of their alcoholic grandparents. Or an adolescent may become indiscriminately trusting in order to master his war-injured parents' "paranoia," but then, after years of feeling hurt and betrayed by others, may revert to his parents' stance and leave the task of healing the family's wounds to his children.

Arrogance is a necessity and a gift of youth. It offers hope against fear. Untested and unwilling to believe in danger, teenagers hide their insecurity behind a mask of bravado. Still unsure that they are able to meet life's challenges on their own, teenagers nonetheless hope that the life they build will be better than their parents'.

Teenagers are both excited by their explorations and afraid of them. By acting out and provoking a response, teens get their parents to express one side of their inner conflict. For example, teenagers may want to stay out late and go to an exciting club, but may actually be worried about potential fights or seductions of attractive people who use alcohol and drugs. They may present their parents with the facts and then argue bitterly when their parents forbid them to go. Teenagers can preserve courage despite their mix of emotions by getting their parents to express their fears for them. By being able to argue just one side of the debate, teenagers feel less conflicted; they can challenge their parents' fears rather than examine their own, and then decide on a course of action for themselves. Already overwhelmed with uncertainty, adolescents feel safer fighting their parents than fighting their own ambivalent feelings. Pushing the envelope of their parents' perceived shortcomings, even "good kids" may get into trouble in adolescence by challenging their parents' fears, constricting rules, and admonitions. Adolescents test the limits of their parents' tolerance; but they must see for themselves what works and what doesn't in order to learn if they can exceed the limits of their parents' achievements and capacity for happiness.

If adolescence is a time of turmoil for teens, it is no less so for their parents. Grappling with their children as they mutate throughout adolescence, parents, too, find the ground shifting beneath their feet. As teenagers experiment with new attitudes, clothing, and behaviors, parents worry. But no one can predict with any certainty which good or bad traits will become dominant and which will recede to the background in the evolving adolescent's character. Meanwhile, as they deal with their uncertainty, parents often find themselves reenacting their own conflicts with their parents, for good or ill. The busy experimentation of adolescents also challenges parents to look within once again—to reevaluate their lives and their perception of their own abilities, interests, and limitations.

THE EFFECTS OF CONFINING ADOLESCENTS

Give me liberty or give me death.
Patrick Henry

The price for inhibiting exploration during adolescence is high. Parents naturally want to keep their teenage children safe from the dangers of the world. Occasionally, family necessity may require some curtailment of a teenager's freedom. But confining an adolescent too severely can leave a lasting wound. Parents need to be mindful of the limits they set to keep adolescents safe, and how much work they ask of them. Without the liberty to make discoveries during adolescence, years of struggle may become necessary in adulthood. An extreme example illustrates this starkly:

After being robbed and beaten, Bill, at forty-three, wanted a life off drugs and off the streets. Being mugged had always been a danger, but the streets were rougher now, more dangerous; street people were younger, more predatory. But off drugs and the streets, Bill's life had no rewards.

Bill had left home at fifteen. The previous year, his father had demanded that he go straight from school to work at the family's gas station. Bill was unable to join in after-school activities or friendships. And all too often, he worked alone at night while his father went "out."

After a year of this, Bill defiantly chose not to go to work after school but stayed out all night drinking with friends. The confrontation with his father was explosive. Bill stopped coming home altogether, preferring the excitement of life on the streets to the prison of home. Now, almost thirty years later, Bill didn't know what else to do with himself. Life on the street was the only life he knew.

Family circumstances and cultural demands that suffocate the energy and exploration of adolescence can make an adolescent's life unbearable and may cripple the adult he becomes. Never having developed sober relationships or interests as an adolescent, Bill was unable to develop normal interests or skills as an adult. Now a middle-aged man, he wanted to try, but he was lost. What adolescents learn so quickly was going to be a long, painful process for Bill.

The story of Janice, a thirty-six-year-old mother, provides a more common example. Although she adored her children, she had felt confined since adolescence, and now she felt nearly suffocated:

The oldest of four children, Janice had taken care of her crippled father and younger siblings from age eleven onward. Her mother worked a 3 to 11 P.M. shift. On weekends, Janice cleaned and stayed with her father while her mother went out to run family errands. Janice was then free to go out, but she was shy and had few friends.

Janice enjoyed school and loved to read, but after graduating from high school, she married a hardworking man who liked staying home. Her mother had wanted Janice to remain home and attend the local college and was opposed to the marriage. After the birth of her first child, Janice became depressed and had violent suicidal fantasies.

Unfairly confining an adolescent is a prescription for enduring hostility. Bill had felt exploited at the gas station and believed he was being suffocated so his father could play. Likewise, Janice had siblings who could have helped more than they did.

Janice had learned duty and loyalty but also feelings of suffocation in caring for others. In taking care of her own children, Janice reexperienced the feelings she'd had taking care of her father and siblings. She hated herself for feeling that way.

Janice longed for the freedom she had never had and therefore never learned to use. Tied to home while growing up, she was a stranger to the world that beckoned to her. Marrying right out of high school allowed Janice the possibility of exploring the world with the security of a companion, but her husband did not share her wish for adventure, and Janice felt too guilty about her yearnings to push the issue. Desire alone never overcame her fear of leaving home, and as an adult, Janice had neither the energy of adolescence to give her the necessary strength nor friends to give her support. The cruel longings for freedom as a teenager never dissipated but instead went underground as Janice silently raged against the circumscribed desires of her husband and the needs of her children. Unable to hold back the intensity of her feelings, and knowing her children and husband were innocents undeserving of her rage, Janice turned those feelings against herself. The violence of her suicidal thoughts reflected the intensity of her feelings.

Medication and therapy were of some help to her, but Janice's real salvation came when she began exploring her world in small manageable increments. For Janice, it started with a book group and the friendships she developed there.

Janice had married young so she could leave home, but in doing so she had unwittingly recreated the very conditions she wanted to leave. Her suicidal fantasies were a protest to feeling condemned to live a life of suffocating constriction. Until she masters the emotions and conditions that confine her, the dominant theme in Janice's life will be her quest for freedom, and the choices that she makes need to be predicated on that awareness, for her own sake and for her children's.

MASTERY AND MOURNING IN ADOLESCENCE

Grief during adolescence interferes with the developmental tasks that teenagers must master, drawing them inward at a time they need to turn their energies outward to explore interests, relationships, and their capabilities. Through death or divorce, the loss of a parent or of a home saps the exuberance from exploration and leaves experimentation flat.

Adolescents often deny the reality of their grief in order to continue the outward march of their lives. The pull of grief excessively confines the adolescent, and as a consequence, there is a tension between his need to grieve and the need to explore. The contradiction cannot be resolved at the time. Younger adolescents who suffer loss may grieve on the run, foreshortening the time needed for grief in an attempt to live "normally," whereas older adolescents already near to the cusp of independence may forsake further exploration to become prematurely responsible.

A parent's death often leaves behind a teenager who has to work hard at having a good time. The teenager may make a life project of trying to rise above the sorrow that threatens him. Alcohol, dangerous adventures, sexual experience, and new freedom can temporarily fill the inner void that remains when a mother or father is gone. But invariably, grief reasserts itself, returning unbidden, often disguised as agitation, anger, or as moments of emptiness that may intrude on intimacy. Such unrecognized grief may leave the children of the next generation feeling an emptiness without a name, a sorrow they cannot attach to a loss. The person who suffers a heavy loss in early adolescence often continues to run from grief as an adult, living on the surface of life. If he does not learn to embrace and express his feelings, he will remain disconnected from his emotions and intolerant of any unhappy expressions. Then, when he becomes a parent, his children may long for a connection he cannot give them.

LIFE'S CHOREOGRAPHY

We are all born with distinct predispositions of temperament to parents whose lives have been shaped by a host of events, some joyful, some tragic. Their injuries consciously or unconsciously determine how we act, love, and raise our children.

Consciously or unconsciously, we replay memories and reenact difficult childhood situations in repeated attempts to heal, even when the primary injury occurred in a parent's life. Until we master these challenges and resolve the old traumas, the hurt remains frozen inside us and directs us to unwittingly manufacture painful situations. We are impelled to overcome the same hurts again and again. Children act out their hurt in their play. We replay our injuries in our dreams, recall them in our sensitivities, and relive them in our actions. Each reenactment offers a triumph that encourages us to repeat it again in various aspects of our lives. These reenactments determine the directions we take in life, the mates we select, the fights we pick, and the way we interact with our children. Until we recognize these patterns for what they are we will be unable to name, understand, and give meaning to the traumatic injuries that compel us. Our lives won't truly be our own to command. Instead, we remain driven by unperceived forces that may steer us into directions we might not otherwise choose.

As a child, the humanitarian physician Albert Schweitzer was separated from his parents for over a year while the kindly staff of a tuberculosis sanitarium took care of him. Later, Schweitzer became highly regarded as a theologian and as an organist and musical scholar. Fellow theologians urged him to concentrate on theology; the musicians urged him to stay with music full-time. Disappointing many, he chose, instead, to become a physician. He later wrote:

> He who has been delivered from pain must not think he is now free again and at liberty to take life up just as it was before, entirely forgetful of the past. He is now a "man whose eyes are open" with regard to pain and anguish, and he must help to overcome those two enemies (so far as a human power can control them) and to bring to others the deliverance which he has himself enjoyed. The man who, with a doctor's help, has been pulled through a severe illness, must aid in providing a helper such as he had himself.[4]

Both Dr. A. and Albert Schweitzer had been hurt and separated from their families as children. Dr. A.'s grief had no end. Albert Schweitzer, however, had been able to return joyously to his family after he got well. As adults, both men devoted their lives to helping others: Dr. A. tried to help heal others' minds, while Dr. Schweitzer tried to heal their physical illnesses.

Helpless and ill as a child, Dr. Schweitzer dedicated his adult life to triumphing over pain and anguish. In devoting himself to others, he transformed his world from a frightening, arbitrary place to one where he could provide hope and healing. Schweitzer achieved mastery over illness by helping others overcome it. By contrast, Dr. A. placed himself in a situation where, again and again, his efforts to heal the chronically mentally ill seemed hopeless. He seemed to reenact his helpless despair with one patient after another. Despite this, however, he was never in fact defeated. We are not defeated as long as we keep trying. Dr. A. was unable to cure, but he was able to help; the very fact of this reenactment spoke to his unconscious hope.

Injuries pass down through the generations until they finally heal. Parents reenact their greatest injuries, and the hurt expressed in the repetition of action, attitude, and feelings affects their children profoundly. In the chain of the generations, children try to emulate their parents' success and struggle to master their parents' failures. But children may also duplicate their parents' failures to heal themselves—to answer lingering questions, to understand, to have compassion for, and to forgive their parents for wounding them—so they can honor and love their parents despite their deficiencies.

Unanswered questions about long-past, harmful situations can unconsciously drive people to answer such questions years later. For example, Maggie, a very genteel Scotswoman, had adored and been hurt by her alcoholic father. He had died over forty years before. Maggie became an alcoholic at the age of sixty-three, to ask and to finally be able to answer the question, "If he knew he was hurting us, why didn't he stop?" Maggie overcame the addiction that had defeated her father. But it was the hardest thing she had ever done, and she learned how difficult and costly it was for her to achieve. Unlike her father, she had the support of a loving family. In finally understanding what her father endured, Maggie could grieve for him as she had not been able to do as a child.

The unconscious reenactment of old feelings in new situations can choreograph a person's future. Reenactments are attempts to heal, but they can also harm, as is the case with adults abused as children who pick abusive partners and recreate an emotional environment they have prepared for since childhood. We are "at home" with the familiar, even when it's unpleasant, and the emotional reactions we carry that are left over from childhood make sense in such an environment. Because we have not mastered it, we pass the hurt on to the children of the next generation.

We also reenact childhood hurts in our relationships, hoping to do better, hoping to heal. Those people who have overcome addictions often become counselors and sponsors for those who are trying to join them in recovery, vicariously healing again and again through their work with patients. With rare exception, the prostitutes I've treated had been sexually abused as children or raped as adolescents; prostitution and promiscuity, however destructive or dangerous, also allowed them to reenact their childhood injuries as the master and not the victim.

KARMIC REENACTMENTS

Freud noticed that this compulsion to repeat old scenarios extended to "normal" people who seem "pursued by malignant fate." He describes a "man whose friendships all end in betrayal," and wondered about the "instance of the woman who married three successive husbands, each of whom fell ill soon afterwards and had to be nursed by her on their deathbeds."[5]

In *Beyond the Pleasure Principle,* Freud writes:

> . . . what is repressed in [the adult], and what he cannot remember may be precisely the essential part of it. . . . He is obliged to repeat the repressed material as a contemporary experience instead of . . . remembering it as something belonging to the past.[6]

For Eddy, a thin, wiry, middle-aged man covered with tattoos and living in prison, one moment of terror as a little boy determined the next forty years of his life. It became his karma, the repeating scenario that seemed his destiny. In the world of violence, pain is reenacted, externalized, and inflicted onto others. Eddy mastered the helplessness of his boyhood terror by placing himself repeatedly in life-and-death situations—in the combat of war and in the gang conflict on the streets, and finally, in the smoldering violence that could erupt at any moment in prison:

> Eddy had grown up with a violent father, and he was proud of his ability to survive. He kept to himself and was always alert for the next attack. He lived in a world of violence and was prepared to run or fight at any time.
>
> Eddy's father had been a loved and respected man who did highly skilled, well-paid work. Eddy had adored him. When Eddy was seven, however, his father suffered a brain injury that left him unable to do anything but the most menial of tasks. Despairing, he began to drink.

A year after the accident, blind drunk and in a jealous rage, his father pointed a rifle to his wife's head as Eddy watched. When his father fell backward and passed out, his mother grabbed Eddy and ran away. Eddy never saw his father again.

Now, years later, Eddy was proud of his many job skills; unlike his father, Eddy had made sure that, if anything happened to him, there would always be some occupation that he could pursue. Eddy was also proud of his ability to survive. While in school, he had survived a race riot; on the streets he survived gang warfare. As a combat soldier in Vietnam, as a gang member, and then later in prison, Eddy had seen many people die. Eddie was always prepared.

At the end of our session, Eddy said, "You know, Doc, I think that my whole life centered around that one minute when my father pointed that rifle at my mother's head."

Eddy's nervous system had become electrified when he was eight, making him more suited for combat than for ordinary life. The camaraderie of combat, gangs, and the dangerous but exciting world of the streets overcame the emptiness of a sad little boy who had lost his father. Prison, too, served that function: though it is an unhappy, every-man-for-himself place, it is also one where the lonely have company, and where walls can keep dangerous, out-of-control reactions from hurting others.

Eddy's task was to master the trauma of two generations: his own and his father's. From childhood, Eddy prepared himself to live in a world of violence and betrayal. As an adult, blaming his father's downfall on his inability to continue to do the only job he knew, Eddy made sure he had many skills. Eddy was determined never to be hurt like his father, nor would he ever be so terrified again.

Reenactments of our traumatic childhood situations are compelling. Abused children often marry abusers, and children of violent homes may be drawn to violence because their nervous systems are prepared to deal with the trauma and are easily stimulated. The uneasy residual feelings tied to the trauma beg for expression, and the successful denouement of the reenactment is triumphant mastery, regardless of how painful it is, since the adult can handle it better than the overwhelmed, helpless child. Grief—for the love that was lost or the possibilities that should have been—underlies such reenactments; but in the moment of reenactment, the nervous system is awash with neurochemical juices that remedy the chemistry of grief.

REENACTING HURT

We reenact old childhood conflicts with those we love until we get them right. Contemporary triggers to old sensitivities recall the intense emotions of the past. Neurobiological reactions associated with the helplessness of early, traumatic experiences are especially keen. Norepinephrine remains high while emotions from the past amplify emotions in the present situation. Achieving mastery becomes imperative for restoring balance, but for the moment, the intimate with whom we are in conflict seems like an enemy. Because the triggered emotions feel current, we may misdirect our anger onto loved ones in the merging of past and present—just as our parents once had, with an intensity we had hoped never to repeat.

When an intimate "pushes our buttons," the raw expression of our immediate emotions hurts the other. The hurt we cause comes back to us. An intimate, feeling hurt and unfairly abused, can get caught up in a parallel process, thereby initiating the very sequence of emotional interchanges that evoke a parent, partner or child's familiar response. In effect, we cause the pain we receive.

REENACTED CONFLICTS

Since conflicts with parents are likely to leave children feeling helpless, it is not surprising that we particularly resent conflicts with our parents. Conflicts between parents and children can seem like never-ending contests of wills where no one yields. As with any conflict, each person feels wronged, believes himself to be in the right, and wants the other to admit it. A child and a parent, two people who care too much to be indifferent to one another, volley hurt back and forth across an invisible net of wounded pride. Self-esteem and emotional well-being are at stake, and the losers are likely to suffer. The intense bond between parents and children—the need each has for the other's love and respect—makes the game obsessive and crucial. There are no winners.

We reenact our conflicts with our parents until we correct our own behavior, not when we force them to change. Although we may feel that a parent's behavior provokes our reaction, we are still responsible for our own response. We can either respond automatically with the hurt, angry reactions familiar from childhood, or in the mature fashion of an adult making a choice. The Fifth Commandment demands that we consciously make an honorable response—and in doing so we begin to end the reenactments of childhood.

Until we are able to persuade ourselves to go against the grain of our powerful childhood emotions and master them, our sensitivities and our pride continue on. The conflicts remain, to seek resolution in other relationships as we reenact old hurts from childhood with our mates, children, and others who are unwillingly conscripted to play. Reenacting our unresolved conflicts with our children transforms the game into a relay we play out through the generations—until someone refuses to play anymore. When "being right" becomes less important than behaving with respect and compassion, and a child or parent refuses to participate, the conflict can finally end.

REVISITING CHILDHOOD

In their raw reactions to events, children amplify the unresolved pain their parents carry, and parents encounter their own unresolved childhood pain as they react to their children's actions and attitudes. Childhood feelings flooding rationality can overwhelm a mature response. Even though parents may strive to be better parents than their own, adult pressures may compromise their ability to remake themselves. Parents often find themselves acting as their own parents once did, hurting their children the way their parents once hurt them.

In raising our own children, we begin to live our parents' experience in raising us. We identify with our parents' and our children's experience simultaneously. We reinterpret our past as we reexperience old emotions from a new vantage point. We revisit our childhoods and in some ways raise ourselves again. We also begin to appreciate our parents' dilemmas. Sharon, for instance, became more tolerant and understanding of her father after she herself had children:

> My father and I fought all through my teens. I felt like he was trying to squash me. He had to know where I was every minute of the day. In high school, there was a time I didn't speak to him for a month.

Once, when I was eleven, we were at Coney Island. My father ran into a friend and started talking, so my brother and I wandered around a while. When we came back, we couldn't find my dad. I knew it was up to me to look after my brother. I was feeling responsible and grown-up. I took him on some rides, bought us ice cream, and was relieved when a policeman finally came up and asked if my name was Sharon. My father was furious. I don't remember what I said, but he slapped me. Something started changing between us then.

Last year, I was in the kitchen. It seemed awfully quiet. My daughter was four then, and I figured she was up to no good. But when I looked, I couldn't find her. I went all through the house and started to panic. I started running out the back door when my neighbor came over with my daughter and said, "Are you looking for this?" I was so relieved, but I had to keep myself from yelling at her. I remembered my father hitting me. It was the first time I started thinking about his side of the story. Now I can understand why my father got so upset any time I was late. I must have given him a pretty hard time. I just didn't know: when you're worried about your kids, there's no peace of mind.

In therapy, William described how teaching his five-year-old to swim led to a reenactment of a childhood trauma:

I was trying to get Tyler to jump in the pool, but he just froze. I told him not to be afraid, that I was there and I would catch him. Tyler didn't move. I got angry with him. No matter what I did, he refused to jump in, and people were starting to look. Finally, I just yelled at him. He started to cry. I was disgusted with him; I actually felt con-tempt for my own son. At that moment, I realized I was acting just like my father when he made me ashamed of how timid I was as a child; and here Tyler was acting the same way. Probably if I had been patient and just taken the pressure off him, he would have been OK. The way I was with him, I know I made him feel like he was a cow-ard. I hurt him.

William loved his son but had loathed timidity ever since his father had condemned him for it years earlier. Seeing the hurt on his son's face, William recalled a time thirty years before when his father was teaching him to swim; he recalled his father's anger and his own spirit crumbling. By stepping back from his childhood emotions, William could see how needless this was. He was determined to protect his son from similar future incidents. The next time his son behaved timidly, William did not pressure him but offered encouragement and reassurance.

William's insight, however, did not immediately relieve his shame, nor did moderating its expression fully insulate his son. That shame was a hundred-headed hydra that had permeated his self-concept and his development as he was growing up; it took years for William to learn to respect himself.

After imagining his father going through an identical experience and seeing his father in more human terms, however, William gradually forgave him. His anger diminished; and in the process of recognizing and reporting emotional flashbacks rather than reacting to them, William gradually healed his relationships as well as his bruised feelings.

Years after the incident at the pool, William described another incident with his oldest daughter, Julie:

We were at my sister's house for Thanksgiving, waiting for Julie to arrive so we could start eating. We were getting pretty frantic by the time she showed up two hours late. She gave a curt "Sorry, I'm late," then introduced this girl no one had ever met before. She acted as if nothing had happened. They were both smelling of marijuana, and I was burning. Nobody said anything at the time. No one wanted a scene, but I was feeling angry, bitter, and rejecting. I felt real contempt for her behavior. It's a good thing I've learned to distrust my feelings when they are like my parents'. I've made it a rule never to react to feelings like that automatically, no matter how justified it seems. When I've done that, it's always screwed me up.

When I got together with Julie afterwards, I made a remark about how much respect my sister had shown by waiting for her even though the dinner was getting cold. Julie agreed and was smiling warmly while I was practically biting my tongue. I really wanted to let her have it. Then she said: "I'm sorry I was so late, Dad, but my friend was all alone and had been smoking marijuana all day. She was talking like she wanted to die and I couldn't get her to stop crying. I didn't feel right bringing her to Aunt Lonnie, but I couldn't remember her phone number. I was feeling so desperate. I knew I was late and was worried about keeping everyone waiting and worrying about me. Thanks for being so understanding, Dad."

I wish my parents could have trusted me like that. But their life was a struggle to survive. For them, what mattered was having enough to eat.

William grappled with his emotions and ultimately mastered himself. Those who have been through the process of recovery know the depth of such a struggle. Like Jacob, in the Bible, we have to wrestle with all of our being:

> And Jacob was left alone; and there wrestled a man with him until the breaking of the day. And when he saw that he prevailed not against him he touched the hollow of his thigh; and the hollow of Jacob's thigh was strained, as he wrestled with him. And he said: "Let me go for the day breaketh." And he said: "I will not let thee go, except thou bless me." And he said unto him: "What is thy name?" And he said: "Jacob." And he said: "Thy name shall be called no more Jacob, but Israel; for thou hast striven with God and with men, and hast prevailed." And Jacob asked him, and said: "Tell me, I pray thee, thy name." And he said: "Wherefore is it that thou dost ask after my name?" And he blessed him there. And Jacob called the name of the place Peniel: "For I have seen God face to face and my life preserved." And the sun rose upon him as he passed over Peniel, and he limped upon his thigh.
>
> Genesis 32:24–31

Jacob's adversary is nameless; his struggle, spiritual. It requires every ounce of his strength; but the struggle transforms him: Jacob is no longer the hurtful pretender who had deceived his dying father and cheated his brother of his inheritance. The change is recognizable and acknowledged. Whenever others address him, he will be addressed differently; when others speak of him, they speak of him differently. The struggle marked him. Before he appeared whole, but his character was crooked. Afterward, Jacob is visibly wounded, but his character has become one to respect. His life is renewed, and it is blessed.

As it was for Jacob, so it is for us. We struggle with ourselves to overcome our flawed response to old injuries. We heal ourselves as we accept our feelings and allow others to witness them, consciously opposing traumatically learned reflexive reactions harmful to others. We bear the scars of the emotional wounds we heal; and we may hobble a bit afterward, but vulnerable, no longer hidden, we can respect ourselves for who we have become. We become wiser, more loving, more compassionate and accessible for the suffering we have chosen to endure and not avoid.

Deeply embedded within a parent's reenactment of an old traumatic scenario is hope for a more profound mastery and a deeper healing. Those who achieve it feel a spiritual triumph. Such a triumph is ultimately a victory over ourselves. To heal the deepest wounds within ourselves, we have to look at ourselves honestly—see our flaws from a loved one's perspective, and unflinchingly look at our feelings in deep introspection. In order to heal our wounds, we must grapple with the pain we cause others, as well as the pain that has been passed on to us.

CHAPTER 10

"AYECKAH?"

Being Honest with Ourselves

And the Lord God called unto the man and said unto him:
"Where art thou?" And he said: "I heard Thy voice in the
garden and I was afraid because I was naked; and I hid myself."

Genesis 3:9–10

To heal we must be unsparingly honest with ourselves. In the Bible, God's first question to man is the one he asks Adam: *"Ayeckah?"*— "Where are you?" Adam answers honestly: he acknowledges his feelings, his vulnerability, his actions, and is willing to accept the outcome of the truth.

"Ayeckah?" The question calls us to consciousness. Throughout our day and throughout our lives, this is the question we must ask ourselves if we are to be aware of our feelings, understand their meaning, and take conscious control over our lives. The question challenges our honesty, but in today's complex world, knowing what honesty is can be difficult. In the rush of an ordinary day, when do we even have the time or quiet to ask *"Ayeckah?"*

Vacations—time off from the workaday life—offer more than a good time. They allow us to get away from our ordinary routine and the stress of our daily obligations. We need to get away from it all periodically—to get outside our circumscribed lives and to look at our lives objectively.

We must look within to understand our feelings, and then must consciously choose our best response to any given situation, whether that response is in accordance with or in opposition to our feelings. Otherwise we are helplessly driven by forces we neither understand nor challenge. Life pushes us first this way and then that. Time rushes by in a blur. When we do not ask *"Ayeckah?"* it is easy to become the victim of circumstance, unable to impose our own will—because we do not know what it is. Without stopping to ask "Where am I?" we waste the valuable moments and years of our lives through evasion. But asking *"Ayeckah?"* is never easy.

Many years ago, while staying with friends, I overheard their end of an intense and lengthy telephone conversation with their son. My friends were reassuring their panic-stricken nineteen-year-old son that they loved him and would stand by him no matter what. He could talk to a therapist if he wanted, but he should not be afraid. Whatever his feelings meant, his parents were and always would be there for him. By the end of the call, they had managed to calm him down. After the call, they explained that he had felt sexual feelings for his roommate while sitting next to him at a movie and was terrified of what that might signify.

I was impressed with the family's trust and honesty, the son's courage, and his parents' immediate, loving presence. His parents did not minimize the import of their son's experience. They did not reassure him that he was not gay. They said nothing that would have kept him from exploring the truth of his feelings but made it clear they would accept whatever was true. The parents expected their son to be honest with himself, and the son could trust that he could be honest with them. The honest asking of *"Ayeckah?"* disregards the needs for acceptable, conventional replies; it only asks what is true, and answering may require great courage.[1]

Answering *"Ayeckah?"*—calling ourselves to consciousness—can be earth-shaking and can reshape the contours of our lives. After the intense, constant self-examination of adolescence and early youth, years may go by before we again challenge ourselves with questions of *"Ayeckah?"* In middle age, however, with our lives established and our child-rearing done, we awaken one day aware that our time on earth is foreseeably limited and ask ourselves, for the first time in years, "Is this how I want to spend the rest of my life?" Like adolescents who want to break through the limits of their parents' lives, adults in their middle years suddenly want to break the bonds of their own conventions. But honest answers are frightening when they threaten the foundations of our lives and the security of our self-understanding.

Feelings of discontent indicate that we should question ourselves, as was the case for Ken, owner of a large construction company. He had originally been a test pilot, then a rising star on the executive fast track at his company. Feeling troubled, Ken asked himself, *"Ayeckah?"* He described his night of reckoning:

I was in turmoil all night. They were considering me for another promotion, and the idea of it felt suffocating to me. I couldn't sleep. I just lay on the lawn, looking at the stars all night. I turned in my resignation the next day. I invested everything I had in my construction company, and I've loved every minute of it.

Another friend described his desperate sense of the need for a new direction in his life, years after a divorce and a dark period of depression. He stopped to pray while jogging:

I felt suffocated with work and obligations. I was begging for a clue to what I should do about my life. I didn't really expect an answer, but suddenly this strange feeling came over me. It shook me. So out loud I said, "Thanks, God, I've got to go now. I'll talk to you later." But I'm still wondering what the answer would have been if I hadn't run away. I was afraid of what I might have been called to do.

He did not have to be so afraid of the truth. The question *"Ayeckah?"* calls us to consciousness, but we choose whether, when, and what action to take. Avoiding the truth is what harms us.

It goes against our grain to ask questions that challenge the rightness of our own actions. During childhood and adolescence when our parents confront us with our behavior and help us form our conscience, it feels like something they are doing *to* us rather than *for* us. To be in command of our lives, however, we need to ask ourselves hard questions from time to time, and then answer with as much depth and honesty as we can manage: "Why do I work so hard and feel so empty?" or "Why do I argue with my children so much?" or "What am I doing to make my parents feel bad?" As we have seen, the answer to the last question holds the key to the pain we reenact and pass on to our partners and children, and we will explore this in depth in Chapter 13.

ASKING *"AYECKAH?"* IN RELATIONSHIPS

Honestly answering *"Ayeckah?"* is particularly difficult when we are in an unhappy relationship. The term "midlife crisis" was initially used to disparage the many men who abandoned their wives in order to revitalize their lives with new romance and younger women. Many of them seemed to have asked *"Ayeckah?"* and then answered by clearing out the stale clutter of their old lives and replacing it with the new clutter of equally superficial ones. Were their answers honest? It's hard to know what is honest after years of living unhappily with someone. We see our partner's shortcomings more easily than our own.

We need to look at and correct our own contribution to an unhappy relationship before we can honestly assess a partner's inadequacy. Without a scrupulous self-examination and a willingness to change our own flaws first, we cannot be certain of a relationship's possibilities. Two major clues that we have to clean our own house first before deciding that a once happy relationship is moribund are a "yes" answer to the question "Am I hiding secrets from my partner?" and a "no" answer to the question "Do I behave honorably with my parents?"

Even if there are no great secrets to reveal, relationships break under the accumulated weight of unexpressed feelings. The turning of a head, the tightening of lips, and the silence of hidden resentments reflect the false peace that arises when one partner seems to accept the other's flaws rather than challenging him to grow. Resignation that arises from one's own disappointed needs pushes away rather than invites love later: "Oh well, what can you do? My wife's just rigid." Or, "This is just a minor annoyance. My husband is sensitive to criticism and it's better to just let the situation slide."

Good relationships break or get stale from the accumulation of dishonest and hidden feelings over time. In Genesis, Adam answers God's question honestly: "I am hiding." But in proclaiming the truth, Adam is no longer hiding. He continues an honest relationship with God.

HIDING

In our daily lives at work, in friendship, in family relations, and in our communities, whether for the sake of freedom or in the wake of intolerance, for the sake of conformity or in hopes of acceptance, we frequently lie and hide. We conceal parts of emotional truth to smooth the path of family relations. We hide the shameful things we do and have done. The reasons we hide are often understandable and sometimes necessary.

Parents who tolerate only a narrow band of conventional behavior or attitudes make honesty, and thus intimacy, hard for their children. Our capacity to be intimate depends on our ability to know ourselves enough and trust others enough to express ourselves honestly in our relationships and in the families we create. The biblical sense of "knowing" requires that we reveal ourselves, and we must trust that we can do so in safety. Like my friends and their son trying to understand the meaning of his sexual feelings, God trusted Adam to tell the truth, and Adam trusted God enough to tell Him the truth. As a consequence, God rewarded Adam with His continued relationship.

HIDING FROM OURSELVES

Pain is as essential and as natural a part of the human experience as joy. To live fully, we must accept and reveal our painful feelings. Should we avoid our pain, we deprive ourselves of our own depth of character and soul, as well as our own history. We will be confused by the persistent return of emotions we do not recognize or accept. Such was the case for Abby, seventeen years old, who came for therapy two years after her mother's death. She had become so "hyper" that she was unable to do her schoolwork.

Abby had always been an active child, but after her mother died, sitting quietly had become impossible for her. Although her grades were still good, she was beginning to drink and hang out with the drug crowd. She was frenetic in her attempts to have fun and was always on the go, rarely stopping for breath.

Abby had been six when her parents divorced, ten when her father remarried, twelve when her mother developed cancer, and not quite fifteen when her mother died. She seemed to manage well initially, but in the two years after her mother's death, she became increasingly agitated. Abby could not understand why she "had these moods all of a sudden, for no reason," as she said. She felt self-conscious with friends, empty and withdrawn. She did not relate her moods to her grief over her mother.

In talking about her mother, Abby began to weep. She had never been able to talk to her mother about her dying. Abby had hoped to have a deep talk with her at some point, but had not realized how sick her mother had been until she fell into a coma.

Abby felt disloyal talking about her mother to her father or stepmother and would not talk about her feelings to her friends. She was afraid that if her friends knew what she was really like inside, she would be left alone.

After weeping for a half hour, Abby seemed calmer and more focused. The calm she felt after expressing her grief demonstrated to Abby how her agitated moods related to her unspoken feelings. She had finally asked herself, "Where am I?" and stopped to listen to the answer.

In times of crisis, children follow their parents' lead. Abby had hidden the imminence of her mother's death from her own awareness; as the cancer progressed, Abby did not allow herself to notice her mother's deterioration, and her mother never called her attention to it. When her mother's death finally came, it was a shock.

Abby never received her mother's blessing nor talked to her about her hopes for the future; and Abby's mother never talked to Abby about the hopes she had for her. Abby never asked her mother about her medical condition or what she was going to do without her. Abby had lost a moment that could have guided her and sustained her in the years ahead. Too much had been left unsaid. It was a great loss for both of them.

The period preceding her mother's death could have been an opportunity for great closeness between Abby and her mother. Instead, they had hidden their feelings from one another, leaving each of them alone to their own fear and grief.

With no one to receive her grief, Abby tried to bury it. But we blunt our own spirits when we bury our feelings, and the feelings we avoid frighten us when they return. Abby tried to put her grief behind her by trying to live the life of a normal teenager. In trying to forget her grief, however, she was unable to make sense of her feelings. Instead, she tried moving faster than her grief, so it would not catch up to her. Though it frightened her to stand still, Abby would have felt even worse had she continued to avoid herself.

Those who run from their feelings remain fugitives from themselves. They can attain no rest, no peace, and no intimacy until they stop—or are stopped—and grapple honestly with the feelings they avoid.

Nathan was another person who was unaware of how much he avoided his feelings. He had not asked *"Ayeckah?"* until his wife evicted him and made him take a look at his life. Nathan and Claire entered couples counseling after she had caught him in an affair. Married for sixteen years and with two children, nine and eleven, they both wanted their marriage to work. But Claire refused to accept Nathan back into their home until she understood the deeper as well as the obvious reasons for his affair. Nearly a year later and several months after Claire had taken him back, Nathan described what that year had been like:

> This has been the worst period of my life, but I'm glad it happened. I felt at the time that the affair with Jean had kept me going, but when Claire threw me out, I realized that nothing else meant anything without her. I pleaded with her to take me back, but she insisted that I be honest about everything I was unhappy about in our marriage. After being in counseling with her, I realized I'd been lonely as a kid and lonely in my marriage. Our routine was oppressive: work, come home, spend time with the kids, go to soccer practice, music lessons, a movie. Claire and I didn't have much time for ourselves: I'd tell her about my day, she'd tell me about hers. We'd talk about the kids. There were so many practical things to take care of. I knew I was bored, but I hadn't realized how empty home was for me.
>
> I've learned a lot these past few months. I never looked at my childhood before. I thought I had long since forgiven my parents for being so distant; I didn't realize how angry I still was. Claire and I are growing closer now, and I'm even getting closer to my parents. I'm beginning to understand them better, too. I'm learning to tell Claire my feelings and put into words what I need from her. It's not easy. I never put my unhappiness in words before. She demands that I pay more attention to her, too. We fight more now, but we have a deal: every night, for an hour, we go for a walk together. Life seems richer than I ever thought it could be.

Claire knew that for their marriage to be a true marriage—a real intimacy—they were both going to have to be more honest than they had been before, with themselves and with each other. There was no turning back the clock. The "normal" relationship they once enjoyed had both failed and been fractured. Their only recourse was to renew their intimacy on a deeper and more honest level. Nathan's affair was not Claire's fault. He was responsible for his own action. But Claire was wise: in addition to asking *"Ayeckah?"* to determine what was important to her and what it was that she wanted to happen, she also asked, despite her great hurt, what part she played in the creation of the painful situation with Nathan. Furthermore, Claire's determination to end the marriage unless there was honesty between them forced Nathan to ask himself, "Where am I in life, what am I doing, and what is important to me?"

Nathan was emotionally raw when he entered therapy. He had been minimizing his discontent since childhood. He realized that if he was going to have a good life, with or without Claire, he had to acknowledge his feelings and not brush them under the rug. For Nathan to understand himself, he had to listen harder to the whispers of his feelings and give them emphasis in expression. To be intimate with Claire or forgive his parents, Nathan had to first acknowledge his anger. Shallow forgiveness cannot forgive deep anger. To live a better life, Nathan had to live a more conscious one. He had to ask *"Ayeckah?"*, determine his feelings, and then express them in the small daily matters that create a couple's intimacy.

EVASIONS OF *"AYECKAH?"*
Addictions

I do not think that all who chose wrong roads perish;
but their rescue consists in being put back on the right road.
A wrong sum can be put right: but only by going back
till you find the error and working it afresh from that point,
never by simply going on.

C. S. Lewis, *The Great Divorce*

Harm to Self

The expression "painfully honest" is especially true for those who have suffered greatly during childhood and adolescence. At war with their emotions, they are also at war with the past that generated them. For them to be honest with their feelings means accepting and not avoiding the feelings they were ill equipped to deal with in youth. In a misguided attempt to "get on with life," they allow unacknowledged pain to become fixed and then inflict it on others.

Alcoholics and other addicts are people in hiding who try to defer or evade the often painful call to consciousness of *"Ayeckah?"* They hide their grief, their needs, and their hurts, pretending to be strong even as they bleed out emotionally. The great majority of serious alcoholics and addicts were repetitively traumatized as children.[2] They began their addictions during adolescence, when they attempted to rescue themselves from bad feelings with self-prescribed doses of drugs and alcohol.

Adolescents who drink and use drugs form quick, loose affiliations with others who will "party" with them. They are children desperately pursuing happiness while fleeing from unexpressed, underlying pain. The chemically induced high permits a grieving, pained, or awkward adolescent to make friends, find peer acceptance, and master the exploratory tasks of adolescence by avoiding painful emotions. In adolescence, when peer friendship is so crucial, alcohol and drugs allow wounded young people to open their world to friends and activity—albeit at a high price. For many, the choice is terrible: become a social cripple or become a drunk. Most people with severe addictions begin them in adolescence. Personal characteristics of being open or of being hidden are usually also established in adolescence.

Regardless of the means or the reasons, when we hide our painful feelings, we cannot heal or grow beyond them; instead, we remain emotionally frozen at the age when we stopped expressing the continuing hurt of the injury. That is why so many alcoholics and drug addicts continue to be adolescents emotionally. Emotional development stops at the age their addictions began. Growth resumes only when they face their pain in sobriety. Otherwise, the wounded child continues to dictate the pattern of the life of the adult, setting the stage for the drama to be played out by the next generation.

Addicts and alcoholics at base are hurt children too ashamed to cry and too scared to trust. In childhood, they learned that they could not rely on others to provide what they needed, and as they moved into adulthood, their lingering hopes were easily disappointed. Their addictions function as the trusted companion, briefly allowing alcoholics and addicts to feel better than bad.

Adults who had needs that went begging in childhood are, in the most literal sense, "childish," and addicts and alcoholics are ashamed of these needs. For them, chemicals prove reliable when people have not been. Drugs and alcohol temporarily alleviate the ache of their unfulfilled childhood needs and permit them the dignity of not having to expose these needs to others. But while chemicals can fill in the gaps when there is a loss of hope for better alternatives, they do not fill the empty heart.

Addictions allow addicts and alcoholics to preserve a status quo in their daily routine and in their relationships that may be unsustainable in the face of true feelings. Feeling alone, but afraid to make themselves vulnerable, addicts try to take control of their lives by modulating their own neurochemistry rather than asking for and relying on others for help. For a time, the addictions do seem to help people control their lives—until the addictions themselves get out of control. It is not uncommon for someone to take a drink or two after work to relieve stress or enliven a boring evening; but it becomes dangerous to drink to fill emptiness or relieve emotional pain.

Afraid to unearth their buried grief, chemically dependent people demand that everyone around them cooperate in the cover-up. In trying to evade pain, they require that friends, lovers, and children avoid the sensitivities they try to hide and take care not to tread on them: "How many times do I have to tell you? I don't like being interrogated with a bunch of questions!" or "Don't you ever tell me what to do!" When intimates inevitably fail in this task, an addict's self-protecting anger surfaces, sometimes violently, to push them away.

In the conflicts inherent in intimacy, addicts make no presumption of a partner's or a child's good faith. Eventually, the addict's close relationships carry an extra burden of increased hostility and failed trust. For those who would love a chemically dependent person, there is always hell to pay. Partners receive the pain and loneliness that addicts and alcoholics avoid.

Harm to Others: the Next Generation

We should not presume to judge people in their addictions. Who knows what is at stake for someone who feels so fundamentally alone? His addiction, bad as it may be, could well be all that stands between him and suicide. Even a father or mother who is dead drunk is better for a child than one who is dead by suicide. In fact, enduring life by any means—including addiction—may be a parent's last-ditch maneuver to protect his children from the ravages of his self-inflicted death.

Nevertheless, the hurt and chaos chemically addicted parents create for their families can be relentless. They damage their children with a host of erratic behaviors they later regret: neglect, failed promises, violence, incest, divorce, abandonment, and attempted or completed suicides are only the most obvious results.

Children of alcoholics and addicts grow up underestimating themselves. They do not perform to the level of their abilities in schools or on IQ tests.[3] This is not hard to understand. It is difficult for a child to concentrate on long division when his drunk father attacked his mother the night before. Without some exceptional ability or some adult to pay him particular attention, the child may find school to be just another place to feel bad. Should the child fall behind, school can become the scene of daily humiliations that prove him stupid before his classmates.

Hurt, needy, and with a wounded sense of self-esteem, children of addicted parents are easy prey for predators and bad influences and often follow their parents into addiction. Having to hide the shameful conditions at home, they are natural secret-keepers and are easily exploited by those who would abuse them.

Unconsciously, and sometimes dangerously, the child of an addict may get himself into trouble to force his dysfunctional parent to behave more normally. A child who gets into trouble with the law, or who attempts suicide, forces the parent to deal with him. The child's problem is an accusation and a summons, a provocative wake-up call that challenges the parent at his healthy evolutionary core—the need to protect the child—and asks the parent, *"Ayeckah?"* The parent standing beside a son or daughter in a court of law is also on trial.

The children of alcoholics and addicts typically grow up without having a good model for intimate relationships and normal parenting. For example, Gordon, a friend, colleague, and a member of Adult Children of Alcoholics, anxiously confided in me before he got married:

> As a child, I'd come home from school, clean the house, pick up after my mother, and try to keep things running. She'd usually be on her ass by the time I got there. Sometimes she'd get all close and gooey and tell me how much she loved me. She'd slur her words, and her breath would make me nauseated. Before they got divorced, my father would come home and hit the roof. Their fights got pretty hairy. I knew I had to get out of there, and I knew I wasn't going to drink and be like them. Now I'm getting married. You've seen what a doll Lucy is. But neither one of us has a clue what's supposed to be normal in a marriage. I just hope the two of us can work things out.

Growing up in the home of hurt parents whose chemically altered emotions distorted reality, Gordon, like other children of addicts, needed help to separate out his normal feelings and expectations from idiosyncratic ones arising from his family situation. Gordon was sincerely asking *"Ayeckah?"* He had to take conscious control over his emotional reactions to keep his disturbed childhood from determining the direction of his life. His marriage and his future depended on the quality of his answers, and Gordon needed help.

Since temperate children raised by alcoholics and addicts do not know what normal feelings or relationships are supposed to be like, they are unable to trust their own feelings as "valid." They often grow up holding on to convention as if to a life preserver. Their children, in turn, often feel constricted by their parents' allegiance to convention and may act out in adolescence to challenge their parents' rigid boundaries. They rail at their parents, defy their restrictions, and fight to live a freer life. Their parents, seeing their children letting go of the life-preserver that has meant so much to them, fear they will drown in the turbulent seas that had once claimed their own parents.

Even when children of alcoholics and addicts avoid becoming addicted themselves, the cycle does not end. Not uncommonly, problems with addictions "skip" a generation. Regardless of any genetic predisposition, the nonaddicted children of alcoholics and addicts had once been traumatized by their parents' behavior. As a consequence, when their children behave as their parents once did, they feel threatened and they may clamp down on their children's normal adolescent explorations. Should they rebel, their unguided, defiant teenage children may fall prey to the mistakes of their grandparents.

Hidden Injuries: Passing On Addictive-Compulsive Eating

Parents who hide their pain with food pass on unresolved emotions to their children. Obesity adds to and is part of a history of unfulfilled need, emblematic of a hunger and desire that is apparent for all to see.

Bulimics hide the honest emblem of obesity. They may appear normal, but bulimic parents try to fill emptiness with food and control their weight with purging. This later transforms into a nausea and an incomprehensible emptiness that their children feel. Food may soothe unhappy emotions, fill in loneliness, and transiently make life seem more rewarding, but emotions derived from a parent's denied or avoided feelings will still pass on to children—and it is usually the most sensitive child who bears the brunt.

Frank, twenty-four, desperate for help with his addictions and marginally psychotic, had at one time or another been addicted to just about everything: alcohol, cocaine, marijuana, psychedelics, amphetamines, and heroin. He found that virtually *any* altered state was better than the way he felt naturally.

These are Frank's words:

I'm feeling pretty weak. I feel sick inside my heart. I always feel sick. Just kind of toasted, like my eyes are dilated. I've felt like hell on earth for the last eight or nine months. I almost killed myself. When my heart kicked in, I was so happy.

My mother was bulimic. She had problems, and maybe I picked up something along the way. My father worked a lot while my mom was always stuck at home taking care of us. Mom kept me up at night telling me her problems. She talked to me a lot more than my brother or sister.

Frank was peculiar in his idiosyncratic expression and his brain was still toxic from the chemicals he had taken. But his language was almost entirely the language of feeling, reflecting an inner war of emotions that bewildered and sickened him. Emotionally porous, he was easily confused, taking in the feelings of anyone who was nearby.

With his father gone so much of the time, and his mother lonely and probably desperate, Frank became her confidant. Confiding unhappiness to children burdens them with feelings they are ill equipped to handle and thus try to block out. Such children often grow up to have difficulty with achieving intimacy and are subject to vast emotional confusion.

At an early age, Frank may have been emotionally older than his mother. A majority of bulimics were sexually abused as children, and nearly 30 percent were physically abused.[4] Who knows what trauma and emotions Frank's mother had to contend with as a child that left her so lonely and needy as an adult? Active bulimics tend to feel sick, desperate, and out of control, often appearing nauseated before and after purging. His mother had probably chosen Frank as her confidant because he was the most sensitive and empathic of the children.

Though he did not become bulimic, Frank absorbed his mother's feelings, and then sought refuge from those feelings in alcohol and drugs. His life has been devoted to a long internal dialogue as he struggles to gain balance and become normal, trying to ask *"Ayeckah?"* and evading his feelings simultaneously. To sort out his confusion, Frank had to stop confusing his feelings, seek help, and gain relief through the healing witness of others. But even though Frank initially expressed sympathy and did not blame his mother, he continued to confuse himself with drugs and alcohol, both as an unacknowledged wish for his mother to witness his confusion and punish her for "messing" him up. Frank had to acknowledge his resentment first before he could forgive her for inducing it; ultimately, he was able to do so.

THE NEXT GENERATION'S QUEST FOR WHOLENESS

Children of alcoholics, addicts, abusive homes, and disturbed families struggle hard to be whole, laboriously correcting one maladaptation at a time as they become aware of it. Healing is a quest; even if they do not know the word, *"Ayeckah?"* becomes their mantra. Having been denied reliable support as children, their strength and independence is their pride, even as it is the source of their loneliness when they grow up. These children have had to battle their way to a healthy maturity without having had a good home to sustain and guide them. Samuel was one such child:

> Samuel's father abandoned him at five, leaving him alone with his depressed, alcoholic mother. She spent most of her days drinking, relying on Samuel to care for her when she wasn't functioning. Samuel cooked for the two of them when he was little, but he didn't learn to brush his teeth until junior high school. His classmates considered him peculiar and ridiculed him. He never drank, however. Instead, he sought out counseling. He finally broke away from home, despite feeling guilty for abandoning his mother.
>
> After moving to the West Coast, Samuel instinctively knew he needed someone to fill in for the father who had abandoned him. Artistically talented and intelligent, Samuel was also honest and courageous. He learned quickly. Responsible at work, he was honest in his relationships. He didn't shrink from conflict and was gentle in his expression. He allowed others the room to be them-

selves. In choosing to grapple with his life, he developed a good one for himself. He married well, and became a good father and good provider.

Samuel had no father to moderate the effects of his mother's dysfunction, but he was born with strengths that served him well. His resilience came from his native intelligence,[5] even disposition,[6] and creative talent.[7] People who are creative or have some kind of enduring passion can make meaning and fill emptiness for themselves.

Samuel never used nonprescriptive chemicals to directly feel better. Instead, he endured, he persevered, and he survived. He transformed his wounds into the sensitivities that allowed him to become a good husband and a father. In matters large and small, whether deciding to move and start a new life, or in everyday relations, a scrupulous honesty guided his life.

Therapy uncovers pain and simultaneously provides consolation, witness, and perspective. For the alcoholic or addict to achieve growth and intimacy, the addiction must first stop and the raw, jagged edges of pain must be exposed to the possibility of comfort. Treating an addiction largely as a chemical problem tacked on to the body of a person misses the point. To struggle with an addiction is to struggle with one's soul.

Adults who grow up in troubled families often spend their lives posing and answering questions of *Ayeckah,* but more than most, they need some guidance to help them make the good lives they long for. As children, they may find surrogate parents to embrace and respect. As adults questing for wholeness, they may find wisdom in close friendships, in books, and support groups like ACOA (Adult Children of Alcoholics), AA, or NA, where they can share their stories of injury and healing.

There is no emotional healing without honesty. In Genesis, Adam answered God's question, *"Ayeckah?,"* with the truth even though he believed he would die for it. Choosing to speak the truth, Adam accepted the consequences of what he had done, and as a result, he was not alone in the universe. His son Cain, on the other hand, hid and answered God's questions with lies and evasions, and lived as a lonely, frightened fugitive.

We know the story well: God approves of his brother, Abel, and not of Cain; Cain, jealous, kills Abel, and God punishes him. In this story, we tend to identify more easily with the victim than with the aggressor, but perhaps we are more like Cain than we would care to admit.

THE FIRST LIE

Cain brought of the fruit of the ground an
offering unto the Lord. And Abel, he also brought
of the firstlings of his flock and of the fat thereof
and the Lord had respect unto Abel and to his offering:
But unto Cain and to his offering He had not respect.
And Cain was very wroth, and his countenance fell.
And the Lord said unto Cain: "Why art thou wroth?
and why is thy countenance fallen? If thou doest well,
shall it not be lifted up? and if thou doest not well,
sin coucheth at the door; and unto thee is its desire,
but thou mayest rule over it." And Cain spoke to Abel
his brother. And it came to pass, when they were in the field,
that Cain rose up against Abel his brother, and slew him.

And the Lord said unto Cain, "Where is Abel thy brother?"
And he said, "I know not: Am I my brother's keeper?"

Genesis 4:3–9

In Hebrew, Abel means "futility, vanity, or breath."[8] The importance we give ourselves is vanity; our efforts and endings are futile; we are like wind, like nothing. Cain means "to lament," or "to chant a dirge." The story shifts when seen from Cain's point of view.

God has rejected his offering. Cain is hurt; his face falls. If we were in Cain's shoes, we would also feel hurt and jealous. Picture the scene: Cain toiling, tilling the earth, Abel in the quiet pastures tending his sheep. The division of labor itself seems unfair. Cain works hard, proudly bringing the fruits of his labors to Him—fruit, bread, vegetables. He expects God to be pleased. Cain has accepted the punishment God had given his father: he is paying for his father's sins with "the sweat of [his brow]" and has to scratch everything out of the earth. In Cain's situation, if we had worked as hard, how would we feel seeing Abel, the little brother, free to live an easier, happier life and not burdened with such grinding labor? It hardly seems fair. Did God not expect Cain to be jealous? How would we feel about our parents had they treated us this way?

True, Abel had given the finest of his flock; and there is no mention that

Cain had done the same. If Cain had not given the best, then he kept it for himself. But so what? Are we any different? It is easy to be generous during times of ease and plenty, but Cain's life was hard. He worked hard and gave what he could. It is understandable that Cain should want to have something to show for his labors. God is sweet to Abel. With Cain, God seems critical, demanding, cold, and intolerant of imperfection. In this story, God seems like a poor father, who is neither compassionate, nor fair, nor just.

But what is just and fair is not necessarily right and good. God holds to the standards necessary for Cain to overcome flaws in his character that would grow if left unchecked. God turns his back to Cain's offering as a statement, an instruction for Cain to meditate upon. Without an event to shake us, we tend to resist looking at ourselves. It is hard to see how we contribute to our own misery. Regretting the consequences of our acts is what often inspires us to change.

Yes, we value what we work for, but after working so hard, Cain clutched at what he produced and refused to part with it even in appreciation for God's shared company. Cain's values were becoming distorted.⁹ God tries again to correct Cain:

> And Hashem said to Cain, "Why are you annoyed, and why has your countenance fallen? Surely, if you improve yourself, you will be forgiven. But if you do not improve yourself, sin rests at the door. Its desire is toward you, yet you can conquer it."
>
> Genesis 4:6–7 (*Bereishis;* ArtScroll translation)

God intends to give Cain encouragement: there is hope for healing and it is in his own hands. He gives the instruction Cain needs to better himself. This is another version of *"Ayeckah?"* with God challenging Cain to look within, examine his darker side—the side he does not ordinarily try to see. But Cain evades the question and avoids self-examination. It's ironic. Taking a longer view despite his pain would have afforded him some comfort; but he is hurt and cannot see the love and regard God demonstrates in trying to help him—the respect He shows for Cain's depth, honesty, and his capacity for self-mastery. Had Cain gone against the grain of his feelings to look at himself honestly, however, his perspective would already have changed. He would have already begun freeing himself from self-centeredness and the narrowness of his own self-interest.

But Cain avoids looking at himself, refusing to see the self-centeredness that shuts out love, hurts him, and fuels his hatred. Instead, he directs his hurt and fury toward a victim. This is a common pattern: when someone is hurt, he feels wronged, and blames a parent, a sibling, or someone else—but does not look beyond himself for a broader understanding that would be a revelation to him. How often do we look beyond our own hurt feelings to try to understand the perspective of a parent, partner, child, or friend who hurts us?

But as we all do, even when there are obvious patterns that seem to repeat in various relationships, Cain justified himself and his own feelings first. Like most hurt children, even adult children, Cain does not fight his feelings in order to see his father's point of view. As is so common in our own lives, Cain remains at the center of his own emotional universe and looks no further than his first emotional reactions. As a consequence, Cain's interpretations only make sense of his own feelings, vindicating him and making God hateful.

As adults, we can make other choices. We have the capacity to look beyond our own feelings to see another's point of view. But that kind of honest examination, accepting the other's perspective in the face of hurt feelings, goes against the grain of our own natural tendencies.

Cain's first lie is implicit and it is to himself. Unless he acknowledges the blemish in his character, it will surely grow, and will only cause him and others pain. Thinking of himself first, stuck in the perspective of a hurt child, Cain goes on to make presumptions that are consistent with it—that God loved him less. Objectively, however, God spends far more time with Cain than with his brother.

Honest introspection would have tempered Cain's hurt and anger. As it was, however, he refused to examine himself and matters got worse. The lies we tell and the truths we keep to ourselves always have a victim. Yet, even after Cain kills Abel, God still gives Cain the opportunity to be honest. He asks, "Where is your brother?" But Cain again hides from himself and hopes to conceal himself from God. He lies once more, and this time his lie is willful and explicit. Cain answers, "I do not know." As one lie leads to another, Cain pretends ignorance and poses man's first question to God: "Am I my brother's keeper?"

"Ayeckah?" calls us to consciousness. The question demands honesty, and that honesty can guide our lives and lead us to healing. We can liberate ourselves and our intimates from the misdirections of our own painful past. We can allow those we love to be close to us—to be our witnesses, healers, and confidants—if we make ourselves vulnerable and risk telling them the truth.

CHAPTER 11

RISKING THE TRUTH

A half truth is a whole lie.
Yiddish proverb

The price is high for the secrets we keep, as well as the secrets that are kept from us. When we keep secrets, the richness of life is lost to loneliness and intimacy is lost to fear; alienated from ourselves, we preserve our pain throughout the time we hide. In keeping secrets, we run the risk that others might uncover what we hide, and our intimates are the ones most likely to penetrate the barriers. To protect secrets, we keep intimates at a distance. Whether the intimate is a partner or a child, we must open ourselves up to those we love, or else we shut them out and extend our loneliness to them.

PROTECTING CHILDREN FROM THE TRUTH

We may try to protect our children from painful family history by keeping secrets, but the skeletons we leave in the closet will speak in their silence, as the following stories illustrate:

Aaron was a sweet-natured adolescent who had a peculiar blank quality about him. His father was a colleague, and I knew Aaron's grandfather had been in Auschwitz. One day, I asked Aaron how old his grandfather had been when he was taken to Auschwitz. Aaron's answer—"What's Auschwitz?"—stunned me.

The lives of the children of Holocaust survivors cannot help but be marked by the emotional pain their parents pass on to them. The stories of the camps themselves are painful to hear, and Aaron's father had wanted to protect his son from knowing about them. And if he had sheltered his son from the stories, I suspected that he had also successfully blanked out his own pain as he related to his son. Thus, Aaron related to blankness rather than to his father's true feelings. Aaron's blank quality suddenly made sense to me.

I understood Aaron's father's impulse. When my children were seven and four years old, their mother and I had been uncertain whether to take them to Yad Vashem, Israel's Holocaust museum. We had never hidden our Holocaust heritage, but because they were so young, we never showed them pictures or made it real to them either. Ultimately, we decided to take them to the museum, and the children seemed to have no difficulty with the horrifying exhibits. But we had to wrestle with ourselves again before permitting them to enter the last room of the museum, which was bare except for a glass case containing the single shoe of an infant. That shoe, more than any other exhibit, took my breath away. That single shoe hammered home the reality of what had occurred.

My children had already spent the morning at the museum, but because I felt overwhelmed, I wanted to protect them. I was afraid of my children's questions, afraid they were too young to learn that people could do such things to children. In the end, however, I took them into the room, they asked questions, and accepted the explanations we offered.

One woman described what it was like for her when her father finally talked about her mother's mental illness:

> My father sat me and my sister down—I was about ten and Sharon was twelve—and he said, "Your mother is mentally ill." It was such a relief when he finally came out and said it. My mother was so bright and beautiful. Maybe my father held on to the hope that she would get better. I know my father's strong impulse was to protect us when she was acting odd or not getting out of bed at all. Maybe he hoped we wouldn't notice. It would have been easier on all of us, though, if he hadn't been so protective. If he had sat me down when I was six and said, "Your mother loves you very much, but sometimes she gets very sick," it would have helped me make sense of what was going on. As it was, we were left wondering why everyone

seemed to be saying the sky was blue when it was clearly green. I missed the way my mother used to be, and I kept away from her when she changed. I felt alone and hurt and I didn't know what to do. After my father spoke to us, I was able to manage better and I wasn't so lonely anymore.

Children seem able to handle the truth when it is presented in an emotionally neutral manner appropriate for their age. Though we would want to protect them, we hurt children when we "protect" them with secrets because until the secrets are revealed, the air is filled with continuous and bewildering tension, to which they cannot help but respond. But revealing the truth alone does not undo the damage. By the time a secret is revealed, the child has already learned to stop asking questions and has accepted the discomfort of emotional ambiguities—as was true for Ben.

Though his usual expression was tense and bewildered, Ben's face was kind. He had suffered from terrible headaches for twenty years and had been addicted to painkillers until he was treated at a pain clinic three years before. As a child, Ben could pick up the most delicate changes in the atmosphere of his family life but couldn't make sense of anything:

> I was fifty when my mother died. At her funeral, a woman came up to me and introduced herself as my half-sister. My mother had left her behind in Europe when she was fleeing the Nazis. She had never told me. I never knew I had a sister, never knew my mother carried such a secret. She must have lived with endless guilt. Was she too ashamed to tell me? Was she afraid I'd reject her? I thought we were close, but it turns out I never really knew my mother.

As Ben told this story, the bewildered look of a little boy crossed his face, and his forehead furrowed with perplexity. In Ben's facial isometrics, I could see the genesis of his tension headaches. Like the constant unnoticed pressure from a long-worn, too-tight watchband, his mother's silent pain became the undifferentiated background to Ben's life. He could feel the pain, but he could not understand or question it and could not locate its source. When parents have secrets to protect, children learn to back off from asking questions.

A person hiding secrets builds a life around a center of pain. The folk belief that "time heals all wounds" is not true. Time only heals wounds that have been expressed to others, not those that are repressed or hidden. When we keep secrets, we bury a part of ourselves in a desolate place where no comfort can reach. So entombed, our pain becomes a shrine visited only by ourselves.

SUBTLE DISTORTIONS AND ORIGINAL SIN
The Real Story

Every secret has consequences, though they may be so subtle that they escape our notice. In our attempt to control the consequences of the truth, we cannot know the ultimate ecology of the act.

Adam and Eve lose Paradise, and in the usual interpretation Eve's weak character is blamed for the loss. But the real blame stems from Adam's dishonesty, which is so subtle that we barely notice. God tells Adam:

> Of every tree of the garden you may freely eat; but of the tree of knowledge of good and bad you must not eat thereof; for on the day you eat of it, you shall surely die."
>
> Genesis 2:17

Adam does not tell Eve everything, nor does he tell everything exactly. Consequently, Eve believes she quotes God when she tells the serpent:

> The woman said to the serpent, "Of the fruit of any tree of the garden we may eat. But of the fruit of the tree which is in the center of the garden God had said: You shall neither eat of it *nor touch it,* lest you die."
>
> Genesis 3:2–3

In fact, God had warned them against eating the fruit, but it was Adam who appended "nor touch it." The Talmud says, "He who adds [to the word of God] subtracts [from it]."[1] Adam tried to keep Eve away from the tree altogether because he was afraid that she might be tempted to eat from it if she got too close. Adam, secretly mistrusting her, did not openly challenge Eve with his doubts.

Adam's lies to Eve made her susceptible to the blandishments of the serpent:

The serpent said to the woman, "You will not surely die; for God knows that on the day you eat of it your eyes will be opened and you will be like God, knowing good and bad."

Genesis 3:4–5

WHITE LIES

The story should be familiar to us from our own experience. It happens every day: we do not tell our mates everything, nor do we tell everything exactly. The act of even subtle lying reveals a lack of faith in a partner and in the eventual good of telling the truth. Eve placed her trust in Adam, and he misled her by giving her false information. In so doing, he left Eve vulnerable to the partial truths of others. Eve's acceptance of the serpent's evil, seductive whisper challenged the foundation of her universe. Eve believed that Adam had repeated God's words. According to the ancient biblical commentaries, the serpent pushed Eve's hand into the tree;[2] when she didn't die, Eve, believing Adam to have been truthful, doubted God.

Implicit in Adam's subtle distortion of the truth was an unexpressed, untested question about the reliability of Eve's character, the strength of their relationship, or perhaps the truth itself.

Why didn't Adam discuss his fears with Eve? Was he afraid of hurting her? Did she have a bad temper? There is a lot more going on here than meets the eye. If couples don't deal with such issues honestly, the unexpressed secrets and attitudes will confuse their relationship and deplete it of life and strength. Adam felt strong and believed he was protecting Eve by shading the truth. The paradox is that what is truly strong and weak is the reverse of what feels strong and weak. Being protective of those we love feels strong, while discussing the thoughts we prefer to conceal leaves us vulnerable to their reaction. But such discussions strengthen relationships. By avoiding that vulnerability, Adam did not give Eve the chance to prove herself to him and thereby deprived himself of the strength he derived from their union. In effect, Adam expelled himself from Paradise before God ever made him leave it.

Family members commonly protect one another from the truth. But how much harm, subtle or otherwise, results from regarding truth as an enemy that would harm others in the family? Who are we protecting: a family member who cannot take the truth, or ourselves from a parent, partner, or child's emotional reaction? We may want to protect children from knowing about a relative's suicide, or an infidelity that is rocking a marriage, yet the notion persists that we become strong by facing the truth. We feel betrayed when someone we trust hides the truth from us.

Children commonly protect their parents from knowing the truth about their activities and their feelings. For some families, telling "white lies" is common—assuming a father won't be able to understand the truth about a son's love life, or that a mother won't be sympathetic with a daughter's desire to spend Thanksgiving skiing instead of at home.

Such assumptions petrify relationships. What seemed true of someone yesterday may not be true today. An intolerant father may have mellowed, the easily hurt mother may be easier to approach, but the child will never know unless he periodically risks the truth and presents his feelings honestly.

Children and parents can spend years together and may believe they know each other inside and out, but the white lies they tell and the secrets they keep from one another can fossilize their image of one another. The truth challenges us to respond to it, and without that challenge we cannot grow to meet it.

Parents and children sometimes have to tell uncomfortable as well as painful truths if they are to be authentic with each other: "Now's not a good time for you to visit, Mom, we're in the middle of a fight," or "We were hoping for a romantic dinner alone," or "It upsets me when you talk about Mom that way, and I don't want to hear it." That kind of honesty is a gift of love that should be welcomed and received for the treasure it is. If the truth is graciously accepted, both children and parents are strengthened for it. Without that kind of honesty, however, and without its acceptance, love fails and conflicts perpetuate.

RISKING THE TRUTH

We learn about who to trust by risking telling the truth. Otherwise, we cannot know for sure how the other person would have responded. When we avoid telling the truth, we are left feeling our way blindly, having had no real test of faith, uncertain who can or cannot be trusted. We learn trust by exercising it. In lying to our intimates, we weaken them, ourselves, and our relationships. This happened to my friend Terry. Dishonesty—his failure to trust—cost him his paradise.

Terry met his wife, Helen, in Vietnam, after he had been wounded in battle. Helen was his nurse, and she knew that Terry was addicted to smoking the cheap heroin that was readily available. After marrying and returning to the States, however, Terry overcame his addiction. Then one night while getting together with some war buddies, Terry smoked marijuana laced with opium:

> I was sure I wouldn't do it again, so I didn't tell Helen. I was wrong. I soon got hooked again and was afraid she'd find out. I didn't want to hurt her and I was afraid to lose her. She trusted me. Each day that passed, I felt like I betrayed her more. The more secrets I had to keep, the more I had to hide. I was getting desperate and my habit was costing me. Seven months after I started using, I was arrested for robbing a convenience store. When I was arrested, I was more afraid of Helen's reaction than prison. When she first saw me in jail, she didn't ask "How could you do this to me?" No anger, guilt trips, demands, accusations. What she said was, "How can I help you?" My parents were mean drunks. Helen taught me what love means. Now I try to pass on the love she gave me.

Terry had not been honest with himself or with Helen. Terry's alcoholic parents had punished him, not forgiving him for his failings. In close relationships, Terry anticipated being hurt and rejected for his failures. So even though Helen loved him and had seen him through treatment for an addiction once, Terry did not trust that she would see him through again. Terry had not been relating to Helen, but reliving the fear of his parents with her. Terry lived in reply to his fear and not to *"Ayeckah?"* Sadly, her words at the jail were her final gift to him. Four years later, while Terry was still in prison, Helen died of cancer.

We must risk telling the truth or we deny ourselves the strength that our intimate relationships provide. The intimacy stops. Stripped of pretense, Terry could finally receive the love Helen gave him—and that changed his universe. After she died, Terry surrendered himself to God and thereby honored Helen's spirit. The love that Helen gave him he now passes on to others. He has become a healer.

TRUST

Stakes are always high in intimate relationships, whether between close friends, parents and children, or partners. In telling painful truths, we risk alienating a partner, but in not telling the truth, we hide ourselves and lose a chance to be known. Jean, who had been in an abusive relationship for fifteen years, despaired even after her life got better. She wondered if she could only love abusers:

> Two years after Jean divorced her first husband, she married a kind, gentle man. But later she became depressed after she realized that she still loved her first husband. Unable to talk about the loving feelings that she had for her ex-husband, Jean tried to hide her feelings from the new one. Her affection for her ex-husband was magnified by the false intimacy she pretended with her new husband.
>
> Hiding grief that she could not express to her husband, she received his affection only with guilt, feeling desperate over the "wrong choice" she had once again made.

When we tailor our truth-telling to avoid conflict, we force a relationship into stereotypical patterns that do not allow for the possibility of working out disagreements. A self-fulfilling prophecy then takes hold, and we condemn the other person to prejudgment, leading to concealed accusations for which there can be no redress.

Jean's not telling her husband what was going on for her emotionally was like being physically unfaithful to him. Alone with feelings she could not express, Jean became lonely in her marriage. She could not love her husband and hide from him at the same time.

I encouraged Jean to tell her husband what she thought and felt, because she had little to lose and much to gain. In not being honest with her husband, she was already living the suffocating alternative—she was living a lie, acting a part, feeling her husband was a threat to her rather than a partner. Even acknowledging this truth, Jean had to take a courageous leap of faith in order to speak. Telling her husband the truth would make her vulnerable, but it would free her from her isolation and grant him an opportunity to respond to her pain. At worst, he might feel jealous, hurt, angry, or insecure. But even then, the two of them would at least have a genuine relationship.

In telling her husband, Jean gained a sympathetic witness for the grief of her prior relationship. She and her husband became closer, and Jean learned something about honesty and intimacy. It was an important lesson—for her and for her children, who had grown up with a father who had beaten and demeaned their mother. Seeing their mother struggling her way through a good relationship gave them hope that it was possible for them to do so, too. Jean's children lived with and saw the frighteningly painful level of honesty that it took to maintain and keep a loving relationship—and the payoff for doing so. Had she not chosen to be so honest, Jean would have believed that her character was too sick for a healthy relationship, and her children would have known nothing about trusting to honesty in the intimacy of a true relationship.

Children learn whether or not it is safe to be emotionally honest by watching their parents relate to one another. Without a good personal example to follow, children may struggle in their future relationships. For a time, the adult child may become too distrustful of his feelings to answer "*Ayeckah?*" This was the case for Charles.

Charles's world of the past thirteen years collapsed after his wife left him. He began to make sense of his marriage when he learned the secret that explained his unhappy childhood. To let him know that she understood and to give him hope that he, too, would be able to endure it, Charles's mother risked the truth and told him about the worst time of her life:

After Marilyn left me, Mom told me about Dad's affair. I was an only child and Mom started working when I was five, because she couldn't stand being home anymore. Mom got bitter. At least once a week, Mom called me over to "have a talk." I was so lonely for her that it made me happy just to be with her, then she'd lash into me: she was ashamed I did this, and how could I do that? My mother could go on and on. I'd tremble and run away crying, sometimes for hours. I began hating her. But what my Mom told me sure puts a different light on the story.

The last five years of our marriage felt hollow. Marilyn was thinking of leaving the whole time, but she kept saying that everything was fine. I thought something was wrong with me. I trusted her feelings more than mine. Now I realize my feelings made sense the whole time—even as a kid.

Charles was desperate to make sense of what happened, but he had to know his own history first. Without knowing his history, his understanding would have merely skimmed along the surface.

When his wife left, it was the second time Charles's world blew apart, but he didn't know it. Charles had grown up in a divorced home even as his parents continued to live together. Unattended, the family died a quiet death and Charles lost the loving support that his parents had once provided him. Their relationship had frozen at the moment of betrayal, leaving Charles to become the recipient of the home's emptiness and anger.

Charles grew up with the lonely, broken heart of a confused five-year-old. When his mother called him close and then reproached him, Charles blamed himself for disappointing her and also began to despise her. In his marriage, Charles didn't believe he deserved the love he so desperately wanted. His wife's attitude and behavior did not erode Charles's self-regard so much as agree that its low state was justified. Unmet childhood needs and a damaged self-image left Charles a weak participant in his marriage. He viewed his own feelings as a scrambled confusion of contradictions. Growing up with secrets, Charles accepted Marilyn's silence and did not think to challenge it. As a child and as an adult, Charles lacked the information he needed to make sense of his feelings. Instead, he distrusted his own feelings and relied on his wife's.

His mother had attempted to protect Charles from the hurt she felt from her sense of his father's betrayal. Her feelings would have burdened her son; Charles might have rejected his father and damaged himself for doing so. But the attempt didn't protect him; she had sacrificed her relationship to him instead.

Unspoken misery will find reasons to express itself. By keeping her silence, his mother made herself alone and left Charles on the outside of her emotional world. Intimates express unhappiness with one another in the hope that something will change. Charles's mother's endless criticism may have been an attempt to get close to him.

It wasn't possible, however, until Charles knew the truth. When his mother told him of his father's infidelity, Charles finally understood his life and he understood his mother. Charles had to reevaluate his whole life; and slowly, he was ready to love again.

INFIDELITY

The unexpressed emotions of our intimates hurt and bewilder us throughout our lives. Consider the dense atmosphere of unexpressed emotions in a home where there is infidelity. The person who is cheating acts as if nothing is wrong, all the while feeling afraid, guilty, ashamed—a host of negative emotions. It becomes an effort to look the partner in the eye. The infidelity must be justified, and should the partner discover it, the truth can end the stability of a life together.

In situations of infidelity, the faithful partner becomes a threat to the unfaithful one and must be diminished. We learn to hate what we fear. One way to diminish the threat is to degrade the innocent partner—directly or to others. No longer a confidant and an intimate, the partner has been negated, negatively judged, and perhaps overtly disparaged. The partnership is over, even if it persists superficially. Once the marriage loses its integrity, the only true relationship becomes the adulterous one.

The innocent partner lives with the effects of the lie, rather than the strength of love and support. Everything may seem all right on the surface, but the information needed to make sense of feelings that are hidden leaves the innocent partner feeling slightly crazy. Children, bathed in the atmosphere of a home filled with hidden emotions, soak up disturbing feelings that will reappear later and still make no sense.

People who have a secret life act a part at great effort to themselves and even greater expense to their would-be intimates. One stodgy-appearing man shopping for a therapist wanted me to tell my history before speaking of his. Reacting mischievously to his stodginess, I gave him a searingly honest autobiographical sketch that would be awkward for any stranger to hear. After a moment's silence, his eyes became tearful and angry. He had just learned that the father he admired and thought he could never live up to had in fact been molesting his sisters for years. He had admired a lie all his life. Now his world had turned upside down.

When a parent hides ongoing impropriety behind a facade of rectitude, the child may idealize someone who is only play-acting his life. Reality can never measure up to the false ideal portrayed by the parent. The child is left to hide the shame, weakness, and vulnerability that he feels in comparing himself to his father. The man who came to consult me wanted to make sure his therapist would not also be playing a part, that I would not hide behind a role the way his father had. He needed truthful reflection to make sense of his world and his feelings.

The word "intimate" is derived from the Latin word for "innermost, to make known." The word "vulnerable" is derived from the Latin word meaning "to wound." We make ourselves vulnerable in order to be intimate. We depend on the care and kindness of our partners to be tender with us. As we will discuss in detail in the next chapter, we cannot build barriers around our feelings and be intimate at the same time.

CHAPTER 12

THE HEALING MARRIAGE

A Second Chance to Master Childhood Trauma

*A married couple is like two rough stones
that take years to grind each other smooth.*

Rabbi Jacob Singer (Seattle, 1977)

We bring the legacies of our childhoods into the new unions we make. In marriage, two individuals—and two families—with all their strengths and weaknesses, come together in the hope of creating a combination as successful as those of the parents, or even more so. Romantic love and sexual excitement are vitalizing, and all couples start out with hope and strength of purpose. Inevitably, however, in every relationship, partners begin to hurt each other as intimacy exposes old pain. As the glow of romance fades, the hurts of childhood are brought to the fore wearing contemporary arguments. Until we challenge old, hurt conceptions from childhood, we habitually bring emotional distortions into other relationships, especially the most intimate.

Arguments between partners, although uncomfortable, can be rich opportunities for healing deep childhood wounds. As long as each partner is willing to take the risk of honest dialogue and self-examination and each partner is willing to look within, the relationship becomes a growing union, a basic unit of human healing, and a positive living example to the next generation.

In arguments, however, each partner wants the other one to see his point of view. The innate self-centeredness of hurt and angry feelings does not easily admit any other person's point of view. But opposing one's first reactions to respect the views of a partner, one of the basic tasks in marriage, allows two people to resolve their disagreements, learn to understand one another, and begin to grow to maturity. Many people would prefer peace at any price, but avoiding conflict by capitulating to a more forceful partner does not end the argument but only buries it alongside other hidden resentments.

In intimate relationships, unexpressed feelings, and memories continually loom in the background, ready to be triggered by a couple's everyday tensions or life's larger struggles. Conflicts, however, can become means of healing once we learn to recognize our own emotional flashbacks—those intense emotions that arise from the past, not the present—and are careful not to injure the other person with feelings that belong more to that painful past than to the present moment.

Emotional flashbacks can be recognized when an emotional response is out of proportion to the current situation. Unfortunately, most flashbacks that occur in marriage at first go unrecognized for what they are and instead are taken at face value. The problem is that the person caught up in the intensity of an emotional flashback usually does not recognize that his feelings have been magnified, does not realize that his reaction is from the past and that the present situation is only a trigger. A partner may perceive and point out the disproportion between the circumstance and the reaction, but not be believed.

Pain triggered from the past seems abusive to the partner who stands wrongly accused of having evoked it. Each person feels hurt, misunderstood, and mistreated, and this inevitably invokes memories of other times and past outrages. It is at this very moment in the argument that *the honor we continue to give or deny our parents in the present is reenacted in the relationship.*

Marriages become stuck or come to an end with reenactments we neither recognize nor understand. Relationships often end in divorce when one or both partners lose hope that the other will do the *self*-examination necessary to acknowledge the true roots of hurt feelings.

As we learn to recognize our emotional flashbacks, our partners become witnesses to our pain rather than enemies causing it. Hurt from the past diminishes and is reenacted less, and relations with parents often improve as a consequence. Conversely, when we restrain ourselves from reacting hurtfully to our parents, when we honor them despite the shortcomings that had wounded us as children, we reenact our childhood pain less. Again, hurt diminishes, and our relationships with our partners often improve. In either case, we answer *"Ayeckah?"* honestly and become conscious.

INTIMACY

As infants, we lived through an Edenic time, when all our needs were encapsulated in warm milk and naked body comfort. In the purity of that first relationship, we learned how life could be if everything was right and we were complete. The restoration we seek in becoming part of a couple strikes us as our most natural state, as the familiar Edenic home from which we were expelled a long time ago. Intimacy heals the grief of childhood loss, fills the emptiness, and assuages old hurt. We search for the partner who will make our life complete again. We experience a fleeting reminder of those early glorious times later in the romance of new love. We feel what it is like not to be alone.

The process of maturation is one of separation, and it is a lonely experience. The first breath we take separates us from the mother womb that protected us and takes us into a new independence. We toddle away, then learn to walk; next we leave for school. In ever further excursions, we explore the world. We challenge our dependence in our parents' home until it is time for us to move to homes of our own.

When we leave home, the arms that clung to our parents in childhood empty, and we seek love again. Loneliness impels us even as sexual need drives us to find ourselves partners. We seek love when we don't have enough of it. We make love not just for sexual pleasure, but in search of the completion others bring us. As we make our first discoveries about a new potential mate, a special glow seems to encompass the world. In the rapture of romance, life feels full and rich with possibility. Worldly concerns pale in significance as we lock eyes with our lover.

The first biblical reference to the human condition tells us that it is not good to be alone. Without love's touch, infants die and adults languish. We hope for love to fill the inmost reaches of our souls. The affection and closeness inherent in true intimacy makes life full. Intimacy is a balm to our souls: in the arms of those we love, we feel secure and content, healed from the emotional wounds of the past. Each couple tries to make a world with each other, and the success or failure of that union determines how well each heals.

To achieve a lasting intimacy, it is necessary for lovers to expose the parts of themselves they have most protected. When partners allow each other to witness their respective hurts, they become closer; they become each other's healer. A couple's most heated arguments occur when one partner's exposed pain uncovers the hidden pain of the other. The most bitter conflicts arise when painful aspects of one partner's past collide with the other's.

Childhood hurts come up disguised within many situations. Two years after she and John had married, for example, Sandra described an incident that led to their worst blowup:

> John accidentally broke my favorite chair when he stood on it to change a lightbulb, and then he didn't tell me. I feel like he lied to me. How am I supposed to trust him if he's not going to tell me the truth? He's so careless with my things. I've had to work hard for everything I have and it's like he could care less. I was furious. He apologized, but I don't think that's really going to change anything. I was mad for days. He promised it wouldn't happen again, but it says something about his character that I don't trust. He moped around with his head down and didn't say anything afterwards. At least he had the decency to be ashamed.

John and Sandra are both honest, honorable, hardworking, and highly accomplished people. They both had problems with their fathers. Being competent, responsible, and a good provider was essential to John. He wanted to be nothing like his father, a binge drinker who left the family worrying about him for days at a time and lost job after job while John's mother desperately tried to keep the family together. When he broke Sandra's chair, John's sense of shame and failure was exaggerated by his childhood memories of his father repeatedly letting his mother down. He knew Sandra would be upset about the broken chair, so like a fearful child, he did not tell her; and then like the honorable adult he was, he felt he had disgraced himself.

In intimate relationships, we cannot help but expose and be exposed to the hurts each partner carries. A chance mishap had exposed John's childhood pain, a pain that he had once defended himself against through exemplary conduct. Then John's defensive reactions tore through Sandra's normal, hard-won composure.

Sandra's father had been domineering, self-centered, verbally abusive, and had refused to help his children financially after divorcing their mother. Sandra had worked her way through school and up the corporate ladder. But for years, she had lived with the insecurity of having no family to back her.

When Sandra became upset, her physiological responses were the intensified ones of an abused child. Hurt by her father's selfishness and lack of support while she was growing up, she was quick to feel the same hurt in her interpretation of the situation with the chair. The story she told herself may have been true for Sandra's father, but John was anything but self-centered. He cared a great deal about his wife's feelings. Sandra overreacted about the broken chair, but she was right to be upset about John's having hidden the accident from her.

John avoided telling Sandra about the broken chair because he surmised, accurately, that she would fly off the handle. That he wanted to avoid the painful confrontation is understandable. But as in the story of Adam and Eve, that avoidance was the beginning of a mistrust between them. John's avoidance also denied Sandra an opportunity to confront her own reactions. John and Sandra were each hurt by each other's blind reactions to emotions from the past intruding on the present. Each felt unseen by the other. Until they worked out their conflict, they were both responding to the ghosts of the past rather than to the real partners they had chosen.

The pain we protect ourselves from is pain we would rather not acknowledge. As their relationship progressed, John and Sandra were quicker to recognize when childhood hurts were being played out in their marriage. Their conflicts taught them a great deal about themselves and each other. In working through their clashes, they slowly grew beyond the loneliness of childhood's frozen pain and began to heal themselves in each other's company.

A wise colleague once said, "A couple has four sets of grandparents. If you had them all to dinner, they wouldn't all get along and wouldn't like the same things. It takes us our whole life to figure it all out."[1] She is right; in marriage, the histories of two families are brought together into one home. The strengths and weaknesses of two families cram together in ill-fitting union. The hurts of several lifetimes are exposed to hurt again and again.

LOOKING WITHIN RATHER THAN BLAMING THE OTHER

Fresh hurt is inflicted when we mistake intense feelings from the past for something current. At the time, our reactions seem to fit the circumstances, but our partner insists that we are being unfair and that our reaction is unjustified. If we persist in our behavior despite our partner's protest, our inappropriate response then triggers our partner's past hurts. One partner hurts the other, the hurt one retaliates, and the fighting continues until there is either resolution or withdrawal.

The painful, stylized fights that recur in any marriage are exactly the places where each partner's painful history intersects with the other's. This is common in intimate relationships. For whatever surface reason, one partner gets angry and the other retreats; hurt by the retreat, the angry partner gets madder still. At these junctures, neither is able to be rational or to recognize that his own response originated in and belongs to a time long past. When pain from the past adds pain to the present, the feelings are so intense that neither person is likely to see the other's point of view. In intimate relationships, the self-protective defensive behavior of one feels like a rejection to the other. The fights continue until each person looks within himself rather than at the partner's shortcomings.

In the story of *Sleeping Beauty,* a prince comes upon a castle locked under a spell. Within its recesses lies a princess who has been asleep for a hundred years. The prince must fight his way through a forest of dense, prickly briars that obstruct all who attempt to wake the princess to life with a kiss. To be truly intimate, we too must fight through the forest of the defenses we've put up to protect ourselves from being hurt by another person. We do not easily open up and become vulnerable. As children, we trust openheartedly. When we have been hurt as children, however, we have to learn to trust again to be open to love.

We easily see our partner's defensive entanglements but may have trouble penetrating the thicket of our own defenses. A wife may complain that her husband shuts down rather than talk about his pain; a husband may regard his wife as an anxious interrogator when she feels she needs answers. Each can immediately see what the other does not in the "overreaction" of one or the "insensitivity" of the other. The effects of pain are seen and negatively judged, but not necessarily recognized as coming from the past. But even when one partner can recognize the source, in the heat of the argument, the other does not—and that blindness can be exasperating as well as hurtful. Should one partner tell the other, "You're acting just like your mother," or "You're treating me like your father," the intended insight is perceived as a vicious attack on the partner and his family. As one partner reenacts his childhood pain in an attempt to master it, the other suffers for it. A partner who acts as a loving witness to the exposed or defended wounds of the other does better than a partner who acts like a victim of the other pathology.

Don and Sally met five years after Don's first wife, Sue, left him. After a few dates, Sally told Don that she could not continue seeing him unless he agreed to be monogamous. Don recoiled:

Before Sue, I'd never been with anyone else, but now the world's like a candy shop. I've had maybe a dozen affairs by now. I've hurt people I cared about. There were two women I might have loved, but they weren't quite right and I wasn't ready for anything heavy; I'm still not. Now there's Sally, my kids' Montessori teacher. I like her, but I'm not sure about her. She hasn't a clue what she's asking me. I seem normal as long as I don't depend on anyone, but if I were just seeing her . . . I'm so hurt and angry. Right now, if a girlfriend's busy, that's cool. I'll see someone else and be adult about it. But if I can't do that, everything inside will explode.

After Sue left, Don needed to reconstruct his world so he would not have to depend on any one woman. To summon up his trust again would have involved retrieving his hurt and rage as well, and this he was unwilling to do. Instead, reenacting the trauma of his abandonment, Don had left one woman after another, diluting the concentration of his pain by dispersing it over a number of people. In their grief, anger, and sense of betrayal, one woman after another expressed Don's feelings.

Don feared that in committing himself to Sally he would be sacrificing too much without any guarantee of being able to get the love he needed to make himself whole. He was afraid of selling himself out again in order to meet his old unfulfilled needs for love. His only precedents for committed relationships had been painful. In the short run, these fleeting trysts of his new bachelorhood were easier; they did not penetrate into his core, where the pain was. But in the longer run, they left Don lonely in his safety.

Don did not trust his own judgment. He often said, "The only thing I trust is my anger." Sally seemed frighteningly familiar. Like his first wife, she was intellectual, sweet, kind, and practical. He did not realize at first that this very repetition of characteristics offered the possibility of healing.

Don and Sally both wanted to be together. Sally moved in, hoping that Don would relax and trust to the evolution of their relationship. She believed that they would come to harmonize as they got to know one another better. She was sure that once Don knew and understood her, he would get over the hurt from Sue's betrayal and be able to trust her. But in closer quarters, the pressures on the pair only intensified.

That first year, Don and Sally's relationship was driven by fear. Don feared he would be lonely in the relationship; Sally feared she would be swallowed up in it. She was determined to maintain her integrity, while Don was determined to have the closeness that eluded him. Don and Sally needed each other's love, but each was afraid of compromising too much to gain it. Their periodic fights became stylized and ritualistic. When Sally maintained the structure of her independence and activities, Don reacted with hurt and escalating anger. But in between their frequent fights, they were tender with each other, respected each other's minds, and trusted each other's honesty. They each asked *"Ayeckah?"* and searched for the truth.

Finally, the two sought the help of a couples counselor to try to make sense of their repetitive conflicts. Sally told the counselor: "I feel like I'm the one paying for Sue's betrayal. Don is so quick to imagine the worst. He's kind to everyone else, but so angry with me. I'm not sure I can take it much longer." Don said: "When we're fighting, Sally gets so reasonable it drives me crazy. She always wants to explain, as if that will take care of everything."

Each partner in a couple readily sees the other's blind spots. But it is the aspects of ourselves that we least recognize that most hurt the ones we love.

Sally gradually became aware of the origin of her "reasonableness" that so bothered Don:

> When I was six, my family was in a car accident. Dad was driving. Mom was in a coma for weeks and was never the same afterwards. She cooked and cleaned, could still be sweet, but she was slower. The first few years, she'd lose control a lot, becoming wild and carrying on. She scared us, but we knew something was wrong with her from the accident. I figured out how to calm her down with my tone of voice. Dad never took charge. All he did was escape to play cards with his buddies. I think he felt defeated and never forgave himself for the accident.

Sally became an anchor for her brother and sister in a home where her mother's behavior was frighteningly unpredictable and her father distant. As a child, she was the most competent and stable person in her home and learned to remain calm and controlled in volatile situations. In the face of irrational anger or behavior, Sally learned to manage, to understand, and to deflect pain.

In hearing all this, Don came to a realization:

I finally understood that when Sally was being so reasonable, she was really hurting. I started taking a time-out from the fight so we could both calm down. Then I'd see Sally's composure crumble and I'd see her panic. I'd leave angry, but tell Sally I'd be back in ten minutes, and that reassured her. Then, when I'd thought things through, from her side and mine, I'd have a better idea of what was right.

Sally, too, was able to make connections:

I began to understand that when Don was angry and upset about something, what was right and what was true wasn't what mattered to him. What he wanted was for me to understand his feelings. When he'd get mad, my heart would start beating hard and I'd think, "If only I can explain, he'll understand and won't be mad anymore." I learned that I have to take a breath and just suppress my inclination to explain. I needed to attend to his feelings. Once Don feels like I've heard him and can understand his feelings, he settles down and we can talk.

Gradually, Don and Sally learned to recognize their flashbacks. In the beginning, it typically took several days before they were able to look back on a fight and understand what had happened between them. This is not unusual: in the heat of emotion, we often do not realize when we are in a mood state belonging to the past. Eventually, however, they began to recognize flashbacks within an hour or two. They hoped someday to be able to notice their old emotions while they were in them.

After a time, their quarrels diminished in frequency and were resolved within hours or minutes rather than days. Little by little, Don and Sally began to understand themselves and then, gradually, to trust one another. Sally described a deep feeling of being home with Don, who was more present than her own father had been. Don glimpsed the possibility of trusting in love at long last.

In the project of building a life together, we must heal each other's wounds or suffer them. Individuals often instinctively choose partners who suffered comparable wounds in childhood because they can each understand and empathize with the other's pain. They then poke and prod at each other's vulnerabilities, trying to wake each other up. In intimate relationships, we force each other to reach for higher levels of self-awareness. Though it can feel terrible, a couple engaging in a struggle about core issues is not necessarily one in trouble, despite the level of conflict involved. The conundrum of conflict is that the times we most hurt each other are also the times when we can most deeply heal.

Like John and Sandra, couples often have parallel sorrows from the past. Sensing the familiar within while seeing the differences without constitutes much of the mutual attraction. However, if couples draw battle lines to protect themselves from one another, these common injuries can entrench them in pain that neither can leave. On the other hand, the mutuality of painful history and a complementary approach can become a couple's joint venture to heal, so long as the injuries partners share become part of their sympathetic understanding of one another. In their similarities, each becomes the other's witness and healer; in their differences, each becomes the other's teacher.

There is an old saying that the three most important events in our lives are birth, death, and marriage. Of the three, we exercise choice in only one. Marriages die, however, if we do not take the time to infuse them with fresh perspective and experience. But modern families, particularly two-income families, are overburdened with obligations, and everyone is familiar with the litany: two careers, separate commutes, young children needing attention, shopping, cooking, cleaning, doing bills, repairs, family illness, legal obligations. There is precious little discretionary time—and time for intimacy feels like discretionary time. Remarriage after divorce sets up new kinship relations that can share in the burden of child-rearing; but good marriages between good people commonly fail because they have no time to breathe with one another. Couples suffocate in their relationships when they are not growing with one another. Seeing through the surface of everyday conflicts to the childhood pain that intensifies them allows one partner to witness and heal the other's pain. There are likely to be no easy solutions to marital troubles, but there may be hard, and perhaps unorthodox, solutions couples can attempt before their relationships become moribund.

TO LEAVE OR TO STAY?

Too many couples relinquish the chance to heal because they have given up on their relationship. It is hard to tell when a relationship is worth fighting for and when it is better for everyone concerned to let it go. Infidelity breaks a basic trust, and even if trust can heal, the relationship still bears the scars. Violence is unacceptable; addictions are often intolerable. But the decision to end a marriage because of the emotional limitations of one's partner is far more difficult to make. It is precisely at the point of crisis, when a couple is often ready to give up, that buried problems come to the fore and there is finally an opportunity to heal core wounds. One woman going through a divorce told me:

> We'd been separated about a month when he came over to see me. He said he couldn't take my complaining anymore, that I wasn't happy no matter how hard he tried. Then he started to sob. He just collapsed and cried so hard his shoulders shook. I put my arms around him and we held each other. That's all I ever wanted, for him to love me and put his arms around me like that. He'd always been so rigid, saying I was too emotional. That day we just held each other like that for a half an hour. It was the closest moment we had in our whole marriage. It was what I'd been wanting, just to get close to him like that.

Too many couples break up just as they reach this point. Declaring an end to the relationship causes their protective armor to drop. At long last, the thick metal that had kept them shielded from one another is battered with holes their partners can see right through. But unless one of them has the guts to say "Wait a minute—I see some hope here," wounded pride can lead them to a divorce lawyer instead of a counselor.

Our pain ultimately reflects back to us as long as we inflict it on others rather than facing it ourselves. We hurt others until we can put our hurt into words. A marriage of equals insures that two people suffer together, at the same depth. Pat was turning forty-five when she decided it was time to leave Dan, her husband of twenty-two years:

> I've put up with Dan's superior attitude way too long. I may not be as smart as he is, but I'm no dummy. I wasn't at the top of my class, but I was an honors student. I'm tired of his talking down to me as

if I'm stupid. It was the same with my mother. No matter what I did, it was never good enough for her. When I married Dan over her objections during our hippie years, she never forgave me for it. I visit her, but she never visits us. With Dan, it's the same as with my mother. Well, the kids are nearly grown and I've had enough.

Dan pleaded with Pat to stay. He had known he was in the wrong for a long time. She agreed to go into therapy with him. At the first session, Dan wept in talking about how lonely he had been in the last several years of their marriage and how lonely he had been as a boy. Dan had been a smart, too-big-for-his-britches little boy with resources his father could neither match nor understand. The disrespect that Dan had brought into his marriage had also been emblematic of the loneliness he had felt with his father. Pat was too hurt to witness Dan's loneliness, and Dan did not acknowledge Pat's hurt.

Unable to please her mother, and too proud to show her hurt feelings, Pat presented Dan with the same stony pride she had shown her mother. With Dan's sense of superiority and Pat's sense of inadequacy, a severe power imbalance evolved between them, one that Dan could trigger with a tone of voice. But Pat's self-respect grew with her accomplishments, and she was less and less willing to tolerate Dan's condescension.

With the threat of separation, each imagining what it would be like to be without the other, Pat and Dan both recognized that they had many rich years of shared history together. They had grown up in each other's company, had had children together, and in moments of grief when she imagined leaving him, Pat recognized that, beneath her anger, she still loved him. Unlike those who divorce, after so many years she was willing to give the marriage more time. But to get back together, they each had to take a hard look at themselves. Unable to forgive a rage that she could not acknowledge, Pat had to hack through her pride to admit how pervasive her own sense of inadequacy had been before she could feel the extent of her rage at Dan's condescension. Her rage was a protest against a childhood belief that had diminished her throughout her life. Pat's demand for respect was a challenge to Dan's condescension.

Acknowledging his condescension as a flaw in himself, Dan began correcting it in his interactions with Pat and with his father. His father in turn became more open with Dan, and Dan learned stories about his father that genuinely impressed him. Pat, feeling more secure with Dan as he attacked her less, also became more open to him. Her anger slowly abated, and she understood her complicity in her own humiliation. Pat now treats her mother with kindness and respect, hoping that one day their relationship will change.

Times of crisis in a relationship are times for taking a new look at our deepest conflicts to determine what we want and need. We can then look within ourselves to see what our own contribution to the problem has been. If we look only at our partner's defects, there is no hope for the relationship.

But by the time most couples go to therapists or mediators, their goodwill has worn quite thin. Some already regard one another as enemies and give up on therapy after only a few months. The trap is that a partner's "shortcomings" are always very evident, while our own are hard to see. When we feel wronged, it goes against the grain of our emotions to examine ourselves rather than our partner—yet this is what both partners must do if their relationship is to be saved.

When we are stripped to the core by a crisis, we have the chance to face the darkest regions of our vulnerability. Unless the sanctity of the union is destroyed by infidelity or violence, the occasions when partners seem most divided are actually when they are most united in passion. Our conflicts only begin feeling like a death grip when we keep fighting the issues on the surface while ignoring the deeper ones that underlie them.

In Genesis 2:18, God says, "It is not good that man should be alone; I will make him an help-meet for him." *K'negdo,* the Hebrew word for "[help]-meet for him," translated literally means "at his side" or "against him." The literal translation is the deeper one: So bonded, we stand by each other, side by side, hoping to face the world together until our last breath. So tethered, we also stand *against* each other, unable to let go, unable to get away, hurting one another as we respond to the traumatic remnants of our separate pasts.

From the first arguments with our partners, our deepest issues from our families are engaged. But in the lock of *K'negdo* we oppose each other until we can see ourselves honestly. The wounds we have suffered at the hands of our parents, the traumas that had injured them, the history of generations past and future are played out before us—and can heal in our relationships.

In healing marriages, partners grow beyond painful childhood reactions, bestowing the gifts of their healing and good examples onto their children.

When marriages end, partners usually condemn one another's fatal flaws of character, blaming them for the expiration of a once precious marriage and for the airless years of hurt without growth.

We must remember, however, that the major flaws in our partner's character derive from old pain reenacted in our presence, pain our partner needs to have us witness in order to heal. If we can be a witness to our partner's pain rather than just react to it, these painful reenactments can become moments of healing. But we need to remember, too, that the recurrent fights we have with our intimates point to our own reenactments as well as theirs; they indicate that we need our partner's witness to heal the pain that underlies our own reenactments. But to have our partner's witness during our moments of pain, we must stop hurting them at those times. To make a healing marriage, we apply all the principles of healing we have learned; we must examine ourselves first to understand our painful relationships. Evasion of honest *self*-scrutiny leads to the stress that a partner must defend against. We must ask ourselves *"Ayeckah?"* to recognize our own reactions for the emotional flashbacks they may be.

In examining ourselves, we must look at our parents' histories as well as our own—seeking to understand their stories to better understand our reactions to them. In imagining our parents as the children they once were, we temper our own hurt with an adult's understanding. Using the guidance and discipline of the Fifth Commandment to honor our parents, we learn to restrain less worthy behaviors and so temper the harshness of our reactions to our partners and our children as well. In our restraint, we feel the full unrelieved force of our emotions, allowing our partners to become witnesses to our pain rather than victims of it—thus breaking a cycle of generational pain and starting a new cycle of generational healing. We stop hurting others to heal ourselves.

CHAPTER 13

THE DISCIPLINE OF THE FIFTH COMMANDMENT

Re-forming Character, Forgiving Our Parents

Honour thy father and thy mother:
that thy days may be long upon the land
which the LORD thy God giveth thee.

Exodus 20:12 (King James Version)

Honour thy father and thy mother,
as the LORD thy God hath commanded thee;
that thy days may be prolonged, and that
it may go well with thee, in the land
which the LORD thy God giveth thee.

Deuteronomy 5:16 (K.J.V.)

When Moses climbed Mt. Sinai to confer with God, he was angry at the behavior of a people who had been damaged by 430 years of brutalization and slavery.[1] The enforced, unceasing labor, whippings, beatings, sexual degradation, and humiliations that had been visited on the Israelites, continued with one another. To heal the effects of trauma that had been endured by generations of parents and children, Moses sought ways to transform the degraded Israelite slaves of Egypt into a people who could live together without the guidance of a whip. After communing with himself and with God for forty days and forty nights, Moses returned with the Ten Commandments—a blueprint for healing the people's emotional scars. If the Jews were to survive as a people, the active cycle of harm had to stop. To free themselves from the past, they had to contain their wounds, not pass them on to others. Only then could the people, as individuals and as a nation, begin to be free.

The first four commandments pertain to man's relationship to God:

> I am the Lord thy God, which have brought thee out of the land of Egypt, out of the house of bondage.
>
> Thou shalt have no other gods before Me. Thou shalt not make unto thee any graven image. . . . Thou shalt not bow down thyself to them, nor serve them: for I the Lord thy God am a jealous God, visiting the iniquity of the fathers upon the children unto the third and fourth generation of them that hate Me; And showing mercy to the thousandth generation of them that love Me and keep My commandments.
>
> Thou shalt not take the name of the Lord thy God in vain; . . .
> Remember the Sabbath to keep it Holy. . . .

The Sixth through Tenth commandments pertain to man's relationship with his fellow man and to society:

> Thou shalt not murder.
> Thou shalt not commit adultery.
> Thou shalt not steal.
> Thou shalt not bear false witness against thy neighbor.
> Thou shalt not covet thy neighbor's house, . . . wife, . . . nor any thing that is thy neighbor's.
>
> Exodus 20:1–17 (K.J.V.)

The significance of the Fifth Commandment—"Honor your father and your mother that your days may be long and that it may go well with you upon the land"—can be measured by its placement at the center of all the commandments.

HONORING OUR PARENTS
DESPITE THEIR FAILURES

We instinctively recognize the importance of the Fifth Commandment. The parent-child relationship is the most basic of human relationships, and it is never easy. No parent is perfect. Emotions get tangled, and children are often conflicted as they and their parents get older; they often feel hurt, or are angry and critical toward their parents for their failures. Whether a child feels mild disappointment, shame, resentment, or utter hatred, the Fifth Commandment is central to healing the wounds that result from hurt parent-child relationships; and it is important to understand what it says. The Fifth Commandment does not command that we love our parents. Love cannot be commanded. Rather, the essence of the Fifth Commandment is that we respect our parents when we can, have sympathy for them when we cannot, and provide care for them if they are unable to care for themselves. No other commandment has an explicit, defined consequence: ". . . so that you may live a long life and so that it may be good for you." Adhering faithfully to the Fifth Commandment compensates for the harm that damaged parents cause their children by promising good for the faithful child. In this way, the future need and dignity of each generation is secured by the generation that follows.

The consequences of not adhering to the principles of the Fifth Commandment can be painful, as the story of Gene and his mother illustrates. Intelligent and good-hearted, Gene entered therapy after his mother died from an overdose of alcohol and pain medication. Whether her death had been an accident or a suicide was uncertain. In describing his mother's life and death, Gene demonstrated an empathy toward her—an empathy that he believed his mother had lacked in regard to her own mother:

My mother lived her whole life trying not to be like her mother. My grandmother was the youngest of eight children and she never stopped being the baby. She had this high-pitched, whiny voice that drove Mom crazy. Mom said that growing up she had to be her mother's mother. Mom hated being dependent and hated having anyone be dependent on her. When I pestered her as a kid, Mom had this tone of voice that made me feel like a worm. I don't know what happened between them after Grandpa died, but at first, when Grandma got sick, Mom used to fly out to care for her. When I was ten, though, Mom came back from a visit and said she was never going back there again.

I've been worried about how lonely Mom was ever since Dad died four years ago. Her visits to us were always very short and she never let me visit her unless it was a vacation and my children could come. Mom must have felt bad at leaving us when we were little to take care of Grandma. The coroner said her death was due to an accidental overdose of alcohol and medicine, but I don't know if it was really accidental. Her arthritis bothered her a lot in the last months. She could have stayed with any one of us. We all wanted her to. I keep thinking about what it was like for her in those last hours. The police found her by the door like she was trying to get out.

Gene's mother had been loved, but she died alone and in pain, never saying goodbye or making her peace with either her mother or her children. She had refused to help her mother years before and refused the help her children offered later.

Gene's mother's life did not have to unfold or end as it did. The ordeals she faced were opportunities to heal the wounds of her childhood. Had she been with her mother as the older woman lay small and dying, the moment might have stripped away her bitterness to reveal the love that existed between them. Her memories of the woman could have been sweet and poignant rather than righteously bitter. Had she allowed her children to care for her when she was alone and in pain, Gene's mother might have taken advantage of another opportunity to heal. Had she allowed herself to depend more on her children and less on alcohol and drugs, the end of her life would have been fuller, more meaningful, and more endurable. Pain endured in loneliness is far worse than pain that is comforted with love and kindness.

Furthermore, allowing herself to depend on her children might have evoked poignant memories of when she herself was little and her mother was still caring for her, before she had reversed roles with her. In the presence of children who loved her and meant well by her, Gene's mother could have grappled with—and perhaps vanquished—the demons of her childhood. Granting her children the privilege of taking care of her in her time of need would have transformed her and allowed the surviving generations a closer, more loving relationship. She would have honored herself and accorded them the respect of trusting them. Long after she died, that respect would have continued into the lives of her grandchildren. But Gene's mother preferred being alone to risking having her children resent her for needing them.

BREAKING THE CYCLE OF HARM

As part of changing our behavior, we reevaluate our lives to accommodate the understanding that comes from the new perspective. When we conduct ourselves honorably despite the provocation of feelings of anger or resentment, we free ourselves from hurt. We act independently of it. We are able to look back and acknowledge our own mistakes and faults, accept responsibility for the harm we have caused, and grieve the wasted years and damaged relationships. Regret is the acceptance of truth and the beginning of healing, a part of the process of maturing and growing up, a prelude to deep, inner change. Unfortunately, the very people who have the most to benefit, like Gene's mother, also have the most to regret, and they often lash out to avoid dealing with painful emotions that are already overwhelming to them.

Destructive cycles of intergenerational harm are interrupted when an adult child makes the effort to honor a hurtful parent with respect, kindness, and appreciation for the good he has done. We go against the grain of adolescent hostility in order to move toward a mature understanding of a wounded parent who had meant to do well for the children. In imagining a parent's life enough to understand and truly forgive, we free ourselves from the harm we perpetrate with our own harsh judgment and wounded pride.

When a parent does something right, all we need to do is emulate him. It is natural to return good for good; we do not need a commandment to tell us to honor parents who treated us well. But when we have parents who did not give us love and respect, or did so imperfectly, then we have to struggle with ourselves to act with goodness rather than to react injuriously.

The Fifth Commandment tells us to honor our parents—despite their failures. We may have good reasons for feeling hostility toward our parents, but until we master it, we will continue to be hurt by it. Continued hostility toward parents indicates our own restricted understanding of them, and indicates, as well, that it is time to apply the Golden Rule—to go against the grain of our self-absorbed emotions and imagine what it would be like to look across a table at the children we raised and imagine being in our parents' shoes with our children behaving as we do. The aversion we feel toward our parents is evidence that misfortune and adversity affected them. Every parent's failure had an origin in a time and place in history. *If we are hostile toward our parents, we can presume that something went wrong in their lives or that something is wrong with our understanding of them.*

The Fifth Commandment tells us to resist the temptation to hurt wounding parents back. A good example is Karla, who was fifty when her seventy-three-year-old mother developed a rapidly progressive cancer. Karla left her family and went to live with her mother in order to take care of her. Despite Karla's sacrifice, however, her mother continued to criticize her as she had all of Karla's life. Karla burned with resentment and bitterness, but she kept her feelings to herself, sharing them only with her husband. Karla was afraid to speak to her mother; if she started, she was sure, she would have unleashed a lifetime's accumulation of hurt and rage on a dying woman:

> My mother was always mean to me. My sister could get anything she wanted, but for me everything was too expensive. I cleaned the house a lot, did the dishes, but my mother would praise my sister and just criticize me. Even when I did well in school, it was always my sister who walked on water. It was different with my father. He adored me, but he was gone most of the time, traveling for work. When he was home, I was always with him. My mother teased me for being "Daddy's girl." It's taken me years to have any confidence in myself.
>
> I saw a therapist who asked me what happened to my mother when she was little. I told him my mother was four when her mom died and six when her stepmother moved in. She never liked her stepmother even though the woman tried to be good to her. My therapist said that every time my father left on a business trip, my mother must have felt like an abandoned four-year-old. I never thought of that before. I imagined my daughter when she was four and I could see how my mother was jealous of me as she had been with her stepmother. I had a flash of me being the older one and my mother having to share my father with me when he came home.
>
> Taking care of my mother was hard to the very last day. Then she was comatose. She looked so small and frail, like a four-year-old. I'd heard that people in comas can still hear what people say to them, so I leaned down to her ear and said, "You've been a good mother." I wanted to comfort her before she went. Her eyes opened and she looked right at me and said, "What a beautiful thing to say." Then she closed her eyes and never opened them again. I wept. A great ache lifted from my heart.

It is a natural human desire to give back measure for measure. But Karla had the courage to speak words that cut against the grain of her feelings, words she herself did not believe at the time. At that moment, all that mattered to her was providing comfort to her dying mother. Karla gave her mother the love and acceptance that her mother had not given to her, a gift that allowed her mother's life to be concluded with peace. And then Karla went back to her own life with a love for her mother she could finally feel inside. The love that Karla sought from her mother was finally hers. It had indeed been "a beautiful thing to say."

Years before, Karla transposed her daughter's face onto her mother's story and saw her mother as a hurt little girl. It helped Karla understand what her mother had endured: When Karla's father returned from a trip, the feelings from her mother's childhood returned, and to her mother, felt contemporary. The pain of her childhood dominated her relationship to Karla.

Karla's mother did not stop hurting her, but with the image of her mother as a four-year-old, Karla was able to moderate the bite of her mother's rejection. When her mother was dying, the insight was there to help her.

Imagining a parent's experience despite mutual hostilities first burns and then humanizes us. Imagining living a parent's life allows us to forgive their failures. Intellectual forgiveness is not enough; forgiveness must be from the heart or it is just an arbitrary principle that sets one person's high-mindedness to contrast against the other's failure. Without true understanding, the act of forgiveness is condescending.

Painful experiences can open our eyes with compassion or shut them in bitterness. It is hard to make ourselves imagine a parent's experience when our hostility blocks empathy; but going against the grain of anger to imagine our parents as children helps us to understand them better and regard them compassionately. In our hearts we may still argue passionately for "justice," but we can love what is real in our parents rather than rage at them for what they have failed to be.

We may not like what we see when we look at ourselves from our parents' perspective, but understanding our parents' lives may help us transform the bitter feelings that poison us into more loving feelings that are healing. But if we try to imagine our parents' reality, we must do so in the compassionate company of a spouse, good friend, or therapist. Recalling feelings of our own experience in order to imagine a parent's can cut through our defenses like a knife. If we imagine it all the way through, it cuts to the heart.

APPRECIATING RESTRAINT

The hurt that parents have inside them often originates from the hurt *their* parents caused them. Paradoxically, the parents who hurt their children are likely to be the ones who most need their children's kindness. They need their children to forgive them so they won't suffer any more deprivation. Children need to forgive their parents for their own sake, so that their bitterness at them does not contaminate their own or their children's future.

As Philip learned, this can be a hard lesson:

Philip is perfectionistic, hardworking, and devoted to his wife and children. Although he has good friends, when most hurt he seeks the solace of his own company. Verbally abused by his father as a child, he is unsure of himself. Since he does not want to be like his father, he controls his anger, concealing his tension beneath an easygoing demeanor. As a teenager, he was rebellious, flirting with alcohol and drugs, but he decided not to go further down the path of juvenile delinquency the way his friends did.

Philip's father had been beaten and disparaged as a child. He never received praise or support—even when he returned home from combat in World War II. Though he was not physically violent as a father, he was emotionally abusive, and Philip was relieved when his mother divorced him. Although his father had the means, he did not help put Philip through college, believing that life is tough and everyone has to make it for himself. Like his father before him, Philip's father rarely expressed anything other than anger and criticism. Unlike his father, he did not hit or drink. For Philip, that made all the difference. He did not have to control physical rage the way his father did; Philip's task was to grapple with his emotions at a more mature level.

Philip had once been quite an angry man. He failed at his first marriage and had trouble with authoritarian employers. Now he is married to a woman who is honest and loving. He treats her respectfully. When he acts harshly, he is troubled and thinks his way through to the truth, apologizing when he realizes he has been wrong. He dotes on his five-year-old son and three-year-old daughter, is gentle and rarely raises his voice with them.

Philip is still in touch with his father. The children love their grandfather's visits. He is funny, playful, and brings them gifts. Philip, however, hates his father's visits. There is still an uncomfortable tension between the two men. When his children are difficult, Philip bristles with concealed rage to see the gloating look of satisfaction on his father's face. However, when Philip expresses his hostility in any way, his father reacts with hurt and bitterness.

Parents must exercise great restraint when they have been brutalized as children; the way a parent hurts a child will likely be the way his child later harms others. Children learn more by example than instruction. If the example is brutal, the child learns brutality; as the Bible acknowledges, "visiting the iniquity of the fathers upon the children unto the third and upon the fourth generation." (Deuteronomy 5:9) If an adult expresses rage as did his elders, then his child learns the ways of his forebears by example.

Children are powerfully affected by the brutality their parents experienced as children. The father who was beaten as a child for dropping a glass of milk must restrain a violent internal emotional reaction when his son does the same thing and the sound of a shattering glass again triggers an adrenaline rush. Even if a father successfully curbs any overtly harsh physical reaction—perhaps not hitting, but still screaming at his child—the child learns to fear, yell, and think badly of himself. This represents progress, however. Though he may resent his father's residual harshness and emotional abuse, the child has not suffered the extremity that his father had to endure. Out of awareness, and by example, the child learns to restrain himself as his father did. He also will adopt his father's determination to be a better father to his children. Since he has not been as damaged as his father, he can struggle in other arenas, initiating a healing process for the next generation.

It requires much more energy to restrain from reacting than simply to react. Children react unthinkingly to hurt; adults must oppose the automatic emotional reactions forged in their own bruised childhoods if they are to stop reacting as children. The more he was hurt as a child, the more restraint the adult must exercise in order not to injure others. But when a person is already pressured with financial difficulties or stress at work, he is more likely to react explosively.

The energy required to contain the reaction to unreasonable harshness is much less than that required to contain reaction to mortal threat. A parent who has been beaten will wrestle with physical restraint, whereas a parent who has been yelled at as a child wrestles with his emotional makeup. However, the child who is living with a raging parent is not likely to appreciate the effort that the parent is making not to be physically abusive. Children are aware only of the parent's failure and not his success at partial restraint.

Resenting their parents for unnecessary harshness, children become judgmental when they become adults. A father who yells all the time is considered "controlling," "authoritarian," "irrational," "infantile." Children who grow up with an emotionally abusive parent are likely to express contempt and resentment, not gratitude; few people say, "Gee, thanks, Dad, for not throwing me against the wall, the way your father threw you against the wall." The children are unlikely to recognize what a great effort the parent had been making.

REPROACHES AND RECIPROCITY

Because we are so used to seeing our parents as powerful, we often fail to see that they are also vulnerable and can be wounded to the core by our dislike, disrespect, and rejection, just as we are wounded by the dislike, disrespect, and rejection of us that they express. If we are to heal the generations, we must break the cycle of repaying dislike and resentment with pain, or hurt with hurt.

Returning to the previous example, we can see that Philip's father was hurt that his son failed to honor him or acknowledge his efforts to be a good father. Already injured by the negative regard he received from his own father, he was further injured by Philip's rejection. *A parent can have no self-respect when crushed between the negative judgments of two generations*—and he cannot pass on respect that he has not experienced.

Though Philip and his father have each grown and changed over the years, they have not yet grown and changed in regard to each other. Looking at the two of them from the outside is like looking at an old snapshot: old wars and old behaviors continue as if frozen in time. The love and respect that might complete the healing of both father and son will continue to be mutually denied until one or the other can manage a better resolution of hurt pride and anger.

We do not truly see our parents as long as we view them as we did when we were children. We must relinquish our own point of view and try to imagine the world through their eyes. This allows us to gain perspective that takes us outside the realm of our childhood reactions and away from our immediate, reflexive response of hurt and anger.

As we have seen, emotional development freezes when a person has been severely traumatized. Philip needed to understand that, inside, his father was a frightened, hurt little boy determined not to batter his children. A child of ten may be emotionally more mature in some realms than a father who was nearly beaten to death at the age of five.

In the company of his children, Philip and his father can see each other without the distortion of old feelings. Philip's children, free from the hurtful history, view their father and grandfather as they are and not as they once were. In watching his children interact with their grandfather, Philip can see a sweetness in his father that would have endeared his father to him had he seen it while he was growing up. And in watching Philip with his children, his father can see his son as a man of worth. Philip and his father each have qualities that they have longed to see in one another; and knowing that makes their hostility with one another all the more painful. Philip and his father can each plainly see that the failure of their own relationship cannot just be attributed to the other person's shortcomings.

The problem is, we prefer not to look so closely. We want to see our parents as parents and not as the children they once were. When a person looks at a parent, he sees an adult and not a child. An amputation of a leg is apparent; an amputation of the spirit is not. If physical appearance were to correspond with emotional age, a grown son or daughter might find it easier to make allowance for the limitations of a parent who is obviously less than fully mature.

Traumatized at home as a child, and by war as a young soldier, Philip's father had been subject to terror and horror that intensified his neuroendocrine response. He did not talk about those experiences. What had happened in his father's life would have been difficult for anyone to communicate, but Philip's father had also grown up in an age when the "strong and silent type" was the ideal for manhood. Philip had grown up with a number of advantages that his father did not have, and that allowed Philip to grow beyond his father's limitations. Having had the support and perspective of friends and the protection of an extended family that his father never had, Philip was able to speak of his feelings.

He also benefited because his father had grappled with his own history of pain. Many children who are angry at wounding parents unconsciously follow in the healing path of their parents' footsteps. As children, we don't necessarily recognize a parent's struggles to grow beyond their own emotional inheritance, but like Philip, we still follow the parent's healing precedent. Philip's father was determined not to make the same mistakes as his father, and Philip did not want to make the same mistakes as his. Still, despite his father's best efforts, Philip was repeatedly traumatized by the repercussions of his father's tortured childhood.

As an adult, Philip continued to react badly, even though he knew that he had matured emotionally beyond his father. He still yearned for something his father could not then have given. However, when he remembered to imagine his father as a hurt little boy, he was able to respond with greater sympathy and patience. Then when his father acted like a child, Philip could react like a father whose child is hurt, communicating with gentle words of explanation rather than harsh words of punishment.

CHOOSING TO BREAK THE CYCLE WITH HONOR

We are not responsible for how our parents behave, but as adults we are responsible for our reply to that behavior. We mold our own characters as we respond to our parents. Although we cannot help but react when hurt, we can modify the expression of that reaction.

Joseph was anxious as a child, and was determined not to be limited by anxiety as an adult. He had grown up in a home that offered no shelter and no safety. His parents had come to hate each other and only stayed together for "the sake of the children." There was no physical violence, but their arguments were ugly and vicious. His father was gentle with the children, but he had emotionally drifted away from the tense atmosphere of the home. Joseph's mother was devoted to her children, and when she felt secure, she was sweet and loving, but she was frequently upset, lashing out to the point where Joseph and his brothers were afraid to tell her if they had gotten hurt or had done badly in school. Joseph often wondered why he "had done so well" and not been as damaged as his younger brothers.

As his parents' marriage deteriorated, Joseph found solace in school. In the face of his mother's increasing anger, he in response learned to be rational and self-controlled. Once after an emotional tirade from his mother, however, Joseph responded with invective of his own. His father took Joseph aside and harshly admonished him: "You are never to speak that way to your mother, no matter what she does!" The intensity of his father's admonition was so uncharacteristic that Joseph never did speak "that way" to his mother again.

In college, during a period of intense emotional upheaval, Joseph called his mother, hoping for support and guidance. She harangued him for managing his life so stupidly. He hung up and wept bitterly, coming to the realization that his mother was "never going to be there" for him when he needed her. Since then, Joseph has continued to call his mother, but no longer expects anything from her in the way of support. Though his friends advised him to stop subjecting himself to his mother's abuse, he knew his mother was a hurt woman and did not want to add to her hurt by abandoning her.

Now, when his mother is loving, he responds with affection. When she is upset, he manages her like the kind father of a child having a temper tantrum. He sets limits, does not engage on the level of anger, and does not react. When he risks exposing himself to his mother's harangues, Joseph is prepared to walk out or hang up the phone. He refuses to let her explosions affect his balance.

The moment when his father chastised him for being disrespectful to his mother had been pivotal for Joseph and in fact contained an answer to his question of why he had done so well. His father had insisted that he treat his mother with respect, regardless of how she herself behaved. Had his father taken the opportunity to ally himself with his son in his war against his wife, Joseph would have had his father's sanction not to restrain himself. Joseph could have had the satisfaction of retaliation, expressing his sense of superiority and contempt toward his mother. He might then have developed an insolence and ugliness in his character that other people would have found provocative and difficult to endure and that would have hurt his chances for stable, positive relationships.

It is our triumph when we can honor a wounding parent. *Those who harm others inevitably have been wounded;* there is no victory in punishing the wounded, nor honor in allowing ourselves to be victimized. Choosing not to respond to emotional provocation by a parent, however, allows us to better separate how we have been treated from who we are. When we can transcend our pain and view a damaged parent with understanding, we are able to accord them respect when on the surface no respect seems due.

Throughout his life, Joseph treated his mother with respect and with honor. He did not abandon her; he does not verbally attack her or try to hurt her back. Though it does no one honor to hang up on a parent, in doing so, Joseph follows another imperative: he is not allowing himself to be a victim. Joseph must carefully balance the ecology of his internal feelings. Should he allow his mother to damage his self-esteem, or abuse him to the point that his hostility rises to unmanageable levels, his anger would overpower his good intentions. He would react vindictively and his mother in turn would react even more abusively to his reactions, each person hurt and feeling justified in the further negative expression of that hurt. If Joseph's self-confidence and self-regard were to decline, his mother would be a toxic presence in his life. She would be poison to him because she could not contain and protect him from the consequences of the traumatic injuries that had damaged her. By setting adult limits to his mother's childish tirades—and thus limiting his own angry responses—Joseph proffers respect to the part of his mother that would want to nurture and strengthen her children. He helps her restrain a virulence that seems justified to her in the passion of the moment. Through the years, Joseph has come to be very respected and dearly loved by his family, community of friends, and colleagues—and through the years his mother has mellowed, showing more flashes of sweetness and affection than in times past.

The sensitivities that Joseph developed in the adverse emotional climate with his mother have grown to be strengths for him. He is patient, tolerant, and keeps his relationships clear of resentment or hostility. He is not vindictive and does not retaliate when wounded, but instead takes pains to work it out. He is sensitive and thoughtful, compassionate, kind, loyal, and forgiving. He respects honesty and insight and takes nothing for granted. He is happy in his life and with himself. *Because Joseph honors his mother, things go well with him.*

REPAIRING THE FABRIC, HEALING THE GENERATIONS

Our lives are woven into the fabric of the generations. When we only examine the span of our own lifetime, we can naively misinterpret the motive and meanings of those who have affected us. As we mature, we must see our lives in a generational context that exceeds the span of our own particular lives in order to have a larger perspective.

In making efforts to understand our parents, we become more patient and accepting with our children, partners, and friends. We see more and judge less. We become more receptive to what a child has to say, more likely to give witness—and thus make it more likely that our children will turn to us, knowing that we will try to help rather than reject and punish when they are troubled.

SEVERED HEARTS, SEVERED LIVES

Ongoing bad relations between a parent and a grown child leave each obsessed with the other. Biologically and emotionally, the parent-child relationship is too highly charged for either to come to rest. Each rejection between parent and child is a minideath of a love that once made life full for each of them. In the anger, accusation, and self-righteousness between them lies their hope for a resolution of the conflict between them—a hope for the other to come to his senses. When neither will budge till the other admits fault, the ongoing hostilities speak badly of each of them; and in the quiet of their own souls, in a place where hostility refuses to look, each feels his own nagging failure to love properly.

When locked in battle, both parent and child divert precious energy to an unwinnable struggle between biological allies. Neither parent nor child can live at full strength so long as the relationship remains conflictual. The karmic justice of hurt children hurting parents back only prolongs the cycle of pain. *The cycle goes round and round until either the parent or the child stops retaliating.*

To move frozen relationships beyond the level of pain, the Fifth Commandment tells us that adult children need to make the first conciliatory move. Wounded adult children take control over their lives, and promote their own healing, as well, by suppressing expressions of feelings that actively hurt others. Adult children of wounding parents do better expressing their hurt to friends and loved ones, getting the witness they need from these sources, rather than by reflexively reacting to parents who persist in harmful old patterns.

Rigid parents are unlikely to change, and flexible ones have already done their best. By the time the children are grown, parents feel they have given and struggled enough, and are ready to resume the lives they put aside to raise the children. In order to continue to grow and so to love, they must confront their own stagnation after so many years of the same routine.

Emotional growth occurs as a byproduct of exploring new directions and new relationships rather than continuing wearying confrontations within old ones. Aging parents are all too aware of time passing. Watching their children come into their own, they can see the imminence of their own decline; and conflict with their children saps their strength at a time when they can no longer take existence for granted.

Adults who sever relations with their parents, regardless of cause or necessity, condemn themselves and their parents to a painful void in their lives. For both parent and child, when there are still unresolved issues, the distance results in a depression that becomes an undercurrent. This was certainly the case for Randy and his mother:

> Randy had grown up in a rough home, but his life had been filled with friends and laughter. Randy was proud of his family and proud of his many accomplishments. His children meant everything to him and he wanted the best for them. But his emotional life unraveled after he broke off his relationship with his mother.
>
> Knowing she was a frightened, needy woman, Randy had forgiven his mother for hurting him in childhood. He played peacemaker between his wife, Eleanor, and his mother. After his father's death, however, Randy believed that his mother had betrayed his trust and cheated him of his father's inheritance. He severed his relationship with his mother—then, for a time, with his sister, for refusing to take sides. Later, despite hearing about how depressed his mother had been, Randy felt too hurt to come to her. Eleanor urged reconciliation, but not forcefully. After so many years of hostility, she, too, felt hurt and angry.
>
> Randy increasingly immersed himself in work and golf as he and Eleanor became more distant. Their conflicts intensified and intimacy became painful. Wanting to protect his children from the hurt inside him, Randy withdrew further from them as well, expressing his love instead by working his heart out for them. But that was not enough. Their relationship with him became strained and distant. Eventually, Randy and Eleanor divorced, leaving Randy alone and bereft.

Randy felt so betrayed by his mother that he did not know how to express his pain. Instead, he cut himself off from the mother love that once nourished his spirit and withdrew into himself and his activities. He put on his armor of wounded pride and then bled to death within it. Randy felt so wounded that even knowing that his mother was still a dependent, frightened little girl inside—that her betrayal was the machinations of a desperate, needy woman suddenly without a husband to protect her—did not help. In order to overcome the enormity of his pain, he needed to do what proved impossible for him at the time: to counter his hurt with an emotional understanding of his mother's fear by imagining what it was like to be in his mother's shoes. He needed real emotional support to do this difficult thing, but his relationship with Eleanor had already been strained.

Emotionally, Randy buried his mother without mourning her. He buried his hurt feelings to get on with life and tried to do the things he enjoyed, but nothing could fill the cavernous emptiness inside him. Emotionally depleted, unhappy, and in pain, Randy gave his children everything but the intimacy of his relationship. Randy's children lost the shelter of their parents' love for one another. Burying his feelings left Randy more and more distant from Eleanor until the weight of emptiness became too much to bear. When Randy cut off his relationship to his mother, everyone got hurt.

And what of Randy's mother? She made herself financially secure in a world that threatened her, but her only emotional attachment became her daughter. Her husband had died and she had to live as if her only son, who had once been the center of her life, had died as well.

Who knows what the consequences might have been—for Randy, for Eleanor, for their children, and for Randy's mother—had Randy been able to hold on to the Fifth Commandment as a life preserver? In honoring the mother who had given him life and who at base did not want to harm her son, he would have offered healing to them both—and perhaps have preserved his marriage as well.

As an example of what it means to honor a parent, the Talmud tells the story of Dana, a respected gentile who was meeting with several of the great men of Rome when his mentally disturbed mother burst into the room, spit at him and slapped him across the face with her shoe. And when her shoe fell to the floor, he bent down, quietly picked it up, handed it to her, and quietly said, "That's enough."[2] He did not shame her, reproach her, or add to her pain. Regardless of his mother's provocation, Dana acted with dignity. Whatever harsh judgments he made about her, or hostility and resentment he felt toward her, he kept to himself.

In responding to his mother, Dana first had to control his automatic reactions. Then he could confront his own emotions. Emotionally, Dana's task was to wrestle with his own hateful feelings so he wouldn't poison himself with them. He needed to temper his harsh judgment of his mother with understanding, make allowances for her limitations, and be grateful for the love she had once given him and the sacrifices she had once made for him. Dana's struggle was with his own wounded reactions, and therein lay his healing and his emotional salvation.

Joseph and Dana both conquered their desire to retaliate and hurt back by honoring their parents, while Randy was not able to do so and paid the price. Joseph recognized the limitations to the amount of injury he was capable of mastering, and evolved strategies to minimize harm to himself so that he could respond kindly and not be overwhelmed by intense reactive emotions. As we practice adhering to the Fifth Commandment, we evolve to maturity. With practice, honoring our parents becomes easier to do.

There is evil in the world and there is an ambiguity as to what it means to "honor." Sadly, children are tortured, raped, exploited, humiliated, and degraded every day. Joseph's mother has her good days and her bad, but there are some parents whose life experiences have left them so grievously damaged and their characters so warped that there is nothing left for their children to honor. What remains for these children is only the understanding that the person who would have been their parent was destroyed many years ago. They can only grieve—for the wounded innocence of the child the parent had once been and for the parent who isn't and is never to be. The best we can do when a parent has become so psychologically deformed is to limit any ongoing damage and not retaliate in kind. Sometimes the best a person can do is disengage or separate from a parent altogether. But cutting off the relationship always carries a heavy price.

UNRESOLVED CONFLICTS

We are wise to conclude conflicts with our loved ones without delay. After a death in the family, unreconciled conflicts can haunt the survivors, the grief persisting to affect the next generation.[3] This is especially true for conflicts with our parents. Without a living parent to fight the unfinished argument through to a conclusion, the survivor is left holding the bad feelings.

Unresolved conflicts complicate relationships in life and then complicate mourning after death. Lingering hostilities make even sincere tears feel hypocritical. Self-accusation intrudes on grief to dull expression and throw doubt on the validity of feelings of love a survivor needs to recall. Within the body of the adult, a child is alone, uncomforted, and cries for the lost parent. The uncomforted grief lingers to suck the vitality from living relationships.

Trapped with unresolved anger toward our parents, we can waste a lifetime trying to be right. If, by contrast, we follow the discipline of the commandment, we heal. The commandment supersedes the argument. Kindness and the dignity of mature conduct assumes priority over the conflicts.

FINDING A LANGUAGE FOR HONOR

Honor must come in a form the parent can receive. Sometimes the key to another's heart is difficult to find and the meaning of honor is unclear. Sometimes we are called upon to be very resourceful as we offer honor to our parents. Raya, a first-generation American born of Russian parents, honored her father by learning to speak Russian:

> Raya had been an exceptional student, but her father objected to her spending so much time reading and so little time helping her mother. He accused Raya of being a princess too good for a father who had only gone through five grades of school. Raya's mother encouraged her studies, however. She knew what it was like to have a good mind and be thwarted from using it.
>
> After Raya's mother died of lymphoma, Raya refused her father's demand that she come home from college to help care for her younger brothers. Raya knew her mother did not want her to sacrifice her future for the sake of her father or brothers.
>
> Her battles with her father became heated. She refused to obey him; she had a full scholarship and was not going to give it up. She studied and her father languished. Hurting her deeply in retaliation for her disobedience, her father did not attend Raya's medical school graduation.
>
> Though Raya later tried to get close to her father, the tension was suffocatingly thick between them. After the birth of her first child, she and her father settled into an uneasy truce, but despite having a

husband, child, and career, Raya felt an inner loneliness she could not define.

One day, while saying goodbye to him in Russian, Raya noticed her father's sad, wistful smile. Raya decided to learn Russian. She began speaking to her father in Russian. He was amused by her accent and helped her with her vocabulary. As the two grew closer over her studies and her child, Raya felt a sweetness that she had not felt since she had been a little girl. Her father had a family again.

Bicultural children straddle two worlds and are outsiders in both of them. They grow up in a world alien to their parents and in a home alien to their friends. Their parents raise a foreigner; children grow up with parents from whom they feel estranged. In the rebellion of adolescence, old-world parents fear they are losing their children. Though Raya tried to honor her father, she could not relate to him, and he did not know how to relate to her. Over time, old hurts and suspicions stole life from both of them. Though both were hurt and angry, they missed each other terribly.

Although Raya's father might have forgiven Raya for hurting him in the past, he could not forgive her for continuing to hurt him in the present—and he continued to be hurt as long as he believed that Raya regarded herself as superior to him. When Raya learned the Russian language, however, the dynamics of their relationship changed. Now her father was the more knowledgeable. In learning Russian, Raya undercut her father's suspicion of her secret condescension; with the gesture of making herself a vulnerable neophyte, she built a bridge for both of them.

Years of hostility and suspicion can make it hard for a parent to accept a child's offering of peace wholeheartedly. But when he can accept the honor a child gives him, he feels as if a long-lost child has finally returned home. Then he can overcome a life-deadening bitterness.

RESPECTING THE WOUNDING PARENT

Wounded adult children want their parents to admit to their past failures. Such admissions help correct the bad experience by acknowledging it. Such acknowledgment is a comfort: the parent becomes a witness to a child's pain, rather than just a perpetrator of it. In acknowledging his pain, the parent accepts the child as a separate person with different sensitivities than his own. The child feels seen and recognized, and the parent shows that he loves his child more than he loves being right.

The mutual acknowledgment of past pain honors both parent and child: the parent is honorable enough to admit truth; the child is honorable enough not to attack in retaliation for the hurt. Even a belated apology allows the relationship to continue without pretense. The relationship then has room to grow.

But clearly though he craves the parent's witness and apology, it may be more realistic for the child to just accept his parents without acknowledgment of past pain. A parent is embittered when a child keeps the focus unendingly on the negative. Already hurt, a wounding parent can feel so defeated by the rejection of the child that there is no room for emotional growth; he is fully occupied in making continuing attempts to recover from the latest attack, and the latest bitter accusation. A parent hurt by the rejection of a child's negative judgment often feels too misunderstood to acknowledge hurtful actions. The parent has spent years of life caring for the child; to him the relationship with an adult child evokes a history of love and self-sacrifice. In return for this self-sacrifice, the parent wants the acknowledgment of respect, gratitude for his good intentions, and the child's generosity in forgiving failures. Parents want their children to understand that, under the circumstances, they gave and loved as much as they could.

Suppressing accusations about the hurts of childhood can interrupt the cycle of a wounding parent's habitual abuse. But this suppression is not easy: the buttons that parents and children can so easily push trigger archaic feelings that can override adult behavior for either of them. But the respect an adult child gives a parent strengthens both of them, as well as the relationship between them. The adult child learns to master the habitually raw, provocative expressions of his childhood, while an emotionally stunted parent, consoled by a caring child, can finally grow up. And in that growth, the child may finally be able to obtain what he had long wanted from the parent.

By making such an effort, Barbara was able to help her father turn his life around and become more like the parent she always wanted:

> Barbara's childhood had been a battleground between a proud, easily hurt father and a physically abusive, self-doubting mother; and Barbara was eleven when her father left the family and moved in with another woman, giving no apology. Until then, Barbara

had been her father's favorite, but after he left, she and her father could not get along. For over twenty years, they took turns hurting each other. Barbara saw her father as swaggeringly macho, demeaning, and petty. After he recovered from a serious illness, however, she realized how vulnerable he was, that she might lose him at any time.

With encouragement, Barbara started to hold her anger in check. Even when provoked, she behaved respectfully toward her father, and then later sorted through her feelings. Barbara refashioned her responses toward him and, in turn, her father softened toward her. In time, Barbara got to know him better and understand him better even though he rarely talked about his life. Gradually, her father became more tender with everyone in the family.

At Barbara's wedding, as she danced with her father, the two of them looked at one another and then looked away. Heads held high, eyes shining, they communicated the richness of a lifetime of love, conflict, and proud reconciliation.

Barbara's father grew up hurt in a hurt family. He left that home with bad feelings and a limited defensive arsenal to protect him emotionally. His macho impenetrability concealed a sensitivity of which he felt ashamed. However, his facade of strength did not provide any of the love he needed and hadn't gotten. Until his second marriage, Barbara's father had been rejected in every intimate relationship of his life.

An emotionally reactive adult child can further wound a parent who is already emotionally crippled. During childhood, parents are the actors, children the acted upon. In reacting to our parents in adulthood the same way we did as children, we deny the power of our own mature volition.

Barbara had admired her father as a child and was so hurt by his betrayal as an adolescent that she had not given him the ordinary consideration she gave to others. Her father's wounded childhood was a story to her, not an actuality. She did not understand how hard he had struggled for love, nor did she sympathize. Unable to see her father in ordinary human terms, Barbara did not see him at all. Blind and hurtful to her father's tender feelings, Barbara also developed a blind spot in relationships with other men. She measured her unrealistic, contradictory images of what she wanted in her partner against an ideal no one could match.

Older and visibly vulnerable after his illness, Barbara's father finally thawed with the warmth of a wife as well as a daughter he secretly adored.

Barbara's father needed love and respect from intimates of two generations in order to assuage the hurt reactions of his childhood.

Had Barbara not reached out to him, her father could have spent his last years reenacting the emotions of his childhood: in growing up, he had survived the attacks of his father; in old age, he would have had to withstand the attacks of his children. But Barbara's deliberate and respectful tenderness allowed her father the consolation he needed to mature and love back. When she was able to receive her father's love and perceive him as an honorable but flawed human being, she was also able to recognize and reach out for real, rather than idealized, love.

What has not been resolved when a parent dies cannot be escaped. Behaving with honor and respect to a parent despite the wounding he has inflicted stops a legacy of hurt from being transmitted from one generation to the next. With enough practice, it becomes natural to be our best selves. Paradoxically, in restraint we find freedom.

TRANSFORMING OURSELVES

The task of Moses is our personal task today. For the sake of our children and the generations beyond, we must free ourselves from the constricting misdirection of our pain, contain our natural response to our wounds, and restrain ourselves from inflicting harm on others. So we do not pass on our bitter legacies, we must struggle with our own reactions to the failures and limitations of our parents, just as we hope our children will struggle with their responses to our failures and limitations. The effort transforms and deepens our character; everyone in our lives benefits.

The love and generosity that parents pass on to their children becomes the honor and kindness that children return to their parents when they get older, and it becomes part of a cycle of goodness that likewise passes on to other relationships and to other generations. But regardless of how parents may have behaved toward us in the past, the compassion that we are able to summon forth and give them when they are old transforms us into people who are more capable of being compassionate, and better able to be giving and loving to our mates and our children.

In Judaism there is a saying, "Do, then understand." If we first change our actions, we begin to understand our lives from a different perspective. As we "clean up our act," the world responds differently to us. We can see how we are responsible for the formation of our own adult lives.

CHAPTER 14

READING BETWEEN THE LINES OF OUR PARENTS' STORIES

No one cares to speak to an unwilling listener.
An arrow never lodges in a stone:
often it recoils upon the sender of it.

Saint Jerome, Letter 52

Without knowing our parents' stories, we limit our perspective to the remembered events of our own histories, and unwittingly perpetuate many of the attitudes and points of view that we had as children. We need to expand our perspective with the understanding and appreciation of our parents' lives to even have a sense of how limited our understanding has been. Unless we know and understand our parents' stories, we cannot understand why we feel one way and not another. Learning more about our parents' lives helps us achieve a greater perspective on our own; it helps us to answer *"Ayeckah?"* with a greater clarity and helps us mature.

We may think we have heard all the family stories many times over, or that we understand our parents and grandparents all too well, but it is more likely that we have taken too much for granted. For instance, a grandson may be aware that his father's father came to this country alone when he was seventeen. This is a simple fact, remembered or forgotten. But *imagining* how his grandfather felt the day he left home, picturing his parting with his parents, brothers and sisters, and friends, expands this one fact into the wrenching emotional experience it probably was. The emotional remnants of his grandfather's parting eventually became embedded within his father's childhood. If the grandson knew and understood the meaning of his grandfather's story, his own father's treatment of him as a child might finally make sense in terms of the lonely ache in his grandfather's heart. And the son's need to ask questions might become more driving. We need to know and understand our parents' childhoods to understand them.

Requesting that parents talk about painful times is asking them to expose feelings they would most likely rather leave alone. Adult children must ask the vulnerable to make themselves more vulnerable still. We imply our good faith and must emotionally prepare ourselves to be genuinely able to offer it. We need to safeguard our parents' trust, for our own sakes as well as theirs.

PRELIMINARY STEPS
Making It Safe for a Parent to Talk

Before asking parents about their lives, we must first overcome obstacles within ourselves: antagonism, hostility, prejudices, and our own paradoxical reluctance to know the truth. We must be willing to do something like the Buddhist practice of *Tonglen*—breathe in dark, breathe out light. We have to be determined not to respond to traditional provocations, and to ask good questions, in the proper spirit, in a good setting. We must be prepared to listen to our parents' words without judgment, argument, or accusation, and to accept unlooked-for answers or even an angry refusal to speak at all. The Fifth Commandment must guide the encounter.

It feels dangerous to bare one's soul in an atmosphere of antagonism. Hostility toward parents prevents adult children from learning about and comprehending their parents' stories even when they are plain to see. This is why parents who are finally ready to talk about a searing memory will be more likely to do so with friends, contemporaries, or their children's friends than with their own children.

Furthermore, even when the child has specifically asked to hear the stories, it may be difficult for an adult child to hear a traumatized parent speak his pain. The intimacy of empathically listening to a parent's raw pain can be overwhelming. Defenses that protected children from a parent's negative feelings while growing up may interfere with their being able to follow a parent's painful story in maturity. For instance, children of

Holocaust survivors have difficulty remembering the stories their parents tell them because they are too intense to hear.

Disclosure requires that parents have confidence that their children will maintain their regard and safeguard their trust. Speaking of painful events requires trust, and the willingness to reveal secrets requires the absolute trust that the listener will love and accept what the secret-holder has rejected in himself. Parents who feel guilt or shame also fear their revelations will diminish the love and respect that their children have for them. A parent will be more willing to risk telling secrets if previous revelations have been met with comfort and reassurance rather than rejection and shame.

Allowing witness is an act of faith. We make ourselves vulnerable when we reveal our pain, leaving ourselves unprotected as we express our most tender feelings, defenseless as we expose sensitivities that hurt or shame us. Dismantling defenses leaves us vulnerable to potentially crippling re-injury. We need to feel we will be understood and not have our revelations used against us.

It is hard to tell who is more vulnerable at times like these: children to their parents or parents to their children. A parent who dares to speak of painful times from the past opens an old wound to a child's gaze, which makes the parent vulnerable. Any adverse judgment at such a juncture can be hurtful; the slightest sign of a child's withdrawal can cause a parent to give up on the hope of getting closer. If we are careful to be compassionate, however, we help our parents heal while we discover something about ourselves.

HONORING A PARENT'S REFUSAL TO SPEAK

Sometimes parents put off discussion until "another time," or refuse to answer questions altogether. Adults are repeatedly surprised at how quickly they regress to childhood feelings when this happens. Triggers to old hurt can quickly overwhelm mature expression, making it feel as if hard-won maturity were merely a veneer. When a parent refuses to talk about the past, it is easy to conclude that the parent's secret matters more to him than the well-being of the child who has asked the questions.

But initial inquiries about parents' painful histories may catch them unprepared, and it may be years before they are ready to speak openly. It is quite possible that the secrets parents protect may be too much for them to reveal. We have to respect our parents' personal standards of integrity, guilt, or shame. For example, the unmarried mother of today lives in a different world than did the unmarried mother of 1955. An antagonistic display toward parents for their reluctance to speak may only further convince them of their good sense in choosing silence, whereas respectful acceptance of the refusal gives a parent time to reconsider his decision. Such acceptance may give the parent hope for the adult child's new maturity and potential for understanding, and even set the stage for the parent speaking later.

GETTING A PARENT TO TALK

Conciliatory actions on the part of the child often must precede deeper personal discussions with parents. Adhering to the Fifth Commandment, "Honor your father and your mother," heals by dropping the question of who is right or wrong, or whether a parent has been loving or hateful. The Commandment requires us to treat our parents respectfully no matter how we see them. Acting in this way, we may make inroads that open up fresh views of our parents. The discipline first corrects our behavior, then our feelings.

In striving to honor formerly hurtful parents, adult children transform their relationship with them. Often, we must go against the grain of powerful feelings in order to move relationships beyond where they have been stuck for years. With practice, however, the discipline of the Fifth Commandment becomes easier, especially as the relationship improves. In time, more loving feelings may come to the fore, stopping a cycle of pain and initiating the healing of generations.

Regardless of the provocation, each of us is responsible for our own contribution to conflict in relationships. Apologizing for this contribution may initiate a process of healing, even if a parent meets an adult child's apology with further accusation. Allowing the parent to express feelings of hurt may clear the way for more constructive and healing discussions later on. Even if a parent does not reciprocate at the time, a shift in his thinking may occur.

A long drive in a car or an extended bus or train trip often provides a good setting for finding out about a parent's history. Time pressures are reduced and there are fewer distractions. There is no one else around to inhibit conversation or interrupt its flow. Being able to avoid eye contact usually makes it easier to express painful emotions.

Asking first about details of a happier time such as "What attracted you to Mom?" or "How did you and Dad meet?" is both informative and helps draw parents out. It allows a parent to gauge the level of a child's sympathy and emotional attunement before delving into other, more painful topics. Or one may use books, movies, and TV shows as springboards to difficult conversations, such as, "You know, Dad, I saw a documentary last week on the Korean War. I never knew how cold it was over there." Reading books and watching movies about the traumatic historical events that had affected a parent's life testifies to a child's interest, caring, and good faith.

Trying to picture the events that a parent describes helps us know how to respond. Imagining what life had been like for a parent as he speaks enables us to ask the kind of questions that invite further revelation, such as, "Didn't you feel lonely while you were growing up?" Or, "How did you manage to get through all that?" Even if a parent does not yet venture new information, future talks might proceed from these preliminary inquiries. A child's sympathetic questions indicate a willingness to learn and understand what life was like from a parent's point of view.

Marty, a father for the first time at twenty-three, learned this lesson when he went to show his father his new grandson:

My dad was always the tough guy except for when he was drunk. Then he'd blubber. I hated being around him, and I couldn't wait to grow up and get away from him. Even after he finally got clean and sober, I was still angry. But when my son was born, I thought, "My dad must have once loved me like this." So I went over to his house to show him his grandson. We started talking, and then he started telling me a story he'd never told anyone.

When he was nine, my dad and his best friend were playing with his mother's gun. It went off and shot his friend in the chest. [His friend] said, "Tell my parents I love them. I forgive you," then died in my father's arms. Afterward, there was a horrible investigation. His friend's family was hateful to him. The friend he killed was the only one who ever forgave him. He and his mom moved away and they never, ever talked about it again. My dad cried telling me all this, and I couldn't help crying right along with him. I could see why he always had to be so tough.

For Marty's father, an innocent, playful moment had transformed into horror; then the devastation of a child had been met with accusation rather than consolation. A nine-year-old looked into the eyes of his best friend's parents and saw hatred, not solace. The boy had been sentenced to a life of uncomforted grief, guilt, and nightmarish secrecy.

When Marty put his new son in his father's arms, he was acknowledging his father's love for him. Until then, Marty had denied his father understanding and compassion, and he kept others at a distance. Marty's recognition of him as a father helped him take the risk of emerging from his long isolation.

DEALING WITH A PARENT'S ANGER

Unfortunately, an angry child of a wounding parent may never find out that a parent has been living with a secret as painful as Marty's father's. The irony is that the great wounds that parents cause their children often originate in incidents that are hidden behind a parent's silence—the very silence which must be broken in order for parent and child to heal within and then with each other.

Parents may protect their secrets with anger, but more than likely the anger points to their own hurt. Parents who are unable to speak freely to their children usually defend a sad, secretive history that they would share if they had the sense that they would not be attacked or be losing respect. They may seem destined to take their secrets to the grave, but we should not stop trying to break through.

Bonnie, for instance, thought her father never would talk about his life. Foul-tempered, bitter, and tyrannical, her father allowed no one to get close. To learn about her father's history, Bonnie spoke with an aunt, who confirmed that his life had been very difficult. Afterward, Bonnie regarded her father a bit more sympathetically. As years passed and her father aged, he gradually became approachable:

I grew up hating my father and avoided him as much as possible. But he mellowed with age, and after he retired he was easier to be with. He probably wasn't as stressed and I wasn't so afraid. A few months before he died, we were walking together when he suddenly said, "Something is wrong with me. I haven't been happy for a long time. I think I need to see a psychiatrist."

It was so out of character. He had always blamed everyone else for his problems. He just started opening up, and we started to get close when he died. There was so much more I wanted to know.

Many people, even those who suspect their parents' memories hold the key to understanding perplexing family dynamics, are reluctant to ask their parents about their hard times, and there are usually good reasons for such reluctance. The peace the parent may have made with the past may be a tenuous one. Questions might prod awake feelings of hurt, guilt, or shame the parent would rather leave alone. Wanting to avoid hurting a parent is legitimate.

Anticipating a bad response, however, may also reflect the depth of an adult child's continued hostility or fear. Perhaps the child can only envision the encounter with the parent as an ugly confrontation rather than as a moment of closeness. But the tone of the encounter he envisions may change if the child figures out a better way of approaching the parent.

FINDING A DIFFERENT PERSPECTIVE, TAKING A DIFFERENT APPROACH

When we are able to create an atmosphere of trust, our parents' histories are usually ours for the asking. But in asking a parent questions, a person is asserting that he can take the honesty of the answers he gets and that he can accept the idea that his parent's life may not have been as it has appeared. The work of getting a parent to open up often reflects a grown child's effort to attain a more objective stance and his readiness to entertain a different slant on family stories.

Mel, for instance, had grown up hating his raging, irrational father for his history of verbal attacks. His mother, on the other hand, had always been sweet, loving, and supportive. Over the years, Mel's antagonistic relationship to his father had settled into an uneasy, unsatisfying, wary truce, until one day, while the two were sitting together at a baseball game, Mel asked, "Why were you so unhappy with Mom?"

When I asked him, my father looked at me in astonishment, and then he told me stuff I had never heard before: How Mom had roped him into getting married, "forgetting" to take her pill, getting pregnant—twice as I came to find out—so that Dad had to give up college and his dream of becoming a doctor. Mom and Dad never really had much of a sex life after that. We talked for about two hours. It was the first time I ever got to know Dad's side of the story. I was forty years old before it ever occurred to me that my father *had* a side to listen to.

Mel adored his mother. He believed that his strength had come from her. To ask his father questions about his parents' marriage, Mel had to risk giving up an idealized image of his mother that had given him comfort since childhood. Having been closer to his mother, Mel had unwittingly continued to see his father from a young boy's point of view. When he was ready to consider that there might be some legitimacy to his father's feelings, he was suddenly speaking to his father man-to-man instead of as a boy protecting his beloved mother from a raging father. As an adult, listening with an open mind, Mel was able to witness his father's pain. It brought the two of them closer together, and something healed inside each of them.

It is not uncommon for a parent to express long-felt bitterness just as his point of view is finally being acknowledged, however. An adult child may make a conciliatory statement of witness to a parent, only to find himself stunned at the vehemence of a parent's response. Under the circumstances, the bitterness is also an expression of pain, and listening compassionately, if possible, despite the apparent rejection, allows the child to witness and acknowledge the parent's pain. Saying "I'm sorry I never understood how much I was hurting you" is better than taking the attack personally. If the adult child is unable to let the rage pass over him, it may be best to apologize for the hurt, with a statement like "I didn't mean to upset you like this. Maybe we can talk again later." Excusing himself thus may set the stage for later, more fruitful talks.

If an adult child has a sense that approaching a parent directly will evoke a more hostile response than he can tolerate or contain within himself, he can write a letter to the parent instead, first having a friend read it to remove the slightest nuance of accusation. Letters allow an adult child to be clear about what he wants to say and a parent to overcome his initial emotional reactions in privacy; a parent has time to compose himself and formulate a better response than the hostile or rejecting one that may come to him first. Sometimes such letters initiate a dialogue that can ultimately reconcile a difficult relationship.

Other relatives may be able to provide information when a parent has died, is too ill, or is unwilling to speak: an aunt, an uncle, or a parent's first cousin who shared the same grandparents. A cousin may also have visited a parent's childhood home and can give an impression of what a parent's home had been like. Usually, there is at least one archivist in the family who has been collecting the family's stories for years. As we will discuss later, the child can also look to historical events for help.

KNOWING MORE THAN WE UNDERSTAND

We should find out the long version of our parents' and grandparents' stories. Those stories provide a framework of history that defines who we are and determines what we perceive. Knowing the truth of who we are and where we came from can change us, alter how we see the world, and bring us closer to ourselves.

But we may know more than we think we know. Often, a parent's story is there, right in front of us, hidden in plain sight. It is our comprehension or our imagination of it that is faulty.

This was the case for Susan, a woman in her thirties. Despite years of therapy, her brusque manner continued to put people off, and she seemed determined to make her own life difficult. Her anger had been honed to a fine edge:

> My mother was a shrew—emotionally abusive, critical, demanding. The one time she ever gave me any praise, I almost fainted; I started to cry. I adored my father, but just when I started high school, he ran off with another woman. I hated him for years, but now that I'm older, I can see why he spent all his time in taverns and why he finally dumped Mom. The only good thing I can say about Mom is that she always encouraged us to follow our dreams.
>
> Mom had always wanted to be a teacher, but she only had a high school diploma. After graduating, she stayed home to help my grandmother with the younger children and help pay her younger brother's way through college. Mom won't talk about it, but I know her brother killed himself five years after graduating.

Susan thought she knew her mother, but her mother and her mother's life story had become so familiar over the years that the details had faded into the background, without enough highlights to make an impression on her as an adult. She had not applied the lens of her mature experience to magnify key facts in her mother's story.

Susan never imagined what it would have been like to live through her mother's experiences. Her anger left no room for such imagining. But Susan's mother had sacrificed her own future to support her brother at a time when a man was automatically the breadwinner and his career was considered more important than a woman's. Hurt and hostility impeded Susan's comprehension that her mother's sacrifice was probably expected, underappreciated, and made with resentment. I suspected that after Susan's mother had children, she continued feeling suffocating resentment for having sacrificed her own dreams for others. She tried to give the best of herself and opposed her true feelings in doing so, because she had wanted her children to have what she was denied—choice.

It must have embittered Susan's mother to have made great sacrifice—not once, but twice—and been unappreciated by everyone. In her youth, her contribution to her brother's education had been taken for granted, then years later, her husband went out to play, giving her neither a break nor companionship, and was adored by the children nonetheless. The intensity of Susan's mother's verbal abuse must have matched the intensity of her feelings of being thwarted and bitter, and Susan's father must have hated coming home to his wife's desperation.

Ironically, everything Susan's mother had worked so hard for seemed to come to nothing: her brother killed himself, her husband deserted her, and her daughter hated her.

After years of feeling "stuck" emotionally, Susan made a real effort to empathize with her mother's life, and her anger diminished as her understanding of the woman grew. Susan's sense of her mother's betrayal vanished—and part of the hurt that had crippled Susan vanished along with it. Though her mother still felt toxic to her, Susan was able to regard her more compassionately. Susan herself became less angry, her face relaxed, and in return, the world responded to her more kindly.

IMAGINING OUR PARENT'S TIMES

Once they outgrow their natural self-centeredness, adult children often forgive their parents for passing on painful legacies, if they are familiar with the historical events that gave rise to them. However, they often do not know about or have not considered or imagined the impact of the historical background to a parent's or grandparent's life story. A parent's life, however, must be imagined against the backdrop of their era. Until a child imagines the times, even major historical events may remain hidden in plain sight.

For example, when I first met Robert, a twenty-six-year-old African-American man, he spoke harshly of his father:

> My father was a minister, and he beat the hell out of us kids if we did anything wrong. If I skipped school or was late to a class, he went nuts on me. I hated school. I was so bored I couldn't breathe in class. When I told him I was dropping out of high school, he looked at me with such rage I thought he was going to kill me. I stayed in school, but I thought, "When this is over, I'm out of here." It seemed like all he cared about was how it would look to his precious congregation.

Robert didn't understand his father's intensity or anger well enough to make sense of it. Instead, Robert condemned him and believed him to be a self-serving hypocrite rather than a father passionately vested in his son's best interest. I urged Robert to ask his father what it was like when he was growing up. Robert had never before asked about his father's youth. When he returned the following week, he was excited to tell me what he had learned:

> I found out that my father was the first black person from his town to ever attend high school. The Negro high school was ten miles away in the next town and he biked each way until a bunch of white people almost beat him to death. They told him that he had no business getting educated and if he couldn't learn his place, they'd kill him. Afterwards, when my grandfather told my dad that he wasn't going to school anymore, they had a terrible fight. My father moved up north, stayed with an uncle, finished school, and then went to college. My father's got a hard head, but no one is going to push him around. I guess I've got a pretty hard head, too.

A child growing up with racism all around him may negate his parents' experience of it by mistakenly equating it with his own. For racism's victims, the caustic effects of its inequities burn. Robert, however, had had his own traumatic encounters with racism, and he thought he understood what his father meant when he spoke of it to him. But a northern-born child whose African-American parents were raised in the segregated South cannot readily imagine what growing up was like for them; the atmosphere cannot be easily explained, and talking about it can expose barely healed sensitivities and scars that many older African-Americans would rather leave alone. For those who did not live in the South before 1964, when segregation was law, the stories are fading into old memories and history books. But without specific knowledge about the racism that wounded a parent, the adult child, left with a restricted understanding, may hurt his parent further with his rejection and add to society's wound by denying him respect.

For Robert, the word "segregation" was an abstraction, not a personal experience; and his assumptions of equivalence—that racism was a singular fact that he and his father both had to endure—blinded him. But as Robert discovered, their experiences were not equivalent. After talking with his father, Robert's attitude toward him shifted dramatically. His father's anger became understandable and, in the light of his father's history, justifiable; and knowing of his father's heroic determination filled Robert with a new pride and admiration. With Robert's new under-standing—and the sincerity of his witness—their relationship had a new beginning.

Gary, too, despite years of therapy, knew little of his father's history, and he didn't take into account the historical events of his father's era. He hated his father for having been cruel to him as a child, but he did not know the answer to the question "What happened to you, Dad, that you would beat your own child so badly?" All Gary knew was that his father was Jewish, in his eighties, the third-born and the second son of a family of eight; he knew that his father had been raised on New York's Lower East Side and that his grandmother, his father's mother, had been unhappy.

But Gary knew more than he understood. Extrapolating from the known historical events of his grandparents' era provided clues about his father's family: Waves of Jewish immigrants had come from Eastern Europe to New York around the turn of the century, seeking to escape pogroms and persecution. Asked when his family had come to the United States, Gary remembered that his grandmother had emigrated to America as a child from a village in Russia. By using his imagination, Gary could dimly envision his grandmother as a child, leaving behind friends, home, and perhaps family to start a new life in America.

To understand a parent's story, we may need to expand on it with questions; but in order to know which questions to ask, we need to try to fill in the details with our imagination. Listening to discussions of past events, which may have significant omissions indicating that there were events too painful to talk about, is the key to figuring out which questions to ask. What had the family suffered during the years before coming to America? What family and what kind of life was left behind? Examining and imagining each detail from each answered question about his grandparents or his parents' lives brought Gary new insights and understanding.

But Gary began to feel more sympathy for his father even before he learned more about the details of his life. In trying to understand his father, he drew on the few details he already knew. He tried picturing his face— that of a middle child, lost in a large family, and raised by the unhappy child who had become Gary's grandmother.

LEARNING TO READ THE CODE

Parents and grandparents often shroud traumatic experience in silence. The stories that they do tell are often meant to protect as much as inform. The stories are often stylized, repetitious, and superficial, presenting a cardboard cutout of a narrative that stands static in time and conceals while pretending to reveal. So much of what we hear is obscure, hidden, or expressed in code. Our parents may allude to terrible experiences, but they do not elaborate. Instead they speak in shorthand. A parent who says, "Boy, my father had a hot temper," may be saying in code, "I was beaten brutally by my father." A parent may say in admiration, "My father was a wonderful man. He worked day and night so we wouldn't have to do without," but he also reveals that his father was unable to spend much time with him.

Untold memories are not preserved well. They condense and distort, returning intermittently, and can die with the passing of time; so we have to listen especially hard to the stories our parents do tell and try to recognize events we may be missing or are taking for granted. We have to make an effort to see beyond our childhood conceptions and a self-protective parent's limitations in order to mature as adults. If we reconsider old stories, panning for telling details from a sympathetic adult perspective, understanding and love can grow for both child and parent.

There are great rewards to both the parent and the child if an adult child can encourage a parent to speak of events that had been previously shrouded in silence. A parent's recounting of a painful experience, however, risks bringing back the feelings. The mind recoils from what it might find within; but our need for solace insists that we cry out and be comforted, no matter how much time has passed. A child witnessing a parent's pain at such moments of tender revelation can heal his parent with his compassion. New expressions of old pain can crack the ice of bitter experience, allowing frozen emotions to come to life again; the past can be mourned to free both parent and child, and allow them each to live and love again.

We all grieve the passing of our own era, the dying of our past. Something is lost to us forever, and the vigor of days past becomes anemic in the telling. To the next generation, the days of their parent's youth are like the ancient history of Sparta and Athens. The meanings of their parents' feelings are not relayed well to children who haven't participated in the experience. Their parents' representations are too thin to capture the fullness of their history, and the memories are too precious to profane with indifference. Parents, however, must tell these stories to keep them alive. These stories are part of the legacy that parents pass on to their children. If children truly listen, no matter how superficial the telling may initially be, their children's witness gives meaning to the joy and suffering of their lives—and sometimes parents may understand their own stories better with the compassionate reflections their adult children's mature perspective provides.

We give honor to our parents when we listen to them, but we are deaf to what we hear when we are sick of a story we have heard "a thousand times already." The fact that a parent tells the story again indicates his need for witness, while an adult child who is tired of hearing the same story again indicates that he probably has not understood it. If we listen to a parent's repetitious story but then ask questions to get beneath the surface—inquire about details to flesh it out, and offer empathic comments as we imagine their experience—we are more than likely to gain new insights that will change our old understanding of our parents and of our own lives. As a consequence, we are likely to fare well, or at least better, in our own lives if we only make the effort.

CHAPTER 15

FINAL WITNESS
AND FINAL MOMENTS

Then shall the dust return to the earth as it was:
and the spirit shall return unto God who gave it.

Ecclesiastes 12:7 (K.J.V.)

We regard our children, parents, and mates as extensions of ourselves—and to a certain point, this is true. We are inextricably entwined, even when we are parted by death.

Love demands sacrifice, and love binds us. Our attachments to those we love constrict us as much as they anchor us. Our parents bound themselves in sacrifice to us when we were young; the Fifth Commandment says we should bind ourselves in allegiance to them when they are old. Children see their worth in their parents' eyes while they are growing up; parents see their worth in their children's eyes as they themselves age. We care for our children when they are young. We hope our children will care for us when we become old. And so it indeed goes if all goes well.

Like the care they give us as children, the care we give our aged and dying parents may come at a high cost. We must call upon ourselves to exercise great compassion and restraint, while questioning and rearranging our priorities. When our parents are ill or dying and need our care, we disrupt our lives and may deny our own children and teenagers the attention they still need. Our intimate relationships may become strained, our sense of freedom may constrict, and for the time, life may become grim. Adult children grieve for a dying parent, but cannot help longing for a return to the freedom of their own lives—freedom that can only be purchased at the cost of the parents' death.

At the end, parents may need their children to sacrifice their lives for them for a time, despite the hardships that their need imposes on them. Parents may recognize that the ties between them and their children now bind too tightly. When we were young, our parents held us, locked eyes with us, and gave us what they could, hoping to make good lives for us. When our parents become too frail to do for themselves, they need us to care for them, comfort them, and give them the best that we can.

As the end of his life nears, a parent may suspect the extent of his child's sacrifice but may not know or want to know the details. If the child is kind and caring and doesn't complain, he protects the parent from knowing the painful truth. While he may long for freedom, the child stays silent, knowing the parent could experience that longing as a wish for his hasty death. For a parent to believe that his child feels this way is too much to bear and too much to acknowledge. The adult child may need to express his feelings, but he does not need to have his parent witness them. The parent may already believe that his child is sacrificing too much. Denial serves to blunt the parent's acute sense of imposition, preserving his dignity at the expense of the son or daughter who cares for him. But denial has a high price. It is painful for a child to care for a parent who seems unappreciative of the sacrifice.

The season of a parent's fragility, his helpless dependence on his children, is a painful trial for everyone. From our own childhood experience, we know that without the kind support from those we depend on, being helpless and dependent can be a bitter, traumatic experience. The conflicting needs of parents and children, during the time when one is dependent on the other, make hostility intrinsic to the relationship. Throughout the ages, parents and children have wrestled with the problems inherent in this first, most passionate and basic relationship—issues and questions that are highlighted in the Bible's haunting and troubling story of Abraham and Isaac.

Love,[1] death, obligation, trust, and sacrifice: the story is a reprise of our relationships to our parents and to our children. The story seems simple: God asks Abraham to sacrifice his son Isaac for Him. Abraham is willing to sacrifice his son, and Isaac is willing to sacrifice his life. The story anticipates the commandment "Honor thy father and thy mother so that life may go well with you upon the land." Providing for a parent who can no longer provide for himself is the very cornerstone of the Fifth Commandment; Abraham, the parent, asks much of his son, and Isaac demonstrates the extreme of filial piety. He is willing to lay down his life for his father.

ABRAHAM AND ISAAC

As we fill in the details, however, and imagine ourselves living the experience, the story is resonant with nuance and complexity—and it disturbs us:

> And it came to pass after these things, that God did tempt Abraham, and said unto him, Abraham: and he said, Behold, here I am.
>
> And he said, Take now thy son, thine only son Isaac, whom thou lovest, and get thee into the land of Moriah; and offer him there for a burnt offering upon one of the mountains which I will tell thee of.
>
> Genesis 22:1–2 (K.J.V.)

God speaks in an uncharacteristically gentled voice. The spare words are riveting. The request is in savage contrast to the gentle tone. But in Hebrew, the words *Kach Nah* are ambiguous. Literally translated, they mean either "take now" or "please take." Abraham has a choice of meaning: he can comply with a command or deny a request.

Abraham does not ask God for any details. Abraham's faith is absolute, and he does not question whether he has the right to offer his son's life. But is Isaac his to give? Apparently, Abraham thinks so; as the story unfolds, Isaac's life seems more Abraham's than his own. Like so many parents, Abraham regards Isaac more as an extension of himself than as a separate person with a distinct life of his own. Abraham expects his son to cooperate with sacrificing his life, and unlike God he does not say "please."

God calls Abraham to consciousness, and Abraham answers as Adam did; his words are identical to Adam's response to *"Ayeckah?"* Abraham shows his devotion by unquestioningly acceding to His authority; he does not protest or bargain as he had over the destruction of Sodom and Gomorrah. Why not?

Does Abraham believe he has the right to sacrifice the life of his child? To Abraham, God is all that matters, and the rightness of his own faith seems to make him blind to any other view or any other person's reality. He is like all of us: our greatest strengths are inextricably bound with our weakness.

> Abraham took the wood for the offering, and placed it on Isaac, his son.

Like most children with parents who can no longer manage for themselves, Isaac carries the burden for his aging father. He makes no complaint or argument. Stronger than his father now, he can see his father's strength diminishing, and he helps him. At this point, Isaac begins to emerge as a distinct character in the story; we can picture him more clearly now.

It is clear that Isaac's father intends a higher ascent: they need to bring their own wood. But where is the sacrificial offering? This cannot be a joyous time. Isaac knows something out of the ordinary is going on and his father is not telling him. The atmosphere is tense.

Isaac, intruding his own reality into his father's distant introspection, asks two questions. The first is all nuance: "Father . . . ?" Abraham's response is gentle and loving, reassuring Isaac that he is not angry with him. Their relationship is intact. From this question, we catch a glimpse of their relationship. Despite his father's shortcomings, Isaac does not rage at his father or hurt him when he is vulnerable. Isaac honors his father, expressing only the utmost respect for him. Despite the tension of their journey, Abraham's gentleness and love for his son is clear. Their relationship seems to be a good one.

The second question is direct: where is the sacrificial offering? Abraham makes it clear that there will be a sacrifice one way or another. Isaac now knows. There are no more secrets. Both father and son can now journey on together, knowing that soon they are each to sacrifice: the father, his son; the son, his life.

If Isaac is upset with his father, Isaac doesn't show it. Isaac knows his father loves him, but would his father still have loved him had Isaac challenged his father's authority? Abraham had not challenged God. Isaac does not challenge his father. Isaac believes he honors his father by submitting to him regardless of the consequences. But should Isaac have refused, his father would have had neither the speed nor strength to subdue him.

They arrived at the place which God designated to him. Abraham built the altar there, and arranged the wood; he bound Isaac, his son, and he placed him on the altar atop the wood. Abraham stretched out his hand, and took the knife to slaughter his son.

Genesis 22:8–10²

At the knife point of separation, we become real to one another. What is Isaac's reality? All his life, Isaac had trusted God to confer blessings upon the faithful. All his life, Isaac had trusted his father. Does he doubt his choice now, as he lies on the altar, helplessly bound, his father standing above him with a knife held high in his whitened fist, ready to plunge? Does he see his father's face twisting in ecstatic contradiction? Does Isaac consider his mother's reality? Does he think of his mother's reaction to hearing of his death? To understand the significance of what we do, we must imagine how others will feel. For those of us who do not speak directly to God, there are always questions.

Human motivation is complex. Can Abraham be so sure of what he is doing or the rightness of his intent? If this is a test, perhaps he is giving the wrong answer. After all, God did not need Abraham to sacrifice his son as a test of Abraham's devotion; God already knew how devoted he was. Nor did God actually command Abraham to slaughter his son—only to offer him up; God doesn't need Abraham's knife to take Isaac's life either. Perhaps He was showing Abraham how much he had abdicated his own moral judgment in submitting to this most heinous request. We learn about ourselves and who we are by how we respond to life's trials.

MAKING DIFFICULT CHOICES

In the scriptural account, the tension breaks in a peculiarly unsatisfying way. At the end, the story of Abraham and Isaac blurs into confused ambiguities and unanswered questions. In the last moment, an angel, not God, pleads with Abraham to stay his hand. We may not realize this at the time, but as we look back and tell our life stories, we see that a few dramatic incidents and the consequences of a few choices seem to have defined our lives.

Did Abraham and Isaac make good choices? What we can understand is so limited; so much of the truth is a matter of interpretation. What if Abraham and Isaac had chosen otherwise? Life is complicated. We make mistakes; we learn as we go along; we often understand only in hindsight. Isaac was willing to sacrifice himself for his father in an act of love and devotion. But did he sacrifice too much? We learn about and create ourselves simultaneously as we reply to the trials that we face in life.

The story of Abraham and Isaac seems to encompass much of the human condition and seems to pose more questions than it answers. We instinctively identify with Isaac. Even the best parents hurt their children. We have all felt innocent and unfairly treated. Our parents once controlled us, and our relationship with our parents must suffer from a conflict of wills through the years. To achieve our independence, especially during our adolescent years, we must oppose our parents' will just as we oppose our children's during their adolescence. The conflicts may get ugly, but as we mature, we tend to resolve our differences with our parents.

Isaac could, respectfully and rightfully, have refused his father. Abraham could, with dignity, have refused to comply with God's request, just as children, in consideration of their own lives and their own integrity, may have to *respectfully* disobey the requests of their parents. The choices are not easy; and even after searching deeply, answering *"Ayeckah?"* is not necessarily clear. What is clear, however, is that we should not answer a parent's antagonism in kind or act cruelly, regardless of provocation, especially in the face of a parent's vulnerability.

Adults in conflict with parents are often blind to the shifting balance of vulnerability and so are sometimes surprised to find that a once powerful parent has become small, fragile, and needy. Not recognizing this, the adult child retaliating for childhood hurts may have far greater impact than he knows. A young child may strike out with a little fist; an adult child may strike out with the same fist but with adult strength and far greater consequences.

INVERSIONS OF DEPENDENCE

Caring for frail or dying parents is the essence of the Fifth Commandment. The parents' time of greatest need is a child's opportunity to repay his parents, express his gratitude, and to confront the demons that have haunted him since childhood. But caring for a dependent parent is a blessing that anoints by fire.

People are not at their best when ill. Grieving the loss of vigor and independence, aging or ill parents often express resentment rather than appreciation for their care. They are grieving too many endings and may begrudge others the ongoing life that is no longer available to themselves. In turn, adult children who have put their lives aside and have entered what feels like a prison of caretaking resent having their sacrifice repaid with complaint and criticism. Remembering our parents once so strong, we grieve the passing of our lives with them. The contentious situation intensifies any old animosity. A child's hostile response to an aging parent's provocation seems to justify the criticism of the parent in an ancient, never ending circle of recrimination. At the end of a parent's life, the unresolved conflicts of two lifetimes come to the fore in high relief.

Applying the discipline of the Fifth Commandment can open doors to final reconciliation, allowing the adult to embrace and finally become the best of himself, but it can also lead to a resurgence of friction within the adult child's family.

Dinah had been married to Paul for twenty-two years, and they had three adolescents living at home. The couple had remained loyal to one another even though their relationship had been strained through years of arguments and reconciliations. Two years after her mother-in-law's death, Dinah described what it had been like living with Paul's mother Mildred in the last six months of her life:

> My hair became grayer. At the time, I felt I may have even lost a year or two of life taking care of her, but it was also a time of richness. I still think about Mildred a lot. We got very close while she was dying. Now when I go for a walk outside my house, I look at the flowers the way we did when we'd walk together. Mildred was appreciating everything in the last few months of her life, and it made me more aware, too. But she was no saint; she could be awful—cold as ice and vicious—when she didn't get her way. There were times I felt my self-esteem eroding. I can't imagine what Paul's life was like when he was a little boy. Now I understand why we fought so much. Paul learned early that he had to fight her or she would have steamed right over him—and I got the brunt of that "lesson."
>
> When she was living with us at the end, I did a lot more of the work. Paul would get too upset with her. For the most part, though, Paul restrained himself and tried to be loving. The kids helped

some, too, but we didn't want them to lock themselves up with their grandmother the way we had to. But as she was dying, we were all with her. You could feel all the love and loyalty in that room. Her death was a beautiful moment. We all learned so much from her in the last months of her life: courage and honesty, and how to die with dignity and honor. Even when they weren't helping us, the children were aware of how much of an ordeal it was, taking care of her. They watched the whole thing and saw what was good and bad. I know they'll be there for us when our time comes.

Paul and I are closer now, too. He's more respectful after seeing me putting my heart out for him and his mom. I protected him when she had gotten really ugly. Once, after his mom was being particularly vicious, Paul turned to me and asked, "Do I do that?" I looked at him and said, "Yes, you do." He's not treated me that way since. He gets close to it at times, but he's aware of it and stops himself.

In taking care of aging or ill parents, adult sons and daughters often must put their own lives on hold. Other family members become isolated, finances are strained, marriages have less time to renew, children and health get neglected. We call to mind the story of Abraham and Isaac and wonder, "How much sacrifice is too much?" What if the caretakers get sick, or their marriage threatens to break up, or their children start getting into trouble, or their genuine love for their parents becomes burdened with resentment? Dinah and Paul endured the trial of it, learned about themselves, each other, and their relationship. They each came out stronger for it, strengthened as a couple, and they set a precedent for their own children—one that will bring them through future trials.

When we have taken on the sacrifice of caring for our parents, we need respite to allow us to regain our composure. We need a network of compassionate family and friends and health-care professionals to spell us and help alleviate the burdens of care. We need to breathe the air outside the sickroom in order to be able to have something to give. In the past, caregiving was diffused within close-knit communities and extended families. Now we need to assemble such a community deliberately, or we risk suffocating in a situation too confining to allow growth.

The emotional crucible of caring for dying parents exposes the strengths and weaknesses of both parents and children; and the end of life pressures everyone to make peace with one another. The impending knife of separation makes the resolution of old conflicts urgent. The promise of imminent separation dissects confused feelings cleanly to reveal the truth. Parent and child are both under pressure to struggle with their wounded and baser selves. No matter what had once been between them, a squeeze of a hand, a kiss, or words of love can prove reconciling; under these circumstances, dying can offer the last healing.

OFFERING COMFORT, MAKING PEACE

Caring for a dying parent can be a great ordeal when an illness is prolonged; old resentments have time to rise to the surface and wound again. In contrast, consciousness of death's imminence sharpens love with the keen edge of grief. Unless leftover hatred threatens to overwhelm the adult child's self-control, caring for a debilitated parent can be a blessing for the healing it allows. In refusing to continue waging war against a parent, the adult child allows the parent the freedom to make peace with life. Parent and child learn to wrestle with the demons within and not just with each other. Under the best of circumstances, they can offer each other honesty, witness, and forgiveness. This is a precious time. What is resolved and what remains unresolved will linger long after the funeral.

Though it may be a trial, reversing roles at the end of a parent's life can begin—or accelerate—the process of healing the generations. The helplessness of an aging, sick, or dying parent forces an inversion of dependence. Parents become like children, and children like parents. If roles had already been reversed in childhood, and the child had to work hard to set limits on a parent's need, his resentment for having to take care of a now legitimately dependent parent can be overwhelming. Difficulties that parents had once had as children reawaken when they become dependent on the care of others. To know how much sacrifice is too much, we must hold ourselves to a rigorously honest standard and continually examine our feelings.

Valerie, a single, attractive, immaculately groomed, and successful woman, was a self-described workaholic in her early thirties when she faced this issue:

My father's almost seventy and he's been a boozer all his life. My mother and I took care of him when I was a kid, and I left home as soon as I could. My mother took care of him by herself for the next forty years, and he's been disgustingly pathetic ever since she died. I get sick watching my father kill himself with booze like some drunk in the gutter. He refuses to get help, and I've decided I'm not helping him anymore unless he gets help for himself. I've thought about it a lot. The idea of not rushing in to rescue him scares the hell out of me, but I'm not doing him or me any good by running over there to pick him up off the floor all the time.

Valerie had lived with a lot of resentment toward her father. To make a life for herself, she had needed to stop worrying about him, and so she tried to harden her heart against the love and pity that she felt for him. She knew that if she did not stop taking care of him, she would be poisoning her life with resentment. But the answer for Valerie was not to harden her heart but to ask "*Ayeckah?*" and look at herself truthfully.

Valerie's father wanted his daughter to help him; he was sick and needed her. But at the same time, when she did rescue him, the healthy part of her father would have loathed himself for his weakness and, like Abraham, a part of him would hope that his daughter would find a way to get out from under his knife.

The only possibility of a healthy resolution for each of them depended on Valerie's father refusing the call of his addiction, and on Valerie not coming to her father's rescue when he drank. She had to look deep into her soul to make sure that vengeance played no part in her choice, or the part of herself that was still young and still loved him would be stained with its ugliness. Valerie was aware that when she stopped helping her father his life would become untenable. But she did not know whether he would then be forced to get help or whether her abandonment would hasten his demise and leave him dying in bitter loneliness. Had her father died at that point, Valerie would have been haunted by hurt and a lingering guilt that returned with every tender memory she yet had of him. To forgive herself for her betrayal, she would have had to reconstruct her defenses a thousand times, trying to exonerate herself for her decision each time.

Sick, old, and impaired, his daughter fully grown, Valerie's father still had a legacy to bequeath to his descendants. Had he not finally agreed to sign himself into a retirement home, his daughter's resentment toward him would have lingered to damage her future relationships. But once her father no longer needed Valerie to rescue him, he stopped actively hurting her.

Valerie was then able to overcome the bad feeling that she had toward him and concentrate on her own life and healing. In the weeks before her father died, Valerie was able to sit by his side; they talked and laughed at the small jokes they made, and they renewed their loving relationship. When he passed away, she could grieve with a clear conscience, letting loving memories of him comfort her.

In caring for parents unable to care for themselves, adult children are confronted with the unresolved conflicts of two generations. Children who have had to struggle hard to separate from their parents the first time find themselves immersed again in a stew of old feelings. Parental standards, once impossible to meet, become more demanding still. Issues of dependence and independence resurface for both parents and children. Neither can bypass the unresolved issues. Parents lose former spheres of competent function, while the usual stress-reducing outlets like going out to dinner, or to the gym, or the movies, become less available to children. Old conflicts become more sharply defined, the ordeal is great, and the rewards may be subtle. But we do best to embrace all of life. Caring for our ailing parents often exposes our own flaws as well as theirs. In the helplessness of the last of their lives, we can offer our parents the strength and consciousness of our maturity.

LAST MOMENTS

Life cuts away at us, piece by piece. At the end, as we look back and calculate what is lost and what is left, we stop taking others for granted. The approach of death, whether our own or our parent's, opens our eyes. If we were consciously aware that any goodbye could be our final one, we would take nothing for granted and be more loving. One man, talking about his father, said:

> When I said goodbye to him at the airport, I didn't think I wouldn't ever see him again. I wouldn't have been so quick to leave. There was so much we could have talked about, so much that I kept putting off till later. At the funeral, seeing him in the casket looking so much like himself, finally at peace—that's when I said goodbye. I spoke to him in my thoughts and wanted to put my arms around him, but I knew he'd be cold. I keep seeing him like that, lying there. More than

any other memory of him, that's the one that comes back to me. It nags at me that I wasn't there with him at the end, that we couldn't say a proper goodbye to each other.

Our last moments with those we love linger in memory. We recall them on our own deathbeds, and we hope to be surrounded by love when our own turn comes. These last moments are what we make them: painful or sweet, hostile or loving. If we know death is imminent, we can say goodbye properly: we recognize that this is our last chance to make peace, to reconcile, and to express love and final words. We see the fleetingness of life and know what is in our hearts. If consciousness permits, it is a time also for final instructions and benedictions, for one generation to bless the next, to bequeath final wisdom and make final bequests. One person responds to the truth of the other, each giving the other comfort and witness.

The knowledge that death is near strips both parent and child of vanity. Old hostilities seem trivial. Parents who have been hurt and bitter since childhood may come to terms with their lives, and find peace in spiritual reconciliation; and parents who trust in God or have lived full lives wish to pass their blessings on to their children. The hierarchy of meaning at last orders itself properly. In the stark light of death's glare, we reevaluate everything. A parent's last breath is the final lesson he passes on in life to his children and grandchildren. And the final witness of children and grandchildren comforts a parent in the fear and grief and wonder of that last moment.

THE DEATH OF A PARENT IN ADULT LIFE

Twenty-six years buried in the deepest,
darkest jungle and I still became my father.
Robin Williams, as the lead character in *Jumanji*

From the time of our ascendance in adolescence, we are witnesses to our parents' decline. But when death comes, it is still emotionally inconceivable. There is an unexpected physical dimension to the parent's sudden absence, as a constant in our universe vanishes. The day of his father's death, one man mused, "I've never not had a father before."

With death, everything seems strange. The gulf between the living and the dead seems so small that we feel we should be able to pick up the phone and call. But with death, time alters irrevocably. The single day, once so lightly thought of and so easily traversed into the future, now comes to represent a chasm in the relentless passing of time.

Sitting with a friend in the hours after his father died, I saw him pick up his father's watch, examine it wistfully, and say: "He must have just wound it. It doesn't seem right. This cheap watch keeps running and my father's heart has stopped."

In fact, with the death of a parent, nothing seems right: Clothes smell of a life as old and familiar as our first breaths. In the deepest recess of animal memory, that smell permeates our sense of security; that smell once surrounded our world. Objects left behind seem to embody a parent and we cling to them. The smell lingers while life has gone.

In our grief, childhood emotions awaken. The feelings are so familiar and vivid that the past seems more real than the present. For a time, feeling as we did as children seems like a return to our truest self. For a moment, the eyes of a child seem to peer out from our adult's body. The child within cries for the mother and father who have always been there before.

In loss, we appreciate what we've previously taken for granted. For a time, bad memories are swept away by grief, and parental instructions that once drove us crazy, such as "Wash the bowl when you give the dog water," return with sweetness. We stop resenting doing tasks we once hated, associating them now with those we loved and have lost. In simple acts—a movement, a gesture—our parents' images grow in us to fill the absent places.

After a parent's death, we can better see life through their eyes; we can see our own failings. Guilt is inevitable, but we honor the generations by changing for the better, by moving further into maturity, not by being mired in regret.

The universe seems vast in its emptiness after our parents no longer fill it. The borders our parents provided are gone. But without having to answer to parents, the ground we walk on truly becomes our own. We perceive our freedom as well as the responsibility for our own actions as never before. We sense that time is something borrowed, and is something most precious. We know, without any doubt, that what life is left is *now*.

In *Counting on Kindness,* Wendy Lustbader writes, "We suspect that the measure of a good life is how we are treated at the end."³ In the end, only family and friends matter. In the end, what matters is how well we have loved, how well we are loved, and how much we have given.

As parent and child face themselves and each other for the last time, they are given a final opportunity to make peace, to heal: the child, making peace with a parent, strengthens the inner reaches of himself; the parent, making peace with a child, strengthens his descendants. In the light of death, the knifepoint of separation glows. There is last locking of eyes, a final benediction.

Following are entries from my journal in the days before my mother's death:

AN AFTERNOON WITH MOM

In her waking moments, Mom is agitated and helpless. She fills these moments with nonstop directives: make warm water (25 percent cool, 75 percent boiled), cook potato, help to bathroom, help to bed. Get Kleenex. Rearrange nasal prongs. Clean room. Make more water. I am her arms and legs.

Having pain. Morphine given. Increased confusion. Trouble communicating. Gets up, gets back to bed, complains that sheet is on wrong. Wants potatoes. Dozes. Run to door to let in the hospice aide. Mom rings to tell me someone is at the door. June comes in and introduces herself, saying sweet things. Mom dismisses her with a wave. June retains sweetness, goes to warm up bath. Mom complains about her and sends me for towels. When I return, Mom is sitting up and had gotten her own water. June bathes Mom and offers to stay so I can go running. Mom glares at her. When I am about to leave, Mom asks me for her potatoes. June offers to cook them. Mom sends me for water. June says she'll get it.

I go running. On return, Mom is telling June that the water is too cold. Mom tells me to make her warm water. June says she'll do it and tells me to take a bath. Mom is asleep when I return. When she wakes up, Mom tells me I am like sunshine.

Mom is dying. Ordering me about tells her she is still in control. I try to keep my negative thoughts to myself, but the flurry of tasks agitates me. Expressing agitation upsets Mom even more. I try to react with reassurance and warmth. I am increasingly the master of my anger.

My standard is to be good and not cruel. Mom matches kindness with meanness and hates herself for it. She cries, "I'm a witch." Dying and demented, she still wrestles with herself. I reassure her. Mom loves me no matter how many layers of confusion she has. I am and forever will be her "little kitten." The feelings she has toward me are the deep, pure feelings I still feel from when I was five. The years of hostility between us are an overlay. Can I be cruel in the face of that?

THE MORNING OF HER DEATH

It took every bit of my strength and much help from friends and family to gentle my mother's final moments. Before she died, when only sincerity was left, my mother blessed me with words. When words were gone, she kissed my face. When I kissed her back, she kissed me again. A little peck. I kissed her again and it was a game. Fifteen, twenty pecks, back and forth. When movement was gone, she looked at me with loving warmth. When I told her that her face was so beautiful to me when she looked at me like that, with wide-open eyes, she gazed at me with everything she had left.

Then her breathing changed. We all gathered. There was a hush in the room. I repeated over and over: I love you. I love you. Thank you. You did good. I could feel life in her body for two or three minutes after she became still.

Our lives have meaning till our last breath. The meaning of that breath can speak for generations. It can bless, curse, and teach. Struggles enlarge us if we look beyond self-interest. Suffering is a teacher that confronts us with ourselves and challenges us to convert injuries into healings rather than actions that harm others. The issues we fail to resolve during our lives leave others to suffer. The healing we do or don't undertake has relevance beyond our particular lives, affecting those around us and the generations that come after us.

NOTES

Introduction
1. *Prisoners of Childhood* (New York: Basic Books, 1981); *For Your Own Good* (New York: Farrar, Straus & Giroux, 1983).

Chapter 1: When Life Doesn't Work
1. Psychoanalysts call this phenomenon "transference": the feelings we have toward our parents are transferred and projected onto others.
2. In psychoanalytic terms, this phenomenon is called "countertransference."
3. In psychoanalytic terms, as we honor our parents, we heal our own "transference neurosis."

Chapter 2: Imagining Another Person's Experience
1. Deuteronomy 5:16, in *Pentateuch and Haftorahs,* trans. and ed. Dr. J. H. Hertz, 2nd ed. (London: Soncino Press, 1981 [5742]) (hereafter cited as *Pentateuch and Haftorahs*); unless otherwise stated, all subsequent citations are to this edition, with the archaic forms "thee," "thy," and "thine" at times changed to "you" and "your."
2. The right hemisphere is the nondominant one in 90 percent of people.
3. Ernest Jones, *The Life and Work of Sigmund Freud* (New York: Basic Books, 1953), 1:7.
4. Ibid., 1:8.
5. Ibid., 2:146.
6. Ibid., 1:7.
7. Martin Freud, *Glory Reflected* (London: Angus & Robertson, 1957), 9–10.
8. Linda A. Chernus, "Marital Treatment Following Early Infant Death," *Clinical Social Work Journal* 10, no. 1 (Spring 1982): 28–38.
9. E. Lewis, "El Impacto del Nacimiento de un Niño Muerto en la Familia" (The Impact of a Stillborn Birth on the Family), trans. J. M. Civeira, *Psicopatologia* 4, no. 3 (July–September 1984): 297–302.
10. Therese A. Rando, ed., *Parental Loss of a Child* (Champaign, Ill.: Research Press, 1986), 14.
11. J. A. Stehbens and A. D. Lascari, "Psychological Follow-up of Families with Childhood Leukemia," *Journal of Clinical Psychology* 30, no. 3 (July 1974): 394–397.
12. Reiko Schwab, "Effects of a Child's Death on the Marital Relationship: A Preliminary Study," *Death Studies* 16, no. 2 (March–April 1992): 141–154.
13. Earl A. Grollman, *Judaism in Sigmund Freud's World* (New York: Bloch Publishing Co., 1965), 50.
14. Ibid.
15. Jones, *Life and Work of Sigmund Freud,* 1:5.

16. Freud compensated for his father's emotional absence with passionate adult friendships with men he initially idealized and often later came to despise. Decrying his own judgment, Freud's hunger for father intimacy was something he reenacted throughout his adult life, even looking up to eccentrics like Wilhelm Fliess, whose sexual theories equated the mucous membrane of the nose with the penis.

17. Hyemeyohsts Storm, *Seven Arrows* (New York: Harper & Row, 1972), 6–7.

18. Rabbi Nosson Scherman, overview to *Bereishis: Genesis,* vol. 2, translated and annotated by Rabbi Meir Zlotowitz (New York: Mesorah Publications, 1978), 367–368.

Chapter 3: Why We Can't "Just Get Over It"

1. Mammals instinctively protect their children, unto death, but mammals may kill their pups under stressful conditions, which, in the wild, translates to scarce resources and overcrowding. Sociobiologist David Barash reports that after an airport opened nearby, the foxes in a commercial fox-raising enterprise began eating their pups. The physiological reactions of the foxes could not differentiate between causes of stress. David Barash, *The Whisperings Within* (New York: Penguin Books, 1981), 95. Like other mammals, human parents may kill their children under great duress or when the stress from a traumatic past returns to make them numb and add stress to the present.

2. William G. Sumner, *Folkways* (1906; reprint, New York: Mentor Books, 1960), 268.

3. The embryologist Ernst Heinrich Haekel believed that an embryo is an accurate record of the evolution of the phylogenetic group from which it arises, and in 1866 he coined the phrase "Ontogeny [the development of the individual] is a brief and rapid recapitulation of phylogeny [the development of the group]." Theodosius Dobzhansky, *Evolution, Genetics, and Man* (New York: John Wiley & Sons, 1955), 236.

4. G. P. Chrousos and P. W. Gold, "Concepts of Stress and Stress Symptom Disorders," *Journal of the American Medical Association* 267, no. 9 (March 4, 1992): 1244–1252; D. E. Redmond et al., "Studies of the Nucleus Locus Coeruleus in Monkeys," in Herbert Y. Meltzer et al., eds., *Psychopharmacology: The Third Generation of Progress* (New York: Raven Press, 1987), 967–975. Animals with lesions in the locus ceruleus do not show a fear response when threatened. Electrical stimulation of the locus ceruleus results in fear.

5. P. E. Gold and R. B. van Buskirk, "Facilitation of Time-Dependent Memory Process with Post-trial Epinephrine Injections," *Behavioral Biology* 13 (1975): 145–153; J. W. Haycock et al., "Enhancement of Retention with Centrally Administered Catecholamine," *Experimental Neurology* 54 (1977): 199–208; R. P. Kesner, "Brain Stimulation: Effects on Memory," *Behavioral and Neural Biology* 36 (1982): 315–367; Gary Lynch, James L. McGaugh, and Norman M. Weinberger, eds., *Neurobiology of Learning and Memory* (New York: Guilford Press, 1984), 125–137.

6. Leo Goldberger and Shlomo Breznitz, eds., *Handbook of Stress,* 2nd ed. (New York: Free Press, 1993), 581; M. J. Scott and S. G. Stradling, "Post-traumatic Stress Disorder Without the Trauma," *British Journal of Clinical Psychology* 33, pt. 1 (February 1994): 71–74.

7. Frederick Petty et al., "Learned Helplessness Sensitizes Hippocampal Norepinephrine to Mild Re-stress," *Biological Psychiatry* 35, no. 12 (June 1994): 903–908; Mardi Horowitz and Nancy Willner, "Stress Films, Emotion, and Cognitive Response," *Archives of General Psychiatry* 30 (1976): 1339–1344; T. I. Belova and K. V. Sudukov, "Morphofunctional Changes in Brain Neurons During Emotional Stress," *Vestnik Akademii Meditsinskikh Nauk USSR* 2 (1990): 11–13; Alan Frazer, Perry Molinoff, and Andrew Winokur, *Biological Bases of Brain Function and Disease* (New York: Raven Press, 1994), 199–201.

8. Leo Goldberger and Shlomo Breznitz, *Handbook of Stress,* 2nd ed. (New York: Free Press, 1993), 581; Lynch, McGaugh, and Weinberger, *Neurobiology of Learning and Memory,* 379. Paul Gold writes: "Hormonal responses . . . regulate neuronal changes responsible for memory storage, [and] initiate long-lasting alterations in neuronal function . . . [with] large effects on memory . . . EEG arousal, cerebral 02 consumption and blood flow, and central release of NE. Epinephrine enhances memory of avoidance responses. . . ." S. M. Southwick et al., "Psychobiologic Research in Posttraumatic Stress Disorder," *Psychiatric Clinics of North America* 17, no. 2 (June 1994): 251–264.

9. Zahava Solomon et al., "Reactivation of Combat-Related Posttraumatic Stress Disorder," *American Journal of Psychiatry* 144, no. 1 (January 1987): 51–55; Edward M. Ornitz and Robert S. Pynoos, "Startle Modulation in Children with Posttraumatic Stress Disorder," *American Journal of Psychiatry* 146, no. 7 (July 1989): 866–870; Southwick et al., "Psychobiologic Research in Posttraumatic Stress Disorder," 251–264. As Southwick observes:

    There is now accumulating evidence to suggest that severe psychological trauma can cause alterations in the organism's neurobiologic response to stress even years after the original insult. . . . For example, increased sensitivity and sensitization of the noradrenergic system may leave the individual in a hyperaroused, vigilant, sleep-deprived, and, at times, explosive state that worsens over time. Being irritable and on edge makes it difficult to interact with family members, friends, coworkers, and employers. To quiet these symptoms of hyperarousal, PTSD patients often withdraw and use substances, particularly central nervous system depressants. . . .

10. The brain dampens the intensity of the physiological and psychological response to norepinephrine by releasing endorphins—internally manufactured opiates. In animals, symptoms of opiate withdrawal occur equally by either withdrawing the animal from the stressful situation or by giving an opiate antagonist. Bessel A. van der Kolk and José Saporta, "Biological Response to Psychic Trauma," *International Handbook of Traumatic Syndromes,* ed. John P. Wilson and Beverly Raphael (New York: Plenum Press, 1993), 29.

11. E. B. Foa, "Arousal, Numbing, and Intrusion: Symptom Structure of PTSD Following Assault," *American Journal of Psychology* 152, no. 1 (1995): 116–120.

12. Some rabbis speculate that the ancient religious injunctions against contact with blood were meant to keep men from becoming hardened to it. They were also to keep the young from developing a liking for violence. *Pentateuch and Haftorahs,* 487.

13. Our streets and prisons are filled with addicts who are unable to cope with the aftermath of their traumatic childhoods. Adults with borderline and multiple personality disorder are traumatized children who suffer from symptoms of PTSD as a result. The majority were sexually abused as children; the rest grew up with the extremes of physical violence or neglect.

14. Michael S. Scheeringa et al., "Two Approaches to the Diagnosis of Posttraumatic Stress Disorder in Infancy and Early Childhood," *Journal of the American Academy of Child and Adolescent Psychiatry* 34, no. 2 (February 1995): 191–200.

15. Catherine Cameron, "Veterans of a Secret War: Survivors of Childhood Sexual Trauma Compared to Vietnam War Veterans with PTSD," *Journal of Interpersonal Violence* 9, no. 1 (1994): 117–132; W. B. McPherson et al., "An Event-Related Brain-Potential Investigation of PTSD and PTSD Symptoms in Abused Children," *Integrative Physiological Behavioral Science* 32, no. 1 (January–March 1997): 31–42.

16. C. A. Glod and M. H. Teicher, "The Relationship Between Early Abuse, Posttraumatic Stress Disorder, and Activity Levels in Prepubertal Children," *Journal of the American Academy of Child and Adolescent Psychiatry* 35, no. 10 (October 1996): 1384–1393.

17. Petty et al., "Learned Helplessness Sensitizes Hippocampal Norepinephrine to Mild Re-stress," 903–908.

18. Ibid.; J. D. Bremner et al., "Noradrenergic Mechanisms in Stress and Anxiety: I. Preclinical Studies," *Synapse* 23, no. 1 (May 1996), 28–38.

19. Alfred Gilman and Louis Goodman et al., *The Pharmacologic Basis of Therapeutics,* ed. Alfred Gilman and Louis Goodman et al. (New York: Macmillan, 1985), 145.

20. This is analogous to the "imprinting" that ethologist Konrad Lorenz observed in ducklings. In the absence of a mother, ducklings will rigidly follow whatever they first see—a box, an object. Konrad Lorenz writes:

    [I]mprinting is the irreversible fixation of a response to a situation which the individual may encounter only a few times in his life.... The remarkable thing about this process is that the permanent association between the behavior pattern and its object becomes established at a time when it is not yet functional (or) ... even traceable. The sensitive period for imprintability often belongs to a very early stage in the development.... [*Behind the Mirror* (New York: Harcourt Brace Jovanovich, 1973), 78.]

21. At birth, the cerebral cortex is still immature; otherwise our heads would not squeeze through the birth canal. Our brains, already disproportionately large for our bodies at birth, almost triple in size by the end of the first year of life. After that, the mature brain will add only another 25 percent to its weight, not

by adding brain cells but by developing more synaptic connections between nerve endings and by myelination. Fully developing the protein/fatty sheaths of myelin that encase the nerves in the cerebral cortex takes years. Like the copper wire that conducts electricity in our homes, these myelin sheaths allow smooth, rapid conduction of electrical impulses.

22. J. L. Conel, *The Postnatal Development of the Human Cortex* (Cambridge: Harvard University Press, 1939), 1939–1955.

23. Ibid.

24. Sigmund Freud, *A General Introduction to Psychoanalysis,* translation of the revised ed. by Joan Riviere (New York: Liveright Publishing Corp., 1935), 243. Unlike modern definitions of posttraumatic stress disorder, Freud did not restrict the definition of "traumatic" to being outside the range of ordinary experience.

25. John Leopold Weil, *Early Deprivation of Empathic Care* (Madison, Conn.: International Universities Press, 1992), 37.

26. Ibid., 37–38.

27. Ibid., 38.

28. Bessel A. van der Kolk, *Psychological Trauma* (Washington, D.C.: American Psychiatric Press, 1987), 43.

29. John Bowlby, *A Secure Base* (New York: Basic Books, 1988), 6–11; T. J. Field et al., "Discrimination and Imitation of Facial Expression by Neonates," *Science* 218 (1982): 179–181.

30. Some parents become addicted to tranquilizers or use alcohol altruistically— less for their own than their family's benefit.

31. Geraldine Dawson et al., "Infants of Depressed Mothers Exhibit Atypical Frontal Brain Activity: A Replication and Extension of Previous Findings," *Journal of Child Psychology and Psychiatry* 38, no. 2 (February 1997): 179–186; Geraldine Dawson et al., "Frontal Lobe Activity and Affective Behavior of Infants of Mothers with Depressive Symptoms," *Child Development* 63, no. 3 (1992): 725–737.

32. Myrna M. Weissman et al., "Offspring of Depressed Parents: Ten Years Later," *Archives of General Psychiatry* (October 1997): 932–939.

33. Margaret S. Stroebe, Wolfgang Stroebe, and Robert O. Hansson, eds., *Handbook of Bereavement* (Cambridge: Cambridge University Press, 1993), 25.

34. Anthony Ambrose, ed., *Stimulation in Early Infancy* (Oxford: Oxford Academic Press, 1969), 48.

> It has been demonstrated that stimulation in early infancy modifies the adult patterns of ACTH secretion and steroidogenesis to stress . . . [with] more rapid and enhanced steroid response in adulthood . . . and in these animals the response tends to persist over much longer periods. (Haltmeyer et al., 1967) Furthermore, the handled animals show a lower steroid response when exposed to novel stimuli as compared with its nonstimulated counterparts. (Levine et al., 1967)

Bessel A. van der Kolk, *Psychological Trauma,* 45, 39–52; Weil, *Early Deprivation of Empathic Care,* 77; G. I. Hockings et al., "Hypersensitivity of the Hypothalamic-Pituitary-Adrenal Axis to Naloxone in Post-traumatic Stress Disorder," *Biological Psychiatry* 33, no. 8–9 (April 15–May 1, 1993): 585–593. Hockings finds:

> [E]xamples of PTSD cases showing full symptomatology . . . in the absence of a single, acute, dramatic trauma. . . . such trauma is thus not a necessary condition for PTSD. . . . It is suggested that the . . . distinction between acute and enduring psychosocial stressors be incorporated into the definition [of PTSD] to distinguish two pathways to stress disorder, post-traumatic and prolonged duress.

35. George Adelman, ed., *Encyclopedia of Neuroscience* (Boston: Birkhauser Press, 1987), 94.

36. Ambrose, *Stimulation in Early Infancy*, 4.

37. Ibid., 4–7.

> [A] single stressful experience . . . to the mother . . . when the offspring is three days of age, permanently alters both avoidance conditioning and the steroid response . . . when it reaches adulthood. Stimulation in the pre-weaning period has consequences that are different from those of equivalent stimulation in adulthood. (Levine, 1956; Seitz, 1954; Spence and Maher, 1962; Wolfe, 1943) . . . [M]any psychophysiological processes are altered by infantile stimulation[:] Brain neurochemistry (Tapp & Markowitz, 1963), neuroendocrine activity, EEG activity, the response to pathogens, rates of survival to severe stress, and the response to brain lesions have all been modified . . . [resulting in] a permanent change in emotional reactivity.

38. Ibid., 32–33.

39. Martin E. Seligman and Steven F. Maier, "Failure to Escape Traumatic Shock," *Journal of Experimental Psychology* 74, no. 1 (1967): 1–9. Psychologist Seligman, in his book *Helplessness: On Depression, Development, and Death,* describes what he learned in his research with animals: "Dogs given inescapable shock . . . seem to wilt. They passively sink to the bottom of the cage, even rolling over and adopting a submissive posture; they do not resist." Martin E. Seligman, *Helplessness: On Depression, Development, and Death* (San Francisco: W. H. Freeman & Co., 1975), 53.

40. A computer search retrieved over sixteen hundred published articles on learned helplessness since 1967.

41. E. M. Eisenstein and A. D. Carlson, "A Comparative Approach to the Behavior Called 'Learned Helplessness,' " *Behavioural Brain Research* 96, no. 2 (July 1997): 149–160.

42. Ambrose, *Stimulation in Early Infancy*, 15.

43. Sighted mothers of blind infants have more difficulty in attaching to them and often find their infants unresponsive. Louise H. Werth, "Synchrony of Cueing Modalities: Communicative Competence Between the Mother and Blind Infant," *Early Child Development & Care* 18, no. 1-2 (1984): 53–60.

44. Kenneth S. Robson, "The Role of Eye-to-Eye Contact in Maternal-Infant Attachment," *Journal of Child Psychology and Psychiatry* 8 (1967): 13–25.

45. Colwin Trevarthen, "Descriptive Analyses of Infant Communicative Behaviour," in *Studies in Mother-Infant Interaction,* ed. H. R. Schaeffer (New York: Academic Press, 1977), 267–268. When mothers immobilized their faces, seven- to twelve-week-old infants initially appeared confused, then dis-

tressed, began crying, acted dejected, and then withdrew. But if another person was distracting the mother, the infant was not so negatively affected by the mother's lack of response.

46. See John Bowlby, *Attachment* (New York: Basic Books, 1969), 27.

47. Seymour Levine, "Psychobiologic Consequences of Disruption in Mother-Infant Relationships," in *Perinatal Development: A Psychobiological Perspective,* ed. Norman A. Krasnegor et al. (Orlando, Fla.: Academic Press, 1987), 359.

48. Looking for an animal model to study the effects of human infant deprivation, pioneering psychologist Harry F. Harlow demonstrated the primacy of the need for "contact comfort." An infant rhesus monkey, fed from a bottle of milk attached to a wire-mesh mother surrogate but deprived of all physical contact comfort, grows up withdrawn and fearful of other monkeys. If the monkey infant is provided a terry-cloth mother surrogate in addition to the wire mesh containing the bottle of milk, the monkey will suckle from the bottle, then cling to the terry-cloth mother. H. F. Harlow and R. R. Zimmerman, "The Affectional Responses in the Infant Monkey," *Science* 130 (1959): 421.

Social isolation of the rhesus monkey in the first six to twelve months of life produces severe, persistent behavioral effects in them as adults. William T. McKinney, "Primate Social Isolation: Psychiatric Implications," *Archives of General Psychiatry* 31, no. 3 (September 1974): 422–426. The monkey becomes more vulnerable to the effects of future separations (McKinney, "Early Stress and Later Response to Separation in Rhesus Monkeys," *American Journal of Psychiatry* 130, no. 4 [April 1973]: 400–405). These monkeys consumed more alcohol during separations and reunions and drank more when given free access to alcohol than other monkeys (Gary W. Kraemer and W. T. McKinney, "Effects of Alcohol on the Despair Response to Peer Separation in Rhesus Monkeys," *Psychopharmacology* 73, no. 4 [May 1981]: 307–310), especially when separations were intermittent rather than for a single prolonged period (Kraemer and McKinney, "Social Separation Increases Alcohol Consumption in Rhesus Monkeys," *Psychopharmacology* 86, no. 1-2 [May–June 1985]: 182–189). Preadolescent rhesus monkeys who seemed adjusted "became acutely violent and killed several of their peers" when stressed with low-dose amphetamine. Their counterparts who had not been socially deprived showed no such behavior (Kraemer and McKinney, "Hypersensitivity to d-Amphetamine Several Years After Early Social Deprivation in Rhesus Monkeys," *Psychopharmacology* 82, no. 3 [1984]: 266–271). Nonthreatening, younger monkeys who initiated contact, however, had a healing effect on older monkeys who had been isolated in their first year of life (S. J. Suomi, H. F. Harlow, and W. T. McKinney, "Monkey Psychiatrists," *American Journal of Psychiatry* 128, no. 8 [February 1972]: 927–932).

49. Wayne H. Green, "Attachment Disorders of Infancy and Early Childhood," in *Comprehensive Textbook of Psychiatry/IV,* 4th ed., ed. Harold Kaplan and Benjamin Sadock (Baltimore: Williams & Wilkins, 1985), 1722.

50. Weil, *Early Deprivation of Empathic Care,* 3.

51. R. A. Spitz, *The Psychoanalytic Study of the Child* 2 (1946): 313–342.

52. Unless otherwise specified, all quotations from the New Testament are from the Authorized King James Version of the Bible.

53. R. Charlton and E. Dolman, "Bereavement: A Protocol for Primary Care," *British Journal of General Practice* (August 1995): 427–430; C. Shaefer et al., "Mortality Following Conjugal Bereavement and the Effects of a Shared Environment," *American Journal of Epidemiology* 141, no. 12 (June 15, 1995): 1142–1152.

54. Stroebe, Stroebe, and Hansson, *Handbook of Bereavement,* 186–193.

55. Ibid.

56. M. L. Spratt and D. R. Denney, "Immune Variables, Depression, and Plasma Cortisol over Time in Suddenly Bereaved Parents," *Journal of Neuropsychiatry and Clinical Neuroscience* 3, no. 3 (Summer 1991): 299–306; L. Hodel and P. J. Grob, "Psyche and Immunity: A Psychoneuroimmunology of Healthy Persons," *Schweizerische Schweig Medizinische Wochenschrift* 123, no. 49 (December 11, 1993): 2323–2341.

57. C. M. Fox et al., "Loneliness, Emotional Repression, Marital Quality, and Major Life Events in Women Who Develop Breast Cancer," *Journal of Community Health* 19, no. 6 (December 1994): 467–482.

58. Stroebe, Stroebe, and Hansson, *Anatomy of Bereavement,* 175–176, 197.

59. Jeffrey Masson and Susan McCarthy, *When Elephants Weep* (New York: Delacourt Press, 1995), 97.

60. Elizabeth Marshall Thomas, *The Hidden Life of Dogs* (New York: Houghton Mifflin Co., 1993), 72.

61. William Styron has written an excellent description of his own depression in *Darkness Visible: A Memoir of Madness* (New York: Random House, 1990).

62. Hans Selye, *The Stress of Life* (New York: McGraw-Hill Books, 1956), 3.

63. The term "depression" can be confusing. It is used in psychiatric classification for a spectrum of mood disorders of differing severity with a variable presentation of symptoms, from a low-grade undercurrent to an incapacitating disorder that immobilizes a person to the point where he longs for death. Furthermore, the term may be used as a description of a prolonged or transitory mood or for feelings of loneliness, sadness, or disappointment, or when mood or energy falls below normal. Then, too, a depressed person does not necessarily feel depressed—he may just have the physical correlates of disturbed sleep and appetite, or he may attribute his diminished interest and pleasure in life to fatigue, a lack of energy, overwork, or a bad relationship. Depression may be masked by addiction or expressed in thrill-seeking, agitation, and anger. Usually, however, negative emotions dominate a depressed person's self-regard, trust in others, and outlook—he withdraws from others and from his engagement with life.

64. *Goodman and Gilman's The Pharmacologic Basis of Therapeutics,* 86.

65. Preston A. West, "Neurobehavioral Studies of Forced Swimming," *Progress in Neuro-Psychopharmacology and Biological Psychiatry* 14, no. 6 (1990): 863–877.

66. J. D. Bremner et al., "MRI-Based Measurement of Hippocampal Volume in Patients with Combat-Related Posttraumatic Stress Disorder," *American Journal of Psychiatry* 152, no. 7 (July 1995): 973–981.

67. J. Wolfe and L. K. Schlesinger, "Performance of PTSD Patients on Standard Tests of Memory: Implications for Trauma," *Annals of the New York Academy of Sciences* 821, no. 21 (June 1997): 208–218.

68. A. Bleich et al., "Post-traumatic Stress Disorder and Depression: An Analysis of Co-morbidity," *British Journal of Psychiatry* 170 (May 1997): 479–482.

69. *Goodman and Gilman's The Pharmacologic Basis of Therapeutics,* 1464.

70. Rachel Yehuda et al., "Low Urinary Cortisol Excretion in Holocaust Survivors with Posttraumatic Stress Disorder," *American Journal of Psychiatry* 152, no. 7 (July 1995): 982–986; Bessel A. van der Kolk, "The Psychobiology of Posttraumatic Stress Disorder," *Journal of Clinical Psychiatry* 58, suppl. no. 9 (1997): 18.

71. Cortisol levels in severe depression may be so high that it does not fluctuate. Without normal rhythmic fluctuations of cortisol, body rhythms disorganize, sleep is disturbed, and eating and elimination may be affected. Sufferers find it difficult to distinguish among their feelings or to make good judgments.

   One woman with Cushing's syndrome, who had an adrenal gland tumor continually pour out high levels of cortisol, had had a bilateral adrenalectomy several years earlier. She said that she felt "terrible" because she didn't "have any feelings." She was wrong. She did have feelings. Her entire expression was infused with the language of emotion, but she had to learn to recognize her feelings without the dimension provided by normally responsive adrenal glands.

72. When a person is depressed, numerous body functions are depressed. With depression, the production of testosterone decreases, as does the desire for sex. Levels of thyroid stimulating hormone (TSH) decrease, and thyroid production is lower; metabolic function drops and the body conserves calories. Levels of growth hormone also subside. Blood sugar decreases, and the body stores fat. Blood clots more quickly, minimizing blood loss in the face of any injury, but resulting in an increased incidence of heart attacks and strokes. Even the immune system is suppressed, impairing the depressed person's ability to fight infection or clean up vagrant cancer cells.

73. M. Cleiren et al., "Mode of Death and Kinship in Bereavement Focusing on Who Rather than How," *Crisis* 15, no. 1 (1994): 22–36. PTSD symptoms following bereavement correlate with the closeness of the relative and not the manner of death.

74. C. S. Lewis, *A Grief Observed* (New York: Seabury Press, 1961).

75. Selby Jacobs et al., "Bereavement and Catecholamines," *Journal of Psychosomatic Research* 30, no. 4 (1986): 489–496; W. T. McKinney, "Primate Separation Studies: Relevance to Bereavement," *Psychiatric Annals* 16, no. 5 (May 1986): 281–287.

76. Jerome Frederick, "The Biochemistry of Bereavement: Possible Basis for Chemotherapy?" *Omega: The Journal of Death and Dying* 13, no. 4 (1982–1983): 295–303. Acute grief has profound effects on the pituitary-adrenal axis and results in the hypersecretion of cortisol, which in turn has the immunosuppressive effect of increasing one's susceptibility to infectious disease and cancer.

77. George Eliot, *The Mill on the Floss* (Boston: Houghton, Mifflin Co., 1961), 241.

78. John Bowlby first noted this in 1961. After much debate, it has since been supported by many studies. Stanley I. Greenspan and George H. Pollock, eds., *The Course of Life*, vol. 1, *Infancy* (Madison, Conn.: International Universities Press, 1989), 243.

79. Kaplan and Sadock, *Comprehensive Textbook of Psychiatry/IV,* 578.

Chapter 4: Moving On After Bad Things Happen

1. I. Fukunishi, M. Kikuchi, and M. Takubo, "Changes in Scores on Alexithymia over a Period of Psychiatric Treatment," *Psychological Reports* 80, no. 2 (April 1997): 483–489.

2. David Rapaport, *Emotions and Memory* (New York: International Universities Press, 1971), 257.

3. T. J. Taiminen et al., "Alexithymia in Suicide Attempters," *Acta Psychiatrica Scandinavica* 93, no. 3 (March 1996): 195–198.

4. Mark Lumley et al., "Alexithymia in Chronic Pain Patients," *Comprehensive Psychiatry* 38, no. 3 (May–June 1997): 160–165.

5. Alfonso Troisi et al., "Nonverbal Behavior and Alexithymic Traits in Normal Subjects: Individual Differences in Encoding Emotions," *Journal of Nervous and Mental Diseases* 184, no. 9 (September 1996): 561–566.

6. Isao Fukunishi et al., "Emotional Disturbances in Trauma Patients During the Rehabilitation Phase: Studies of Posttraumatic Stress Disorder and Alexithymia," *General Hospital Psychiatry* 18, no. 2 (March 1996): 121–127.

7. Lumley et al., "Alexithymia in Chronic Pain Patients," 160–165.

8. Arthur Kleinman, *The Illness Narratives: Suffering, Healing, and the Human Condition* (New York: Basic Books, 1988), xi–xii.

9. Comparing the lives of those who survived the Nazi camps, R. G. Roden found those who later committed suicide had detached from their experiences. R. G. Roden, "Suicide and Holocaust Survivors," *Israel Journal of Psychiatry and Related Sciences* 19, no. 2 (1982): 129–135. This was true for writers Primo Levi and Bruno Bettelheim, survivors of the Holocaust, who remained distant from their emotional experience and from others; they killed themselves decades later. Detached expressions of hurt allow no healing and elude comfort. These writers did not invite others to respond. Likewise, before her suicide, Virginia Woolf had decided not to trouble her husband with her last descent into depression.

10. John Berryman, *Recovery/Delusions, Etc.,* quote taken from the foreword by Saul Bellow (New York: Delta Books, 1974), xii–xiii.

11. John Haffenden, *The Life of John Berryman* (Boston: Ark Paperbacks, 1982), 29.

12. John Berryman, *Recovery/Delusions, Etc.,* 45–50. To keep treatment as Berryman's first priority, the counselor opposed the wishes of a physician who would have given Berryman leave to teach his classes. The counselor weathered Berryman's anger and offered to teach the class for him.

13. The use of alcohol, drugs, and other addictions preserves the stalemate by temporarily alleviating the pressure from intrusive memories.

14. False memories of abuse accuse and damn the innocent, destroy love, and destroy families. Those who follow the trail of false memories find themselves lost in a nightmare. Progressively darker flights of imagination pose as memories. If molested after five years of age, most people have some remnants of memory and do not entirely forget the experience. This is often the case for children as young as two years old when molested. Recovering memories in the absence of corroborating evidence is unreliable. We can remember what we see in our dreams and imagination. False memories may be planted by the unconscious suggestion of a therapist. Hypnosis can help a person remember what was once repressed, but half of the time the retrieved memories are false. Even without hypnosis, a therapist's suggestion can be so subtle that the therapist himself is unaware of it.

    For further discussion of this, see: Stan Abrams, "False Memory Syndrome vs. Total Repression," *Psychiatry and the Law* 23, no. 2 (Summer 1995): 283–293; Elizabeth F. Loftus and Jacqueline E. Pickrell, "The Formation of False Memories," *Psychiatric Annals* 25, no. 12 (December 1995): 720–725; Maryanne Garry, Elizabeth E. Loftus, and Scott W. Brown, "Memory: A River Runs Through It," in a special issue, "The Recovered Memory–False Memory Debate," of *Consciousness and Cognition, an International Journal* 3, no. 3-4 (September–December 1994): 438–451; Michael D. Yapko, "Suggestibility and Repressed Memories of Abuse: A Survey of Psychotherapists' Beliefs," *American Journal of Clinical Hypnosis* 36, no. 3 (January 1994): 185–187; Susan L. McElroy and Paul E. Keck, "Recovered Memory Therapy: False Memory Syndrome and Other Complications," *Psychiatric Annals* 25, no. 12 (December 1995): 731–735.

15. Wendy Lustbader reported this anecdote from a speech given by Elie Wiesel at Wesleyan University, Middletown, Connecticut, 1974.

16. Also described by Robert McAfee Brown in the preface to Elie Wiesel, *Night* (New York: Bantam Books, 1986), v–vi.

Chapter 5: How the Wars of Our Forebears Relate to Our Lives Today

1. Robert Krell, "Children Who Survived the Japanese Concentration Camps," *Canadian Journal of Psychiatry* 35, no. 2 (March 1990): 149–152.

2. Yolanda Gampel, from *Generations of the Holocaust,* Martin S. Bergmann and Milton E. Jucovy, eds. (New York: Basic Books, 1982), 120–121.
3. Ibid., 267.

Chapter 6: Needing to Let Others Know

1. Alfred Lange et al., "Childhood Unwanted Sexual Events and Degree of Psychopathology of Psychiatric Patients: Research with a New Anamnestic Questionnaire," *Acta Psychiatrica Scandinavica* 92, no. 6 (December 1995): 441–446.
2. Children are not only confused by the lies their predators tell them; they are further confused by the lies the predators tell themselves about the meaning of the child's response. One giant of a man argued that what he did with the five-year-old girls he preferred was not wrong because they liked what he did:

   I never bully them or hurt them in any way. I give them a choice. If they say "Stop!" I stop for a little while and try again later. I know they'll like it because I'm attentive and I always give them orgasms. . . . I'd tell them it would be our little secret because their parents would be upset with them if they told.
3. People traumatized as children are sometimes regarded as "hysterics."
4. Mother-son incest is the least common form of incest. Studies among rhesus monkeys and ape colonies demonstrate that a biological inhibition exists, preventing sexual activities between primate mothers and their sons. During estrus, when female monkeys freely give themselves to other males in the colony, mothers scrupulously avoid intercourse with their sons. A. M. Arkin, "A Hypothesis Concerning the Incest Taboo," *Psychoanalytic Review* 71, no. 3 (November 1984): 375–381.

   In my own experience, I have seen only two cases of mother-son incest. Both had problems with addictions, interpersonal relationships, and the law.
5. Among 465 incarcerated pedophiles, using phallometric testing, the ratio of heterosexually to homosexually oriented pedophiles is 11:1. Kurt Freud and Robin J. Watson, "The Proportions of Heterosexual and Homosexual Pedophiles Among Sex Offenders Against Children: An Exploratory Study," *Journal of Sex and Marital Therapy* 18, no. 1 (Spring 1992): 34–43.
6. Janet Teets, "Childhood Sexual Trauma of Chemically Dependent Women," *Journal of Psychoactive Drugs* 27, no. 3 (July–September 1995): 231–238. According to Teets's study of sixty chemically dependent women in a long-term treatment facility, 68 percent said they had been the recipients of unwanted sexual contacts from perpetrators. Those who had been sexually abused began drinking and using drugs earlier and had a higher incidence of chemically dependent family members, they had been raped at some time in their life, and were more often African-American. Among 947 of my patients in a residential alcohol and drug treatment facility, 58 percent of the women and 19 percent of the men reported severe sexual abuse in childhood.
7. At Cedar Hills residential alcohol and drug treatment program, 65 percent of the residents who admitted to having been sexually abused had children.

8. Boys who have been molested by sexually mature males tend to be more sexually anxious than other adolescent males and, in my experience, frequently believe they are poorly endowed and sexually inadequate as adults. I suspect that, having been sexually abused as children, they experience flashbacks, feeling small upon seeing the mature genitalia of others. The feeling of being small is so compelling, they often cannot be convinced of their normality.

9. Many women who have been sexually abused as children have difficulty finding pleasure in heterosexual relationships afterward, and individual psychotherapy by itself is less effective than conjoint therapy with couples, and behavioral strategies employed by sex therapists.

10. Ronda had been given a diagnosis of multiple personality (MPD) at the hospital, but I treated her for having been badly traumatized as a little girl, rather than for dissociative disorder, borderline personality, or MPD. I find the diagnosis of MPD suspect in the overwhelming majority of patients with that diagnosis. Furthermore, those who have accepted the diagnosis of MPD seem to have relinquished a certain degree of responsibility for their actions. Those diagnosed with MPD have suffered the severest abuse, but the disorder has become mythologized with approaches that seductively elevate therapists to a position of special knowledge: the therapist becomes the only one who knows, understands, and can heal the "multiple" and the "alters." What reintegrates MPD patients, in my opinion, is a trusting, long-term, honest, clearly defined relationship with a caring therapist who offers support, guidance, and witness.

   Had Ronda continued in her development as an MPD patient, she would have refined her sickness and lost her children. Had she given up her children, as her therapist had urged, neither she nor her children would ever have recovered from the grief of it. After receiving her therapist's approval then, Ronda's "career" as a mental patient would have come to be the only reward in a hopelessly crippled life. Ronda, however, finally came to protest her hospitalization and her diagnosis and wisely left the hospital.

Chapter 7: Giving Grief Its Due

1. Jean F. Saucier, "Anthropology and Psychodynamics of Mourning," *Canadian Psychiatric Association Journal* 12, no. 5 (1967): 477–496; George P. Murdock, "Universals of Culture," in *Readings in Anthropology*, ed. E. Adamson Hoebel, Jesse D. Jennings, and Elmer R. Smith (New York: McGraw-Hill Book Co., 1955), 5–6.

2. Elman R. Service, *Profiles in Ethnology*, 3rd ed. (New York: Harper & Row, 1978), 62–63.

3. Ibid., 344.

4. Kaj Birket-Smith, *The Paths of Culture* (Madison: University of Wisconsin Press, 1965), 196.

5. Ibid., 314–316.

6. Donald J. Cohen, "Enduring Sadness: Early Loss, Vulnerability, and the Shaping of Character," *Psychoanalytic Study of the Child* 45 (1990): 157–178.

7. Russell Baker, *Growing Up* (New York: Signet Books, 1982), 79.

8. Ibid., 81.

9. Donald S. Zall, "The Long-term Effects of Childhood Bereavement: Impact on Roles as Mothers," *Omega* 29, no. 3 (1994): 219–230; S. B. Patten, "The Loss of a Parent During Childhood as a Risk Factor for Depression," *Canadian Journal of Psychiatry* 36, no. 10 (December 1991): 706–711; Bernhard Bron, "The Significance of Loss of Parents in Childhood for Depressive and Suicidal Patients," *Praxis der Kinderpsychologie und Kinderpsychiatrie* 40, no. 9 (November 1991): 322–327; T. Harris et al., "Loss of a Parent in Childhood and Adult Psychiatric Disorders: A Tentative Overall Model," *Development and Psychopathology* 2, no. 3 (1990): 311–328; A. T. Bifulco, "Childhood Loss of a Parent, Lack of Adequate Parental Care, and Adult Depression: A Replication," *Journal of Affective Disorder* 12, no. 2 (March–April 1987): 115–128; R. A. O'Connell, "Psychosocial Factors in a Model of Manic Depressive Disease," *Integrative Psychiatry* 4, no. 3 (September 1986): 150–154; Camille Lloyd, "Life Events and Depressive Disorder Reviewed: I. Events as Predisposing Factors," *Archives of General Psychiatry* 37, no. 5 (May 1980): 529–539; John Bowlby, "Disruption of Affectional Bonds and Its Effects on Behavior," *Journal of Contemporary Psychotherapy* 2, no. 2 (Winter 1970): 75–86; Sidney Zisook and Lucy Lyons, "Bereavement and Unresolved Grief in Psychiatric Outpatients," *Omega* 20, no. 4 (1989–1990): 307–332; G. Parker and V. Manicavasagar, "Childhood Bereavement Circumstances Associated with Adult Depression," *British Journal of Medical Psychology* 59, no. 4 (December 1986): 387–394; A. Munroe and A. B. Griffiths, "Some Psychiatric Nonsequelae of Childhood Bereavement," *British Journal of Psychiatry* 115, no. 520 (1969): 305–311.

 Although there have been studies that dispute the contention that early loss predisposes to depression, those studies have been challenged on methodological grounds, or have used academic definitions of depression that do not include the more subtle criteria used by practicing clinician-researchers. Rating scales, which are used to assess depression among "normal" and non-hospitalized people, rely on self-reporting in a population that must wall off grief in order to continue to live and develop. Furthermore, rating scales are unable to capture wounds that are reflected in a person's eyes and posture. In individual histories, the loss of a parent is a dominating theme pervading a person's life. Those effects can be lost to a science that must separate fact from folklore and must depend on replicable quantification.

10. John M. Petitto et al., "Relationship of Object Loss (Death of Parent) During Development to Hypothalamic-Pituitary Adrenal Axis Function During Major Affective Illness Later in Life," *Psychiatry Research* 44, no. 3 (December 1992): 227–236.

11. Beverly Raphael, *The Anatomy of Bereavement* (New York: Basic Books, 1983), 199.

12. Stroebe, Stroebe, and Hansson, *Handbook of Bereavement*, 196–201.

13. Ibid., 197.

14. Bessel A. van der Kolk, *Psychological Trauma* (Washington, D.C.: American Psychiatric Press, 1987), 38–39.

15. Anna Freud, "Adolescence," *Psychoanalytic Study of the Child* 13 (1958): 258–278.

16. Hope Edelman, *Motherless Daughters* (New York: Dell Publishing Co., 1994), 238.

17. Ibid., 256.

18. Ibid., 39–40.

19. Ibid., 202.

20. Ibid., 186–187.

21. Ibid.

22. Herbert C. Northcott, "Widowhood and Remarriage Trends in Canada, 1956 to 1981," *Canadian Journal on Aging* 3, no. 2 (Summer 1984): 63–77.

23. Edelman, *Motherless Daughters*, 116.

24. Elyce Wakerman, *Father Loss* (New York: Doubleday & Co., 1984), 8.

25. Stroebe, Stroebe, and Hansson, *Handbook of Bereavement*, 315.

26. Gordon Parker and Pavlovic Dusan Hadzi, "Modification of Levels of Depression in Mother-Bereaved Women by Parental and Marital Relationships," *Psychological Medicine* 14, no. 1 (February 1984): 125–135. The variable that was most highly correlated with depression among seventy-nine women whose mothers died when they were between eight and twelve years of age, and whose fathers remarried, was the lack of care from fathers and step-mothers. Almost all the women who had uncaring parents had an episode of depression. Those who married affectionate husbands, however, corrected this tendency to depression. On the other hand, unaffectionate husbands undid the protective effects of caring parenting.

27. Robert A. Furman, "The Child's Reaction to Death in the Family," in *Loss and Grief: Psychological Management in Medical Practice*, ed. Bernard Schoenberg et al. (New York: Columbia University Press, 1970), 76.

28. Helen Epstein's *Children of the Holocaust: Conversations with Sons and Daughters of Survivors* (New York: G. P. Putnam's Sons, 1979) was the first popular book examining the issues of the children of Holocaust survivors, and it spurred a movement across America for the children to gather together and talk of their experiences.

29. Under the ancient rituals of Orthodox Judaism, a convocation of rabbis closely questions a divorcing couple to ascertain that there is no hope for reconciliation. Although the husband makes the formal petition, either party is entitled to a divorce if there is no hope for happiness. Maimonides had written, "If a woman says, 'My husband is repulsive to me, and I cannot live with him,' the husband is compelled to divorce her, because she is not like a captive woman that she should be forced to consort with a man whom she hates." *Pentateuch and Haftorahs*, 933. A scribe then carefully letters the details of the

divorce onto parchment; a mistake requires him to start over. When everyone is satisfied that the document is perfect, the officiating rabbi slashes it with a knife or razor.

30. G. I. Hockings et al., "Hypersensitivity of the Hypothalamic-Pituitary-Adrenal Axis to Naloxone in Post-traumatic Stress Disorder," *Biological Psychiatry* 33, no. 8–9 (April 15–May 1, 1993): 585–593. Hockings finds:

> examples of PTSD cases showing full symptomatology . . . in the absence of a single, acute, dramatic trauma." Hockings et al. concluded that "such trauma is thus not a necessary condition for PTSD and other evidence shows it to be not a sufficient condition. It is suggested that the . . . distinction between acute and enduring psychosocial stressors be incorporated into the definition to distinguish two pathways to stress disorder, post-traumatic and prolonged duress.

31. P. S. Webster and A. R. Herzog, "Effects of Parental Divorce and Memories of Family Problems on Relationships Between Adult Children and Their Parents," *Journal of Gerontology: Series B: Psychological Sciences and Social Sciences* 50B, no. 1 (January 1995): S24–S34.

32. Judith Mishne, "The Grieving Child: Manifest and Hidden Losses in Childhood and Adolescence," *Child and Adolescent Social Work Journal* 9, no. 6 (December 1992): 471–490; S. H. Henley, "Bereavement Following Suicide: A Review of the Literature," *Current Psychological Research and Reviews* 3, no. 2 (Summer 1984): 53–61.

33. John W. Jacobs, "The Effect of Divorce on Fathers: An Overview of the Literature," *American Journal of Psychiatry* 139, no. 10 (October 1982): 1235–1241.

34. Richard Rhodes, *A Hole in the World: An American Boyhood* (New York: Touchstone Books, Simon & Schuster, 1990), 15.

35. Ibid., 21.

36. A person who kills himself may not write a note, but in the act, he always leaves a last expression of his true feelings. A person tormented by his thoughts does not stab himself in the heart, nor does a person whose heart is breaking shoot himself in the head. An asthma patient suffocated herself by stuffing Kleenex down her throat. One physician known as an "ice queen" for her cold unapproachability ended her life by shutting herself in a freezer. Whether one drifts off to sleep with an overdose, drowns, self-immolates, or hurtles oneself off of a building, the act speaks to the pain.

37. Raphael, *The Anatomy of Bereavement,* 145.

38. Such is the case when a loved one dies. The threat is great, the death is forever, and we are helpless. After an initial outpouring of emotions, and subsequent bursts of emotions later, we shut down. We wrap ourselves in a cortisol cocoon and are comforted by others, if they are available. Then, with repeated expression of emotions to those who can offer solace, grief begins to lose its force. This is the same way we heal from other kinds of trauma.

Chapter 8: Protecting Against Dangers That Are No Longer There

1. Norman A. Krasnegor et al., eds., *Perinatal Development: A Psychobiological Perspective* (Orlando, Fla.: Academic Press, 1987), 402–409. Although reactivity is highly heritable, in the company of the mother, differences of reactivity disappeared and reflected more the mother's temperament.

2. G. M. Brown, S. H. Koslow, and S. Reichlin, eds., *Neuroendocrinology and Psychiatric Disorders* (New York: Raven Press, 1984), 108. Catecholamine responses do not extinguish as rapidly upon reexposure to stressful stimulus as do those of cortisol. Thomas Millman et al., "Sleep Events Among Veterans with Combat-Related Posttraumatic Stress Disorder," *American Journal of Psychiatry* 152, no. 1 (January 1995): 110–115.

3. Anthony Ambrose, ed., *Stimulation in Early Infancy* (Oxford: Oxford Academic Press, 1969), 48.

4. Psychologist Simon S. Rubin writes: "The bereaved [parents] as a group [function] with greater impairment . . . for many years. . . . [T]he tendency to idealize the deceased following loss is pronounced and characteristic of many cultures and age groups. . . . The excessive valuation over living children is recognized as a major source of tension in bereaved families." Raphael, *Handbook of Bereavement*, 295–298.

5. Reported in an interview by Wendy Lustbader.

6. Krasnegor et al., *Perinatal Development*, 402–409.

7. Using the expanded criteria of Hagop S. Akiskal.

Chapter 9: Mastery and Reenactment

1. Martin E. Seligman, *Helplessness: On Depression, Development, and Death* (San Francisco: W. H. Freeman & Co., 1975), 53.

2. P. Martin, "Thyroid Function and Reversal by Antidepressant Drugs of Depressive-Like Behavior (Escape Deficits) in Rats," *Neuropsychobiology* 18, no. 1 (1987): 21–26; P. Martin, "The Effect of Monoamine Oxidase Inhibitors Compared with Classical Tricyclic Antidepressants on Learned Helplessness Paradigm," *Progress in Neuro-Psychopharmacology and Biological Psychiatry* 11, no. 1 (1987): 1–7.

3. M. E. Seligman and S. F. Maier, "Alleviation of Learned Helplessness in the Dog," *Journal of Abnormal Psychology* 73, no. 3, pt. 1 (1968): 256–262.

4. Albert Schweitzer, *Albert Schweitzer: An Anthology*, ed. C. R. Joy (Boston: Beacon Press, 1947), 288.

5. Sigmund Freud, *Beyond the Pleasure Principle*, trans. James Strachey (New York: Bantam Books, 1959), 44–45.

6. Ibid., 38–39.

Chapter 10: "Ayeckah?"

1. Those who react hatefully to homosexuals may be uncertain about their own sexuality; their attacks deflect their fears. In measurements of penile circumference, sexually explicit homosexual videotapes of men are more arous-

ing to homophobic than to nonhomophobic heterosexuals. H. E. Adams, L. W. Wright, Jr., and B. A. Lohr, "Is Homophobia Associated with Homosexual Arousal?" *Journal of Abnormal Psychology* 105, no. 3 (August 1996): 440–445. In a world of intolerance, we need courage to answer questions of self-definition. In a condemning society, "Am I gay?" is a brave question, and an answer of "Yes" is a heroic reply. Freud fainted on two occasions after catching himself with a latent homosexual thought. Frank J. Sulloway, *Freud, Biologist of the Mind* (New York: Basic Books, 1979), 232. Punishing those who answer *"Ayeckah?"* honestly, we do violence to ourselves and each other. Adolescents generally patrol their sexuality for signs of deviation, and the undercurrent of anxiety lingers for years.

2. William S. Aron, "Family Background and Personal Trauma Among Drug Addicts in the United States: Implications for Treatment," *British Journal of Addiction* 70, no. 3 (September 1975): 295–305. The majority of addicted parents were once hurt children who grew up in troubled homes.

3. Cynthia Perez and Cathy Spatz Widom, "Childhood Victimization and Long-term Intellectual and Academic Outcomes," *Childhood Abuse and Neglect* 18, no. 8 (August 1994): 617–633.

4. Arthur Green, "Childhood Sexual and Physical Abuse," *International Handbook of Traumatic Stress Syndromes,* ed. John P. Wilson and Beverly Raphael (New York: Plenum Press, 1993), 582.

5. David M. Fergusson and Michael T. Lynskey, "Adolescent Resiliency to Family Adversity," *Journal of Child Psychology and Psychiatry and Allied Disciplines* 37, no. 3 (March 1996): 281–292. Resilient teenagers were defined as having to face a high degree of family adversity during childhood and showing an absence of external problems, such as substance abuse, delinquency, and school problems. These teenagers had a significantly higher IQ, engaged in fewer novelty-seeking behaviors, and had fewer friendships with delinquent peers.

6. Jan Smith and Margaret Prior, "Temperament and Stress Resilience in School-Age Children: A Within-Families Study," *Journal of the American Academy of Child and Adolescent Psychiatry* 34, no. 2 (February 1995): 168–179.

7. Mary D. Laney, "Multiple Personality Disorder: Resilience and Creativity in the Preservation of the Self," *Individual Psychology: Journal of Adlerian Theory, Research, and Practice* 51, no. 4 (December 1995): 35–49.

8. *Bereishis: Genesis,* translated and annotated by Rabbi Meir Zlotowitz (New York: Mesorah Publications, 1978), 1: 143.

9. Rabbi Meir Zlotowitz, in his commentaries on the Cain and Abel story in *Bereishis,* 1: 143, notes:

> " . . . man becomes attached to the soil, fertilizing it with his own sweat. . . . man comes to worship the forces of nature and to enslave other men to labor for him in the effort to attain property. The agricultural peoples were the first to beget slavery and polytheism."

Chapter 11: Risking the Truth
1. *Talmud* (Sanhedrin, 29a), quoted in *Bereishis,* 1: 116.
2. *Bereishis,* 1: 116.

Chapter 12: The Healing Marriage
1. Courtesy of Darlene Yuna.

Chapter 13: The Discipline of the Fifth Commandment
1. Exodus 2:41.
2. Gerald Blidstein, *Honor Thy Father and Mother: Filial Responsibility in Jewish Law and Ethics* (New York: Ktav Publishing House, 1975), 43–44.
3. Therese A. Rando, *Treatment of Complicated Mourning* (Champaign, Ill.: Research Press, 1993), 10; Holly G. Prigerson et al., "Complicated Grief as a Disorder Distinct from Bereavement-Related Depression and Anxiety: A Replication Study," *American Journal of Psychiatry* 153, no. 11 (November 1996): 1484–1486.

Chapter 15: Final Witness and Final Moments
1. The first time the word "love" appears in the Bible is God's acknowledgment of Abraham's love for his son Isaac.
2. This and the subsequent biblical quotations used in the Abraham and Isaac story are from the ArtScroll Tanach series, *Bereishis,* vol. 2.
3. Wendy Lustbader, *Counting on Kindness* (New York: Free Press, 1991), 180.

INDEX

Author's Note

Forgive Your Parents, Heal Yourself was the title given this book by the original publisher; but the actual title has always been *Healing the Generations*. Although I wrote this book to help all seekers of inner healing, I also hoped to deepen the work of those in the healing professions. The book emphasizes understanding rather than forgiving.

My wife Wendy Lustbader and I have produced an audiotape, "Healing the Generations," based on the themes of this book. You can obtain the two-hour, two-tape set by sending $14 to Okama Press at the address below. You can also contact me at the same address.

Okama Press
P.O. Box 22956
Seattle, WA 98122